Bernard O'Reilly

Novissima

Where do our Departed go?

Bernard O'Reilly

Novissima
Where do our Departed go?

ISBN/EAN: 9783744653213

Printed in Europe, USA, Canada, Australia, Japan

Cover: Foto ©Thomas Meinert / pixelio.de

More available books at **www.hansebooks.com**

NOVISSIMA;

OR,

WHERE DO OUR DEPARTED GO?

— BY —

BERNARD O'REILLY, D.D.,

D. LIT., "LAVAL."

"*Thou hast made us, O Lord, for Thee; and our heart knoweth not rest till it repose in Thee.*"—ST. AUGUSTINE.

NEW YORK:
P. J. KENEDY,
PUBLISHER TO THE HOLY APOSTOLIC SEE,
EXCELSIOR CATHOLIC PUBLISHING HOUSE,
5 BARCLAY STREET.
1896.

THE AUTHOR'S PREFACE.

THE subject of this little book has long haunted me. A portion of it was written on my return from Spain to the United States over two years ago. The rest was the result of an interval of comparative repose during my stay in Ireland. It is natural that, as I approach the limit assigned by Scripture to the ordinary life of man, I should think a little of the "eternal years," and of the goal toward which I am traveling.

If I have, in answering the question, "Where do our departed go?" only treated of everlasting rewards, it is not because I feared to consider the subject of eternal punishment. The title given to this work * would have been misleading had it not been my purpose to verify it by treating in a future volume both of the punishment and purification to be undergone after death.

Fra Angelico, in painting his exquisite "Last Judgment," lavished all the splendor of his genius and the affection of his gentle nature on the representation of his Saints and angels. They are truly heavenly, divine. It is evident that he recoiled with horror from the uncongenial task of painting hell, with its demons and lost souls.

I confess that the labor of writing about the supernatural destiny of man, about God's infinite generosity, and "the unsearchable riches of Christ"—bestowed on us in part in this

---
* NOVISSIMA—"The Last Things."

life, but more especially reserved for the life to come—has been to me a more congenial work than that of fathoming the divine justice in its awards to the wicked.

If the germs of thought I have presumed to present to the reader in the following pages, can afford him a small portion of the comfort they have given me, or if, by meditating on them in a leisure moment, he can lift heart and mind nearer to heaven and its glorious realities, my pains shall be amply repaid.

Whatever the un-Christian or the half-Christian world may dream or dare to say about eternal punishment, a calm consideration of the magnificence of God's rewards, and of the fitness of the heavenly beatitude to satisfy all the tendencies, aspirations, and cravings of human nature at its noblest, must result in acknowledging the truth, the beauty, the harmony, and the completeness of the revealed doctrine concerning the life to come.

I have avoided controversy, and exposed the teaching of the Bible and the Church—the interpreter of the Bible—because I wished this little volume to bring light, consolation, strength, and rest to the homes that might welcome it, and the troubled of heart who would chance to peruse its pages.

BERNARD O'REILLY.

DUBLIN, September 29, 1885,
Feast of St. Michael the Archangel.

CONTENTS.

CHAPTER I.
INTRODUCTORY, ... 1

CHAPTER II.
WITH CHRIST, ... 18

CHAPTER III.
"TO BE DISSOLVED AND BE WITH CHRIST"—THE YEARNING, 34

CHAPTER IV.
WITH CHRIST AT THE FOUNT OF LIFE—THE REALIZATION, . 52

CHAPTER V.
WITHIN THE OCEAN DEPTHS OF LIGHT AND LIFE, . . 69

CHAPTER VI.
STILL AMONG THE DEPTHS, ... 83

CHAPTER VII.
THE SOCIETY ENJOYED IN GOD'S HEAVENLY EMPIRE, . 100

CHAPTER VIII.
AMONG THE MULTITUDES OF THE BLESSED IN CHRIST'S HUMAN KINGDOM, ... 111

CHAPTER IX.
LOST AMONG THE HUMAN WORLD OF HEAVEN, . . 121

CHAPTER X.
AN HOUR IN HEAVEN WITH THE ANGELS, . . . 138

CHAPTER XI.
The Place Itself, ... 153

CHAPTER XII.
The Place Itself—Its Physical Conditions, . . 168

CHAPTER XIII.
The Empire of Charity, ... 185

CHAPTER XIV.
The Belief in the Resurrection of the Body, . . 200

CHAPTER XV.
The New Birth of Mankind, ... 217

CHAPTER XVI.
The General Judgment, ... 233

CHAPTER XVII.
Christ's Human Empire After the Resurrection, . 250

CHAPTER XVIII.
The Triumph of Christ, ... 265

CHAPTER XIX.
The Utmost Goal of Human Aspiration and Progress, 285

CHAPTER XX.
How to Find Heaven on Earth, ... 302

CHAPTER XXI.
The Eternity of Heaven, ... 321

SYNOPSIS.

CHAPTER I.
INTRODUCTORY.

We all ask ourselves the question: "Where do our departed go?" It has been asked by all mankind in the past, as it is at present—A belief in the survival of the soul and in a future state underlying this question—The pagans believed in a future life—Glorious witnesses of this truth and of a belief in the resurrection of the body among the Hebrew race—The seven Machabee martyrs and their mother—St. Paul attests the faith of his race—Apostolic testimony to the Christian belief—Christian heroism and self-sacrifice founded on the hope of eternal rewards—Armies of the self-sacrificing in both hemispheres—"The perfect way" and "the treasure in heaven."

CHAPTER II.
WITH CHRIST.

The rest which death gives to the weary—The rest which the true Christian looks forward to—To be with Christ everlastingly—Christ gave us a foretaste of our destiny in being on earth our Emmanuel, "God with us"—In heaven we are to be "with God"—"God with us"—Preludes to the incarnation in the old law—The angel Jehovah—God's intercourse with Moses, and His abiding with the Hebrew people—"Show me Thy glory," spoke the yearning of the human soul—Our Emmanuel coming among us "in a cloud"—How He made His divinity to be felt by those who approached Him—His Spirit communicated to Mary and Joseph, and to other personages—The ecstasy of the transfiguration a foretaste of paradise—The risen Christ "walking with" the disciples of Emmaus.

CHAPTER III.
"TO BE DISSOLVED AND BE WITH CHRIST"—THE YEARNING.

St. Paul before and after his conversion—Raised up to paradise while still in the body—Preaching "the unsearchable riches of

Christ," "the charity of Christ which surpasseth all knowledge"—"Desiring to be dissolved and be with Christ"—The idea of "dissolution" to the Christian is the welcome permission to depart for home—Examples: The poor fever-stricken immigrant woman and her son; St. Ferdinand, the conqueror of Cordova and Seville.

CHAPTER IV.

WITH CHRIST AT THE FOUNT OF LIFE—THE REALIZATION.

What constitutes the life eternal? The possession of God by clear knowledge and love—The Eucharistic Sacrament and sacrifice a pledge and foretaste of the eternal possession—The banquet of earth and the banquet of heaven—The particular judgment after death—The first meeting of Christ with the holy soul on the frontier of His everlasting kingdom—The "peace be to you!" on passing out of the shadow of the valley of death—The sight of His glorified human countenance a preliminary to the Beatific Vision—What the "Fount of Life" is—In heaven we are not absorbed in the abyss of the Godhead: we preserve our personal identity and exercise our proper vital acts—What God gives us in heaven—The heaven of Eastern pantheism and the Christian heaven—The yearning for the clear sight of God, as expressed in the Old Testament—Christ's explicit declaration and definition of life eternal—The Beatific Vision—What the council of Florence decrees it to be—The great dogmatic fact concerning the bliss of the life to come affirms that the blessed "see God as He is in Himself"—No sleep of the soul after death—A passage from a lower to the highest life.

CHAPTER V.

WITHIN THE OCEAN DEPTHS OF LIGHT AND LIFE—SEEING AND POSSESSING GOD.

We are tried by faith in this life, and rewarded by clear sight in the next—This, probably, was also the trial imposed on the angels in the beginning—Harmonies, anticipations, and aspirations in our nature and in the duties of human society—Apostolic testimonies bearing on the Beatific Vision—The pursuit and possession of knowledge, the tendency and felicity of the human mind—The supreme good the necessary object of the heart's desires—Both of these necessary aspirations and appetites of rational nature fulfilled in the Beatific Vision—Supernaturalness of this Vision and the consequent felicity—Illustrations—St. Paul explains our present imperfect knowledge and longings, and their fulfillment—What takes place in the Beatific Vision—The embrace of God our Father—Illustrations.

CHAPTER VI.
STILL AMONG THE DEPTHS.

The doctrine of the clear sight of God immediately after death, the belief of the early Christian ages—St. Irenæus, martyr—St. Gregory Nazianzen—St. Gregory of Nyssa—St. John Chrysostom—St. Augustine—St. John Damascene—How the "light of glory" elevates and enlarges the mind—Analogies from the natural world and science—The will or affections simultaneously and harmoniously elevated, enlarged, perfected—The love or charity of heaven proportioned to the knowledge there given—Scope of the knowledge conveyed in the Beatific Vision—Helps and illustrations toward understanding its immensity—Its blissfulness derived from the perfect insight into the nature and operations of the Godhead—Inability of the human intellect in our present state to sound these divine depths—Besides God, the primary object of this clear sight, all outside of God, are known and seen perfectly—His mysteries and the whole course of His providence—The heavenly empire, its worlds and inhabitants—The material universe, its substances and laws.

CHAPTER VII.
THE SOCIETY ENJOYED IN HEAVEN.

I. The parents of regenerated humanity—The companionship of Christ and of those who were upon earth called His parents—Bliss arising from the clear sight of Christ in heaven, and from intercourse with Him—His beautiful character, as known through the gospels, the object of intense and enthusiastic study in our day—Incomparably greater the knowledge of Him enjoyed by the blessed—St. Bonaventure's ecstatic prayer to Christ—We cannot study Christ in His earthly career without finding by His side the Blessed Mother and St. Joseph—We cannot dissociate them from Him in heaven—They are near Him where He thrones as King and Head over the elect of our race.

CHAPTER VIII.
AMONG THE MULTITUDES OF THE BLESSED.

II. The society of the Saints and elect—Theirs is the assemblage of the truest, best, and loveliest—The friendship of such an assemblage—A pause to consider what is this moral perfection which renders the Saints in heaven so admirable—Transfiguration of the entire man in the life to come—Analogies and illustrations—The present life too short for the earnest worker to attain perfection in anything—The mighty moral growth witnessed here a guarantee of the perfection attained hereafter—St. Paul's witness—Glimpses of paradise.

CHAPTER IX.
LOST AMONG THE HUMAN WORLD IN HEAVEN—ITS IMMENSITY.

1. Christ's human kingdom in heaven—Intoxicating effect of beholding such countless numbers of the glorious and the good—The felicity derived from the friendship, the love, and merited praise of such a kingdom—The holy ties of earth bind souls together in heaven—Examples: Who those are who "shine like stars" among these multitudes of the good and great—Holy families—Holy Patriarchs—Peoples who have kept the faith—The ancient Hebrews—Modern peoples.

2. Population of Christ's human kingdom in heaven—What may be, at present, their real numbers—Bases for forming an estimate—How we are to interpret the words of Christ about "the small number of the elect" and the "narrow gate"—Those who labor among the masses know how many there are who are faithful to God—If we may compute the number of the elect at *one thousand millions*, the present estimated population of the globe—If so, what glory and felicity to be one of such a kingdom!—Illustrations—The real nature and source of social happiness: To feel that those we are with are our own; loving us, beloved by us, and deserving of our utmost love.

CHAPTER X.
FROM THE HUMAN TO THE ANGELIC SOCIETY—AN HOUR WITH THE ANGELS IN HEAVEN.

1. Lingering to count accurately the millions of the blessed—Everything in eternity partakes of the infinite—In the Middle

Ages all men sought to die well—Men then remembered Christ's bestowing from the cross paradise on the penitent criminal crucified with Him—In these Christian ages the oppressed and suffering multitudes were not all excluded from Christ's grace and love—We may, without exceeding, estimate Christ's kingdom on high at *three thousand millions*.

2. Christ's Angelic Empire—It is that of our brethren and friends; our own also—Its population—Testimonies from Scripture—The Book of Job asks if there "is any numbering" of them?—The "scientific imagination" of the theologian and the Christian readily adopts the grandest views of God's works—St. Denis, the Areopagite, and St. Thomas Aquinas—The latter's doctrine and estimates most worthy of our acceptance—The angelic world numbering more substances than the whole inferior creation—We are safe in estimating the population of the angelic empire as incomparably superior to the human—St. John's vision of both of these worlds—Catholic theologians adopt the theory of the Areopagite about the division of the angels into three hierarchies, each including three orders: nine divisions in all—Nine concentric and subordinate worlds—Such is the angelic society—Magnificence of this subject of study on earth and contemplation in heaven—Glory and bliss of this fellowship.

CHAPTER XI.

THE PLACE ITSELF—THE LAND OF THE LIVING.

The Prophet Baruch's sublime conception of it—Ideas of the location of heaven—A world created apart—Bellarmine's conception of it—The immensity of the heavenly world and the Beatific Vision—St. Ignatius Loyola sees God in all things—We need to expand our minds in thinking of divine things—Every part of this heavenly empire accessible to the blessed—How easy intercourse with all its parts will be even after the resurrection—Illustrations—Magnificence of this empire—It is called in Scripture the bride, and, sometimes, the dwelling place of the bride—This argues the utmost magnificence the Bridegroom can display—It is the country and home of God's beloved children—Illustration from parental love—The paradise and garden of delights—Magnificence and glory of its inhabitants.

CHAPTER XII.
PHYSICAL CONDITIONS OF THE HEAVENLY EMPIRE.

These conditions are in harmony with the final perfection of the inhabitants—Analogy founded on the conditions for life on earth—Everything in the supernal world will satisfy the exalted imagination and the purified sensibility of man—St. John's descriptions imply all this—Comparison of the earthly Paradise with the heavenly—The heavenly prepared as a reward for the Saints—Social condition in harmony—Unspeakable happiness and greatness of this empire—God willed man from the beginning to set his heart on it—Impulses—Comparison with the greatest and happiest of earthly realms—Solomon's wisdom and folly—David's aspirations.

CHAPTER XIII.
HEAVEN BEFORE THE RESURRECTION—THE EMPIRE OF CHARITY.

The Church of heaven and the Church on earth—What is seen in the blessed city of God: The altar of the Lamb—What is seen in the Church on earth: "All nations and tribes" around the altar of the Lamb—Wherever the children of the Church are encamped, the armies of angels ascending and descending—Divine security and unchangeableness of the city of God on earth—"God in her midst—She shall not be moved"—The charity which is the soul of the communion of Saints—Heaven "the kingdom of perfect charity"—"The charity of Christ presseth us" also—The two great armies of charity here below—Their labors and creations—Charity of men and women in the world—Example.

CHAPTER XIV.
BELIEF IN THE RESURRECTION OF THE BODY.

The Christian religion founded on the fact of Christ's Resurrection—Witnesses to the fact: The dogma of the resurrection before Christ; Christ's teaching; Facts of resurrection before Christ; Persons restored to life by Christ; Moses and Elias at the Transfiguration; Resurrection of Lazarus; The question, "Who has come back to tell us of the life to come?" Christ has; Miracles of the Apostles in confirmation of this fact; Stephen dying beholds Christ in heaven; The world has accepted Christianity founded on this fact, and on the belief in the resurrection—St. Paul's testimony: He saw Christ last of all the Apostles and Disciples; His doctrine on the resurrection—The plea of "impossibility" put in by unbelievers—Magnificent horizons opened up by our belief.

CHAPTER XV.
THE NEW BIRTH OF MANKIND.

St. Paul—Gospel of the resurrection—Christ's prediction—Events preceding the general resurrection—St. Paul's teaching and description of the event itself—The consummation of the Creator's work in the physical world—Clothing a barren continent with verdure and filling it with animal life, a work of Omnipotence, helping us to understand the new birth of mankind—With Him is the secret and the fount of life—St. Paul on the new bodily life—Objection: The total material changes occurring periodically in the human frame—Which body shall we rise in? Most probably the body consigned to the grave—The veneration of all ages and races for the remains of the dead—Violation of tombs by the Reformers and the Roundheads—Their example imitated by the French Revolutionists—French scientists desecrating Egyptian tombs—Desecration now openly practiced in the name of science—Reverence of the Church for the human body—Anointed temples of the Holy Ghost—Christian burial, a depositing in the furrows the seed for the future springtide—God giveth life and increase—St. Paul's text further examined—Coming down from heaven of the angelic and human spirits—Souls from the Limbus or intermediate world: fallen angels and fallen men—The sounding of the trumpet—The fairest sight ever beheld by the Creator Himself.

CHAPTER XVI.
THE RESURRECTION OF JUDGMENT.

God's triumph—A favorite subject with artists in the Christian ages—The mystery of free-will and divine providence cleared up—Man enlightened from the beginning about his supernatural destiny—Free to serve or not to serve God and gain heaven—Helps toward securing his eternal happiness—God, through Christ Crucified, taught the world the infinite value of the heavenly treasure, and the infinite loss entailed by its forfeiture—

The book of the crucifix—The book of judgment—Hell is the loss of Christ—The judgment—Preliminaries—The scene as described by Christ—The two-fold law of charity, the soul of all divine legislation—Why Christ bases on its observance or violation the award He pronounces—God wills us to pay the debt we owe Himself to the poor and suffering who hold His place—Timeliness and necessity of insisting on this divine law of brotherly charity in our age—How and where we can find on our road Christ in the persons of the needy and suffering—Golden opportunities—Example of St. Francis of Assisi—Confirmation of the Christian doctrine on heaven and hell from ancient Persian literature.

CHAPTER XVII.

THE TRANSFIGURATION OF THE BLESSED.

Christ's glorious human empire—We must take the infallible Church's interpretation of the Scriptural doctrine of the Resurrection—Christ makes of each blessed human soul, on the last day, a "quickening spirit" like His own—The risen bodies of the blessed must bear "the image" of the heavenly Adam—Qualities or "gifts" of these bodies: Incorruption or impassibility; lightsomeness; agility or power; explanations of the holy Father's subtility or spirituality; analogies borrowed from the teachings of modern science; imponderable fluids, their subtility, energy, velocity; universal ether and its agency and spirit-like substance and qualities; the Transfiguration of Christ, and that of each of His blessed—Peculiar happiness of soul and body arising from this re-union and this Transfiguration—This happiness a compensation for bodily privations and sufferings in this life—Christ's triumphant ascension.

CHAPTER XVIII.

THE TRIUMPH OF CHRIST.

The preludes to the Wedding Feast—Exaltation after humiliation—Spoils won by the cross—Numbers added to the elect by the Church—The flock gathered into heaven by the Good Shepherd—The regal progress of our King—The select bands in the army of Saints—They sing *Te Deum Laudamus* as they go—The LXXXVIII Psalm—Joys of eternity and joys of earth—In heaven all have the perfect power to enjoy—The divine harmonies of heaven—Human feet treading the soil of the heavenly empire—It blooms afresh beneath the feet of Christ triumphant—Beautiful legends about St. Francis of Assisi—"I have said, ye are gods, and all sons of the Most High"—The Bridegroom and the Bride—"King of kings and Lord of lords."

CHAPTER XIX.
THE SUPPER OF THE LAMB.

A royal wedding feast the ideal on earth of magnificence and enjoyment—Even among the poor a wedding means sumptuosity and hospitality unbounded—What we know it to be among the wealthy—The banquets of Assuerus—What we are to understand by the Supper of the Lamb—It inaugurates a new era in heaven—Members of the elect to whom heaven is new—Magnificent pageant of their arrival at the Feast—True conception of the banqueting place—Two worlds, the angelic and human, seated at the Banquet—The heavenly fare at that Supper—Anticipations on earth of that divine Food: "I am the Bread of Life." "Take ye and eat: This is My Body." "Drink ye all of this: For this is My Blood." "I will not drink from henceforth of this fruit of the vine, until that day when I shall drink it with you new in the kingdom of My Father"—What "this fruit of the vine" is—Partaking of the Divinity—Christ's instruction to His Disciples: "I am the Vine. . . . You the branches"—The cup which man and angel drink at that Feast—The Father's joy in giving; the children's bliss in receiving—In what consists the "newness" of the wine given at that Feast—1. Man in heaven only a spiritual being before the Resurrection; now he lives there in body—After the resurrection the wine of the Beatific Vision intoxicates body and soul—New transports of that hour—The sight of Christ with our bodily eyes—2. Intoxicating effect of beholding with the bodily sense the new heavens and their angelic and human inhabitants—It will be new for the parents of regenerated humanity to have their family around them there. . . . New for the Eternal Father to welcome to His kingdom the entire family of the elect—Joy, like "the rush of a river, inundating the city of God."

CHAPTER XX.

HOW TO FIND HEAVEN ON EARTH.

The end in heaven; "God all in all"—Divine love finds means to be "all in all" to us, even in this life.

I. God present in all things—He fills heaven and earth: the immense and infinite—Present in all things as Creator, Preserver, Ruler—Easy to find Him—Present in man.

II. God works for us in all the energies and activities of the material, intellectual, social, and religious world—St. Paul to the Corinthians: "All things are yours;" "the sufferings of time;" the glory to come"—God directs all things toward our good—Human infirmity supplemented by almighty power and divine generosity—The Three divine Persons working for us—The mystery of free-will—How man may work divinely for God—St. Francis Xavier—A docile instrument in the hand of God—Human weakness transformed into divine energy—How attentive meditation can help us—The "Ladder of Jacob" not yet withdrawn—The angelic world working for us—And the Saints in heaven—St. Paul's example: "Who shall separate us from the love of Christ?"—To die for Christ the privilege of the few—To live and labor for Christ that of many—We should be spurred on to work by the prospect of winning an everlasting inheritance—What we see gold-seekers daring and enduring.

CHAPTER XXI.

THE ETERNITY OF HEAVEN.

Precautions taken by business men to invest and secure money—Stability and perpetuity a great ground of confidence—Vain to seek either outside of God—Two memorable examples—The Christian's foundation—God and His eternity—Eternal life as explained in the light of revealed truth—The last article of the Creed—Utterances of our Lord and His Apostles on eternal or everlasting life—The Beatific Vision and the partaking of God's own life in heaven imply eternity—Conclusion: Everything divine in the heavenly life; therefore its duration should be divine, eternal—The everlasting society of God, His angels and Saints—The eternity of the heavenly universe; all our own, for evermore—The eternal God possessed eternally.

NOVISSIMA.

CHAPTER I.

INTRODUCTORY.

> Where are they gone, of yore
> My best delight,
> Dear and more dear, though now
> Hidden from sight?
> —*Lady Nairn.*

"Let not your heart be troubled. You believe in God; believe also in Me."—*St. John*, xiv, 1.

THE QUESTION ASKED BY ALL MEN.

WHERE is the man or woman whose heart has not been troubled by the thought of that dread and mysterious *hereafter*, toward which the stream of life irresistibly hurries them?

Around us, while the skeptic's doubts come out of the darkness, and take shape like the phantoms of a horrible dream, we hear our contemporaries asking aloud, with concern and with fear: Whether the generations which preceded us have been as utterly blotted out of life, of all personal existence, as the grass of the prairie over which the flames have passed destroying the very roots of every green thing, as the races of geological monsters which have left behind no living representative?

We who, arrived near the limit assigned to human life, behold the shadows fast lengthening on our road, and the sun about to disappear into a world to us unknown, cannot help seeing in his setting the image of our own existence. With troubled hearts we, too, ask ourselves: What sphere will receive our spirit when our day is ended? Into what company shall we be ushered in parting with this body of clay?

For we know that all living peoples, as well as those who have gone before us, are unanimous in believing that the soul survives the dissolution of the body. And we know as well, that they asked themselves in their day, as we do now, with anxiety not unmixed with fear: Where do our departed go?

The question, and the grave thoughts it suggests, will not be put away, in the evening of life especially. Like travelers who have climbed a steep hill after a long road, we look back to find those who started with us, and perceive, with a shudder, that few, very few indeed, are by our side. Where are they?

We remember the aged to whom we looked up for guidance and counsel on beginning life's journey; the strong, the wise, the venerable, on whom our soul leaned for support; they dropped away, one after the other, like ripe fruit from the overladen tree. Does the earth cover all that we loved and revered in them?

Our own parents too—the father who taught us all generosity of aim and deed; the mother whose tenderness was deeper than the springs of ocean, whose pure and loving soul was to us as God's angel in human form; they, too, in their turn, closed their race of devotion and suffering, with their eyes looking fondly for the dawn of a better life, in which we should be reunited with them. Is this reunion in a blissful eternity only a delusion sent by nature to deceive the hopes of earth's dearest and best? Have we lost forever the sweet companionship of those who first discoursed with us on immortality? Are we never again to be folded within those dear arms? Shall their loved voices never more make music in our souls?

Every day, as we advance toward the goal, we hear fond parents mourning by our side over the grave of children cut off in the springtide of lovely womanhood, or a manhood full of brilliant promise. They were rearing children for heaven; they watched over them as if they had to keep angels in the body free from earthly stain, while training them to all earthly heroism. Is there no heaven, then, for the bright, pure spirits departed from their home?

Within the Christian home, as outside of it, the young are called to watch by the death-bed of their best beloved; nothing soothes for them the pang of separation but the faith in a better life, and the certain hope of meeting there those who are a part of themselves. Is there, then, to be no reunion hereafter?

Has all mankind conspired to cheat themselves with this magnificent dream of a future life and a better world? Let us meditate seriously on this thought at the very threshold of our inquiry.

Has all mankind, therefore, believed, and believed firmly, in a future state? Yes; all!

ATTESTING VOICES FROM THE TOMB.

Examine, in every portion of the habitable globe, the records and monuments of the most ancient empires; consult the religious beliefs and the funereal customs of races the most civilized or the most savage; from every land and age, from the literatures of the pagan world and the world worshiping the one true God, from the tombs of Egypt, Assyria, India, China, and Japan, as well as from the sepulchres of Palestine and Etruria, come solemn voices attesting the soul's immortality—everlasting rewards for the good, everlasting punishments for the wicked. From the reverently preserved remains of the half-famished tribes wandering around Hudson's Bay or through the forests of Alaska, from the sepulchral mounds of races long extinguished, scattered over the valleys of the Ohio and the Mississippi, down through Mexico and Central America, and the vast regions of the Southern Continent to Cape Horn—the care bestowed on the dead of yesterday, as well as the love and respect paid to the bodies of those who died thousands of years ago, alike proclaim that all these races believed in the survival of the soul.

More than that. The care taken by men, while living, to secure for their remains after death a safe and inviolable resting-place, as well as the sentiment in the survivors prompting to carry out the wish of the dying, and impelling children to give to parents the honorable sepulture which they hoped for in return—all spoke of the primitive revelation promising not only the life to come, but the revival of, the body to partake thereof.

SURVIVAL OF THE SOUL.

Leaving all discussion of "the resurrection of the flesh" to a future chapter, we insist upon this unanimity with which mankind in the past, as in the present, all civilizations and religions, affirm the immortality of the soul, its future accountability to its Maker and Judge, and the everlasting happiness of the good, as an offset to the proud, pretentious and shallow few, who put out the eyes of their own intelligence lest they should see the necessity of the life to come, the magnificence of its rewards, and the salutary terrors of its threatened punishments.

The pagan Cicero and the pagan Plato revolted in their day against the few Materialists whose practice and teaching aimed at depriving the toiling and suffering masses—as well as all who set virtue and conscience above the honors, enjoyments, and happiness of the present life—of the comforting hope of a blissful immortality. And so, even now, heathen philosophy and heathen religions rebuke the purblindness of the false science, which, seated in the chair at Oxford, from which Roger Bacon taught, seeks to extinguish in men's souls, one after the other, the lights and the hopes which made Bacon's life so bright and happy amid toil, and obloquy, and persecution.

He only gave utterance to this article of the universal pagan creed who wrote:

> 'Tis the Divinity that stirs within us,
> 'Tis Heaven itself that points out an hereafter,
> And intimates eternity to man.
> . . . . . If there's a Power above us
> (And that there is, all nature cries aloud
> Through all her works), He must delight in virtue;
> And that which He delights in must be happy.*

GLORIOUS WITNESSES AMONG THE HEBREW RACE.

But whatever doubt obscured or weakened the traditional faith of the heathen nations, among the

---

*Addison.

Hebrew race, holding fast to revealed truth, there was no doubt on the cardinal doctrine of the life to come. From the lips of none, among this chosen people, may we learn a lesson on this matter more profitably than from the glorious martyrs, who, amid torments, testified to their belief in the life eternal and its rewards.

Let us seat ourselves, therefore, in spirit among the half-pagan, half-Jewish crowd, which surrounds the mother of the Machabees and her seven sons, as the children first and then the mother, each in succession sacrifices limb and life rather than sin against the law of God. The oldest has already suffered his long agony and triumphed beneath the eyes of the heroic mother. The second, undismayed, has endured tortures unspeakable. "When he was at the last gasp," the sacred historian tells us, "he said thus (to King Antiochus): 'O most wicked man, thou indeed destroyest us out of this present life. But the King of the world will raise us up, who die for His laws, in the resurrection of eternal life.'"*

The third son, in like manner, allowed the executioners to torture and mutilate as their ingenuity taught them. Limb after limb was cut off. "And when he was required, he quickly put forth his tongue and courageously stretched out his hands, and said with confidence: 'These I have from Heaven, but for the laws of God I now make little of them, because I hope to receive them again from Him.'"†

Even so the fourth: "When he was now ready to die, he spoke thus: 'It is better, being put to death by men, to look for hope from God, to be raised up

---

*2 Machabees, vii. 9.   † Ibidem, 10-11.

again by Him. For, as to thee, (King Antiochus), thou shalt have no resurrection unto life.'"*

We must pause in the midst of this fearful tragedy to listen to the words of that heroic mother, whose sublime spirit suffered and triumphed in each of her boys. It was she who had instilled into them, with the milk of infancy, the fear and love of God—that constancy which no torture and no bribe could move. Hear how she repeats before Antiochus and his satellites the lesson so often taught before:

"Now the mother was to be admired above measure, and worthy to be remembered by good men, who beheld her seven sons slain in the space of one day, and bore it with a good courage for the hope that she had in God. And she bravely exhorted every one of them in her own language, being filled with wisdom, and joining a man's heart to a woman's thought: '*I neither gave you breath, nor soul, nor life,*' she says; 'neither did I frame the limbs of every one of you. But the Creator of the world, that formed the nativity of man, and that found out the origin of all, He will restore to you again in His mercy both breath and life, as now you deprive yourselves for the sake of His laws.'" †

The martyrdom of the seventh and the youngest raised to a pitch of sublimity never heard of in the ancient world, or conceived of by Plato or Æschylus, the courage and constancy of mother and son. Antiochus, baffled and beaten in his impious design by the unconquerable spirit of parent and children, endeavors to win the only survivor by cajolery and the promise of wealth, honor and royal favor. He failed. He then turned to the mother. "The king

---

* Machabees, vii, 14-15. † Ibidem, 20-23.

called the mother, and counselled her to deal with the young man to save his life. . . . She promised that she would counsel her son."

The interest of the courtiers and the crowd is excited to the highest degree. Is she going to give up to the maddened ferocity of king and executioners her only remaining one? Listen again: "I beseech thee, my son, look upon heaven and earth, and all that is in them; and consider that God made them out of nothing, and mankind also. So thou shalt not fear this tormentor; but, being made a worthy partner with thy brethren, *receive death*, that in that mercy *I may receive thee again with thy brethren.*" *

Such is, among the people of God, and before the coming of Christ, the most glorious testimony borne to the belief in the life to come, the resurrection of the dead, the bliss of heaven, and the fearful retribution in store for the wicked.

As we meditate together, in the light of such examples, the answer to the question, "Where do our dead go?" we may well exult at the heroic faith of these saints of the Old Testament. Of them, St. Paul, the Apostle of this faith, enlarged and perfected by Christ, wrote to the Christian Hebrews of his day:

ST. PAUL CONFIRMS THAT TESTIMONY.

"Now, of the things which we have spoken, this is the sum: We have such a High Priest, who is set on the right hand of the throne of Majesty in the heavens, a Minister of the Holies, and of the true Tabernacle, which the Lord hath pitched, and not man.† . . . Having, therefore, a confidence, brethren, in the entering into the Holies by the

---
* Machabees, vii, 25-29.   † Hebrews, viii, 1-2.

blood of *Christ,* a new and living way which He hath dedicated for us through the veil, that is to say, His flesh, and a High Priest over the House of God, let us draw near with a true heart in fullness of faith. . . . Let us hold fast the confession of our hope without wavering, for He is faithful that hath promised." *

Be comforted, troubled hearts; and let the light from above break gradually, sweetly on your darkness. See you not that all the faith and hope of the world before Christ pointed to heaven, to the true Holy of Holies, to the House of God, unbuilt by man, and over which Christ our Lord is King? Into that house and home the blood of Christ has opened to us "a new and living way."

Now, from the cradle of our race in Eden down to this day, survey the generations of believers, who have lived, labored, suffered, and died, fixing their eyes on the promise of that Redeemer, Restorer, and King—on the Hope of the Heaven which His blood was to reopen; on the glorious prospect of the Resurrection so openly proclaimed in Antioch by the seven Machabee Martyrs and their mother.

"Now, faith is the substance of things to be hoped for; the evidence of things that appear not. . . . By faith Abel offered to God a sacrifice exceeding that of Cain, by which he obtained a testimony that he was just, God giving testimony to his gifts, and by it being dead yet speaketh. By faith Henoch was translated, that he should not see death, and he was not found because God had translated him. For before his translation he had testimony that he pleased God. But without faith it is impos-

---
* Hebrews, x, 19-23.

sible to please God. For he that cometh to God must believe that He is, and is a Rewarder to them that seek Him. . . . . .

"By faith he that is called Abraham obeyed to go out into a place which he was to receive for an inheritance; and he went out, not knowing whither he went. By faith he abode in the land, dwelling in cottages, with Isaac and Jacob, the co-heirs of the same promise. For he looked for a *City* that hath foundations, whose builder and maker is God. . . . All these died according to faith, not having received the promises, but beholding them afar off, and saluting them, and confessing that they are pilgrims and strangers on the earth. For they that say these things do signify that they seek a country. And truly if they had been mindful of that from whence they came out, they had doubtless time to return. But now they desire a better, that is to say, *a Heavenly Country*. Therefore, God is not ashamed to be called their God; for He hath prepared for them a *City*." *

Such is the living faith of that chosen Hebrew race, who were the predecessors and spiritual parents of the Christian people. Among them the belief in the life and the world to come shines like a stream of light along the entire path of their history down to Christ; and since His teaching has only made the existence of the "Heavenly Country," of the "City" with eternal foundations, "whose builder and maker is God," a more distinct and glorious Reality.

---

* Hebrews, xi, 1-16.

"LIFE AND INCORRUPTION BROUGHT TO LIGHT BY THE GOSPEL.

"I know whom I have believed,"* writes St. Paul from his prison in Rome; "our Saviour Jesus Christ, who hath destroyed death, and hath brought to light *Life and Incorruption* by the Gospel." † It was this heroic Apostle of the perfected Revelation, who, in penning the sublime eulogy of Hebrew faith in the past, wished to nourish that of the new-born Christian Church, composed so largely of Hebrew converts.

Persecution and suffering had been the lot of believers in the long ages before Christ; persecution and suffering are the inheritance held forth to Christ's followers; and all this to be accounted as nothing in view of the eternal reward. The Hebrew Church was personified in Moses, who, "when he was grown up, denied himself to be the son of Pharoah's daughter, rather choosing to be afflicted with the people of God than to have the pleasure of sin for a time, esteeming the reproach of Christ greater riches than the treasure of the Egyptians. For he looked unto the *Reward*. By faith he left Egypt, not fearing the fierceness of the king; for he endured *as seeing Him that is invisible*.‡

This Unseen God and the invisible world in which He lives and reigns with His faithful servants, the angelic spirits and the spirits of just men, is precisely what modern unbelief, under the usurped name of science, would have us look upon as the *Unknowable*. With St. Paul, each of us Christians must reply to the skeptic and the mate-

* 2 Timothy, 1, 12. ‡ Hebrews, xi, 24-27.
† Ibidem, 10.

rialist: "I *know* whom I have believed! . . Our Saviour *Jesus* Christ, who hath destroyed death."

Therefore, while turning to the very best account this short mortal life in glorifying our Maker, in helping our brethren, and in sanctifying ourselves, we account earth and all things temporal as of little moment, because we, too, look forward to the Reward, to that "Life and Incorruption" brought to light by the Gospel.

ATTESTED BY THE HOSTS OF THE SELF-SACRIFICING.

Were we not sure of this prospect, St. Paul's words to the Corinthian Christians of his day might literally apply to Christians the whole world over at the close of this nineteenth century: "If in this life only we have faith in Christ, we are of all men the most miserable." *

Look around you, inside and outside your homes, and count those of your acquaintance who try earnestly and consistently to serve God with their whole heart and soul—men and women who, while living in the world, and fulfilling every duty of their station with scrupulous fidelity, endeavor to follow Christ Crucified by self-denial and self-sacrifice. We speak not of churchmen, or persons bound by monastic vows to special abnegation, but of the secular crowd traveling along the common road of life. How many beautiful souls there are among the toiling, travel-soiled, over-burdened multitudes?

Is their faithful service to go unrewarded? Is their hope of immortality and its repose all vain? Is there for these indefatigable toilers, these patient, uncomplaining sufferers, these devoted lovers of the

---
* 1 Cor., xv, 19.

poor and the afflicted, no greater assurance of a life beyond the grave than there is for the horse, the ass, or the mule, that falls down dead by the roadside? Is there no more certainty of survival and everlasting honor for the martyr who gladly bares his breast to the persecutor's steel in China or Tonquin than there is for the ox or the sheep slaughtered in the shambles?

Suffering, persecution, martyrdom have not yet ceased to be the portion on earth of those who are dearest to Christ. It is to all such, in our days, that another Apostle also writes from prison and from the verge of the grave: "Dearly beloved, think not strange the burning heat which is to try you, as if some new thing happened to you. But if you partake of the suffering of Christ, rejoice that when His glory shall appear you may also be glad with exceeding joy." * Are we now to believe that the future reality will give the lie to both Peter and Paul?

Look abroad into the world and count these mighty armies of men and women who have torn themselves from home, from all the satisfaction and bliss of domestic life, from all the pursuits and noble rewards that a legitimate or praiseworthy ambition opens up to the well-born, the educated, the gifted, and accomplished; they have chosen to share Christ's poor and laborious life, while doing for the bodies and souls of His people all that the experience of nineteen centuries of Christianity points out as most needful, most salutary, most glorious, and most heroic in self-sacrificing devotion. Do you doubt that He desires such imitators or

---

* 1 St. Peter, iv, 12-13.

holds out to them all that a God can give in the life to come? Then listen to the Gospel narrative:

"When He was gone forth into the way, a certain man, running up and kneeling before Him, asked Him: 'Good Master, what shall I do that I may receive life everlasting?'

"And Jesus said to him: 'Why callest thou Me good? None is good but one—God. Thou knowest the Commandments: *Do not commit adultery, do not kill, do not steal, bear not false witness, do no fraud, honor thy father and mother.*'

SELF-SACRIFICE AND THE TREASURE IN HEAVEN.

"But he answering, said to Him: 'Master, all these things I have observed from my youth.' And *Jesus*, looking on him, loved him, and said to him: 'One thing is wanting unto thee; go, sell whatsoever thou hast, and give to the poor, and thou shalt have treasure in heaven; and come, follow Me!' Who, being struck sad at that saying, went away sorrowful, for he had great possessions." *

In St. Matthew's narrative of the same incident, our Lord says to the young man: "If thou wilt be perfect, go, sell what thou hast, . . . and come, follow Me." †

This, then, is the "perfect way" of evangelical poverty and self-sacrifice to which Christ invites heroic souls, holding out to them, after death, the "life everlasting," the mighty "treasure in heaven," which is to compensate for all that the most heroic can renounce and undergo in this life. Hence the pregnant sequel in the next verses. "And Peter began to say unto Him: 'Behold, we

---

*St. Mark, x, 17-30. †St. Matthew, xix, 21.

have left all things, and have followed Thee.' *Jesus* answering, said : 'Amen, I say to you, there is no man who hath left house, or brethren, or sisters, or father, or mother, or children, or lands for My sake and for the Gospel who shall not receive an hundred times as much, now in this time; houses, and brethren, and sisters, and mothers, and children, and lands, with persecutions; and in the world to come life everlasting.'"

The rich young man of the Gospel, frightened by the thought of all he should have to give up to follow the Master into the narrow way, turned back sad and "sorrowful" from his quest. He could not, then at least, in spite of his earnest desire of attaining to the life without end, renounce all the good things of the present. If he could have seriously reflected on the eternal possession of that "treasure in heaven," how paltry had appeared to him the price demanded!

But the little band among whom Peter was spokesman had given up their all at Christ's first call to follow Him. And now, when the young man had gone his way, and they are assured of the "persecutions" that await them in the future, their heroism is still further tested by the prophecy of Christ's near crucifixion.

It is not perfect renouncement only, or perfect self-denial, which is demanded of those who follow Him in the better way, but self-sacrifice and self-crucifixion. Oh, what hosts of those noble men and women, all through both hemispheres, rise up before our mind's eye, ever toiling, like their Master and Model, to make earth the foretaste of heaven, and the children of man the true children of God!

> "O lives beloved wherein once mine did live,
>   Thinking your thoughts, and walking in your ways,
>   On your dear presence pasturing all my days,
> In pleasantness and peace; whose moods did give
> The measure to my own! how vainly strive
>   Poor fancy's fingers, numbed by time, to raise
>   The veil of woven years, that from my gaze
> To hide what now you are doth still contrive!"

What hosts of these, the glory and the crown of our humanity, have gone to their rest and their reward; other legions, more numerous still, filling up the void in their blessed ranks, and continuing to sow this earth of ours with the seed of all divine virtues!

Have these—have all who, since this world came into existence, devoted and sacrificed their lives to the good of others, prompted by the instincts and the hope of their immortality—have they been following only the light of a "will-o'-the-wisp," which went out in utter and eternal darkness on the grave?

No! On the contrary. In presence of these "clouds of witnesses" to the nobleness of self-renouncement, and the divinity of self-sacrifice—witnesses whose shining ranks stretch back to Calvary and beyond it—we solemnly profess our belief that charity, the heaven-born love of God, and the self-devoting, self-denying, self-sacrificing love of the brotherhood, shall have its exceeding great reward beyond the grave.

Our soul may be filled with grief and anxiety when, in the midst of a Christian society, whose moral laws and loftiest virtues all repose on the belief in the soul's immortality, and in the eternity of rewards and punishments for deeds done in the flesh, false teachers' voices, like notes of discord in the divinest of harmonies, are heard denying the existence of the life to come.

THE MASTER'S ANSWER TO THE QUESTION.

We, who cling with mind and heart to Christ our Master, as we do to the certainty of our own existence; we, who mourn for the dear ones sent before us, and see ourselves brought near the end of our pilgrimage—we must not allow materialistic or anti-Christian doubts to trouble the serenity of the evening of life, or to cloud the eye of our soul as it looks upward to the everlasting hills. We must place ourselves in spirit at the feet of the Master and drink in His dear words:

"Let not your heart be troubled. You believe in God, believe also in Me. In My Father's house are many mansions. If *it were* not so I would have told you. I go to prepare a place for you. And if I go and prepare a place for you, I will come again, and will take you to Myself; that *where I am* you also may be."*

We know, then, "where our departed go." Not in vain do we place all our trust in Him who alone is the Way, the Truth, and the Life. Even on this side of the grave, and while the cold mists of earth fall thick and chilling around our path, we feel that "this is eternal life to know Thee, the only true God, and *Jesus Christ* whom thou hast sent."† The firm faith of the present is only the prelude and the pledge of the clear knowledge of the future. We know that He, who is the Way, hath gone before us,

---
* St. John, xiv, 1, 2, 3.   † St. John, xvii, 3.

and taken possession of the Father's house with its many mansions, of the land of the living with its vast empire and its unfading glories. We know that those who, either yesterday or long ago, parted with us on the road, and died believing in Him, trusting in His promises, and loving Him with the last pulsation of their hearts, *are with Him.*

> Where they rejoice to be,
> There is the land for me;
> Fly time, fly speedily;
> Come life and light!

CHAPTER II.

WITH CHRIST.

> My feet are wearied and my hands are tired,
> My soul oppressed;
> And with desire have I long desired
> Rest—only Rest.
> —*Ryan.*

To the half-believing multitude, weary of bootless toil, weighed down by oppression and care, despairing of seeing wrong righted, or the earth yielding to their sweat even a sufficiency, death, the seeming end of all things, might be looked forward to and welcomed for the rest it brings to hand, and head, and heart. And there are many, very many, among the wealthy, the fortunate, and the great, to whom life, with all its advantages, is so full of bitterness, so intolerable a burthen, that they long to be at rest in the grave.

THE REST FOR WHICH THE CHRISTIAN YEARNS.

But, the true Christian, whether the poorest peasant, the most ill-requited laborer, or the man or woman placed in the highest position, and conscious of the heaviest responsibility, the rest which comes with the end of present toil and care, is not the mere cessation from labor, nor the mere relief from sorrow and trouble.

It is, above all things, for pure and lofty souls the release from all the moral dangers—from the fear of temptation and sin, from the terrors of the judgment following speedily after death, and from the uncertainty of one's eternal fate. For the man or the woman who look their last upon earth, who have kept the faith, fought the good fight, and been true to the God of their salvation, the Judge has comforts in store for the last hour, and sweet sentiments of filial trust, enabling the departing soul to look forward to meeting, on the frontier of His kingdom, with the Creator, the Father, the Saviour, in whose hand is peace, and rest, and length of days.

We know in whom we believe, in whom we trust, and whom we serve. we strive to live, to labor, to suffer for Him here; we make His will our own. Is it not from His lips we shall hear:

"Well done, thou good and faithful servant! . . . Enter into the joy of thy Lord!"

Our rest is to be with Christ, to be with Him everlastingly, in the joys of His most glorious and most blissful existence.

Who has ever thought out fully and explained to the world what it is to be *with Christ* in His kingdom—to be *with Him everlastingly?*

This companionship and union is the supernatural

destiny for which man was created and redeemed. It is the end of all God's providence and government here below. It is to secure this companionship, this union with Christ, and with the glorious society of angels and saints, forming one moral person with Him, that God disposes all things, counting on man's free co-operation with His grace.

THE DESTINY FOR WHICH MAN WAS CREATED.

To be with Christ, with God everlastingly, is our destiny. The following chapters will set forth the meaning of these words, and tell the reader something of the mighty and blissful reality.

In this present chapter, we would fain have you meditate with us how that same Eternal Word and Wisdom by whom God created all things and through whom He disposeth all things in conformity with that sublime end, wished by the Incarnation to be "God with us" upon earth, in order to teach us to be worthy of being ourselves, as it were, God's, the adopted sons of God, *with Him* eternally in Heaven.

I.

GOD WITH US.

What was that near and sensible presence, that familiar, almost, and friendly intercourse, with which God honored Moses all through the course of the latter's long mission and arduous labors of freeing and guiding God's people toward the Promised Land? The interpreters of Holy Writ have seen in the Angel-Jehovah, through whose ministry the miracles were performed in Egypt, the Law delivered on the Mount, and the constitutions of the Twelve Confederated Tribes were framed, the Person of the Eternal Word thus veiling His Majesty under the appearance of an angel and preluding the Incarnation. Be that as it may, and whether it be really Jehovah Himself who spoke directly to the Hebrew deliverer, or an angel commissioned to speak in His name and act with His power and authority, Moses, so far as we can judge, reverenced and worshiped the Speaker, Revealer, and Guide as very God. The nearness to that veiled Majesty, from the day when the vision appeared amid the burning bush to Mount Sinai, with its alternate scenes of abject terror and insolent idol-worship, produced in Moses not only resistless yearning to see, without cloud or veil, the divine Being who spoke to him, but also unbounded love for God's people.

When the idolators have been signally punished for their sin, this love of charity for the people breaks forth in the touching prayer: "'I beseech Thee, this people hath sinned a heinous sin, and they have made themselves gods of gold. Either forgive this trespass, or, if Thou do not, strike me out of the book which Thou hast written.' And the Lord answered him: 'He that hath sinned against Me, him will I strike out of My book; but go thou and lead this people whither I have told thee; My angel shall go before thee.'"*

Here it is plainly intimated that it is the Lord of Angels Himself who has been the Revealer; that He it is against whom, while in communication

---

* Exodus, xxxii, 31-34.

with Moses on the near mountain-top, the sin of idolatry was committed. He is unwilling further to continue this nearness to "a stiff-necked people."

"And Moses said to the Lord: 'Thou commandest me to lead forth this people, and Thou dost not let me know whom Thou wilt send with me, especially whereas Thou hast said: "I know thee by name, and thou hast found favor in My sight." If, therefore, I have found favor in Thy sight, show me Thy face, that I may know Thee, and may find grace before Thy eyes. Look upon Thy people, this nation.'

"SHEW ME THY FACE."

"And the Lord said: 'My face shall go before thee, and I will give thee rest.' And Moses said: 'If Thou Thyself dost not go before, bring us not out of this place. For how shall we be able to know, I and Thy people, that we have found grace in Thy sight *unless Thou walk with us*, that we may be glorified by all the people that dwell upon the earth?'" *

Then follows the ardent request that the Godhead should unveil Himself to Moses, and the answer, "I will show thee *all good*."

So, as we see in this pregnant prophetic passage, the Hebrew leader would not be satisfied to have, in the fulfillment of his mission, the assurance that God would be with them by His presence in power, by the terror of His might, as shown in Egypt, and signified by the words, "My *face* shall go before thee." He wanted an indwelling of the Godhead with His people; He was to "walk with them;"

---
* Exodus, xxxiii, 12-16.

He whose being is "all good," the infinite truth and the infinite perfection and loveliness, must be in their midst as their very own to satisfy the craving of the true of heart and noble of soul among them.

WE YEARN TO BEHOLD GOD FACE TO FACE.

Moses spoke the yearning of the human soul enlightened by faith and undismayed by conscious sin: "Shew me Thy glory!" But the privilege of beholding in its essence the unveiled and awful majesty of God is one reserved to the supernatural perfection of man in the life to come. Neither our bodily eyes in this mortal state, nor the eyes of our soul can look upon the divine Being as He is in Himself. To be raised to the divine condition and endowed with the almost divine powers fitting us for the Beatific Vision, is the reward of our present merits through His grace, who is the Author, Repairer, and Perfecter of our nature.

Listen then to what the Hebrew lawgiver relates of the manner in which God fulfilled, in a certain measure, the ardent prayer of His servant:

"And when the Lord was come down in a cloud, Moses stood with Him, calling upon the name of the Lord. And when He passed before him, he said, 'O Lord! the Lord God! merciful and gracious, patient and of much compassion, and *true;* who keepest mercy unto thousands; who takest away iniquity, and wickedness, and sin; and no man of himself is innocent before Thee.' . . . And Moses, making haste, bowed down prostrate upon the earth, and adoring." *

---

* Exodus, xxxiv, 5-8.

OUR EMMANUEL—OUR "GOD WITH US."

Aye, we can only look upon the Sun of Righteousness, as through a cloud, with these bodily and unhallowed eyes of ours. We may feel that He is near us; that He comes as He did in the Tabernacle of Moses, or in the Temple of Solomon, veiled in a cloud to dwell with us and be our Emmanuel. He is "God with us," our Helper, our Healer, merciful, patient, compassionate of our sufferings and misery, taking away iniquity and sin; *true* to us in His promises, and true in His teachings, our faithful and infallible Guide.

All this He is while "walking *with us* in the way," and abiding as our Guest in our tabernacles. But what shall it be, when the journey is over, and He takes us to Himself, to be where He is, *with Himself* inseparably and eternally?

FORESHADOWING.

This is the sweet mystery of the life to come, the shoreless ocean of light, of truth supernal, of heavenly bliss, whose abysses we have to explore in these chapters—as a son and heir after long wandering from the glorious patrimony and the splendid halls of his ancestors is allowed by night to enter stealthily, and to be led by some devoted old servant through every portion of the noble mansion which is one day to be his own. He can only pass through rapidly, fearfully; for he is but the unreconciled, unacknowledged prodigal; while outside the regal home all is shrouded in the darkness of night.

Even so may we in spirit, guided by the light of the divine oracles, and directed by the teaching of the Church, soar above those heights, descend into those depths, where all is so radiant with the divinest hope, so well defined in every detail by the Spirit of God.

But, in studying what light and what warmth the near Presence of God in the Old Law shed upon His people, upon His chosen servants, and those who sought Him with their whole heart, we are led necessarily to the very feet of the Incarnate God in the New Law, to that Home in Nazareth, where He abode as the Carpenter's Son during thirty years of His life among us.

THE WORK OUR EMMANUEL DID AMONG US.

Surely, the Only-Begotten Son, in coming down among us, came also "in a cloud;" and while He dwelt among us, He busied Himself in taking away iniquity and sin. The saintly precursor, whose light was only the forerunner of our Day-Star, said of Him, as he pointed Him out to the multitudes at the Jordan: "Behold the Lamb of God, who taketh away the sins of the world!"

Not merely did He busy Himself with paying the ransom of our sins, and expiating our guilt, but He, the merciful, the compassionate, and the *true*, applied Himself to repairing the consequences of sin. More than that. He sought to banish from our hearts and our lives the fruitful causes of sin—pride, vanity, sensuality, the lust of pleasure, and the lust of gold. He sought to kindle in our souls the fire of divinest generosity, by filling them with the supernatural love of His Father and Himself, as well as with the love of the human brotherhood as the inseparable fruit of the love of the Father. His grace—that is, the influence of His teaching and example, aided by special inspirations enlightening our mind and a corresponding impulse to the heart—tends to make us practice toward God and our brethren the humility which He practiced by embracing ignominy, shame, and suffering, in order to glorify God and save the world.

He lived among us in obscurity, poverty, toil and persecution, and died crowned with thorns and nailed to a cross between malefactors, that we might learn the secret of His hidden wisdom, which chooses the weakest instruments to accomplish the mightiest purposes; vanquishes sin, death and hell by the shame of the cross; lifts man to heaven, and enables him to sanctify and lift up the world with himself by self-denial and self-sacrifice.

THE VIRTUE THAT WENT OUT OF HIM.

See how all who were nearest and dearest to our *Emmanuel* learned this lesson of a wisdom all hidden and divine, from the influence of His grace, the reading of His life, the light which escaped from within the cloud, and the secret fire which the nearness of that mighty Heart kindled in theirs. Of Joseph's death we know nothing from the Gospels. But we may guess the rest, from the generosity displayed, at the divine command, in silencing his own scruples,* in flying into exile at a moment's warning with Mother and Babe, in abiding there amid dangers, poverty, and obscurity till warned to return, and then returning forthwith to face new dangers, new persecutions, hardship and obloquy, in fulfillment of the divine trust. Such a man showed that the Holy Ghost had taught him to "esteem the

---
* St. Matthew, 1, 19-24.

reproach of Christ greater riches than the treasure of the Egyptians." *

He, had he been among the living, would have stood with the Blessed Mother and St. John beneath the wood which bore our Ransom, as His shame and suffering paid the price of all our pride and sensuality. But by following Him to the cross she, as well as the holy women who had been in Galilee the companions of her ministrations to Christ, showed how they had "learned Christ." So did John; and so, in a different measure, did presently the other Apostles and Disciples. Who could enable men to "learn Christ, and Christ Crucified," but the Spirit of Christ?

After the Ascension that Spirit will be poured down on Apostles and Disciples, and divine generosity, manifesting itself in self-denial and self-sacrifice, in glorying in the cross, and in being crucified for the love and the name of Christ, will be like the rush of inundating waters, flooding the whole earth.

Such was the first result of Christ's stay upon earth; such fruits followed the first hidden husbandry of our Emmanuel, working silently, obscurely upon the minds, the hearts, the lives of men and women around them at Nazareth, at Bethlehem, in Jerusalem, in Samaria, among the "hundred towns of Galilee," and even in Egypt, where the stay of the divine Babe, like the central heat of the earth, when winter has passed with her thick overlying snows, covers hill and plain with verdure and bloom, burst later into the glories of Alexandria and the Thebaid.

---
* Hebrews, xi, 26.

To Joseph and Mary; to Elizabeth and Zachary; to John the Baptist; to holy Simeon and Anna; to the shepherds of Bethlehem, as they worshiped at His crib; to the Apostles attracted to His Person by the spell of a hidden magnetism, as to the multitudes who flocked to hear Him around Genesareth, and followed Him across the lake and into the wilderness; to the crowds of the afflicted, the suffering, the sick, and the maimed, "a virtue went out of Him," healing, creating anew, enlightening the mind, purifying the heart and firing it, exalting and sanctifying the whole nature of man. The unborn babe felt that virtue as the hidden God was borne across his parent's threshold. The mothers of both precursor and Redeemer are filled with His Spirit, and pour forth their soul in adoration, praise and prophecy, when their Emmanuel brings them for the first time together.

THE CLOUD LIFTED A MOMENT MAKES EARTH HEAVEN.

When, on the Mount of Transfiguration, He allows some of the hidden glory to shine forth and irradiate the body about to be spit upon, scourged, and crucified, as the hill-top on which He thus appeared was suddenly changed into heaven, Peter, in the name of his two companions, could only exclaim in the excess of his rapture: "Lord, it is good to be here!" And he would fain have pitched his tent and fixed his abode forever amid these splendors and the intoxicating spiritual delights of this new Presence.

It was a foretaste of heaven, so to be *with Christ*.

But, oh, the difference between the glory and delight of Tabor and the clear vision and bliss of Paradise!

Only that once did our Emmanuel treat those who were to promulgate His law to the nations and be His witnesses to the ends of the earth as He had treated Moses in the passage quoted above. Moses and Elias were both there to bear their testimony to His divinity. Thus did the Old Testament affirm the divinity of the New—the Law and the Prophets point to Christ as the fulfillment of all. Moses could only gaze upon the cloud which concealed the inaccessible brightness of the divine Majesty, or, when the Vision had passed from before the place where he was hidden in the rock, catch a glimpse of the vanishing glory, as one can bear to look at the western horizon, on the fiery radiance which the just sinking sun leaves upon earth and sky. But Moses was privileged in the New Testament to look upon the glorified face of Him who was very God in the flesh, Him on whose face we shall first look in Heaven ere the clear splendors of the Beatic Vision burst upon our sight. "In His light we shall see the *Light*."

WALKING WITH US IN THE WAY.

The secret but powerful and sweet action of our "hidden God and Saviour" on all to whom He drew near upon earth is well exemplified in what is related by St. Luke of the two Disciples journeying toward Emmaus on the day of our Lord's Resurrection.

They were "talking together of all these things which had happened. And it came to pass, that while they talked and reasoned with themselves, *Jesus* Himself also drawing near went with them. But their eyes were held that they should not know Him." *

Their minds, their hearts, were full of Him. Their faith, as yet, was only in its germinal state, like the bud on the fruit tree in early spring, ready to burst its enclosure, but fearing the nipping frost. He sets about teaching them, laying before them the entire scheme of Redemption and enlightening their eyes to perceive the necessary completion of the divine whole in the Crucifixion and Resurrection of Jesus Christ. Our Emmanuel had " walked with them" the remainder of the way. The spell of His presence and word was on them. They could not bear to part with such a Teacher and Comforter. "Stay with us, because it is toward evening, and the day is now far spent."

He yields, enters their present abode, seats Himself at their table, "took bread, and blessed and brake, and gave to them. And their eyes were opened, and they knew Him, and He vanished out of their sight. And they said one to the other: 'Was not our heart burning within us, whilst He spoke in the way, and opened to us the Scriptures?'

"And rising up the same hour, they went back to Jerusalem; and they found the eleven gathered together, and those that were with them, saying: 'The Lord is risen, indeed, and hath appeared to Simon.' And *they* (the two Disciples) told what things were done in the way; and how they knew Him in the breaking of bread. Now, while they were speaking these things, *Jesus* stood in the midst of them, and saith to them : ' *Peace be to you. It is I. Fear not.*'

---
*St. Luke, xxiv, 14-16.

"But they being troubled and frighted, supposed that they saw a spirit. And he said to them: 'Why are you troubled, and why do thoughts arise in your hearts? See My hands and feet, that it is Myself; handle, and see: for a spirit hath not flesh and bones, as you see Me to have.' And when He said this, He showed them His hands and feet."*

O Adonai, Emmanuel—Thou sweet Son of the Virgin Mary, Thou who .condescendest to become bone of our bone, and flesh of our flesh—how we still need that Thou shouldst be what Thou art indeed—God very near and dear to us—*the God of our heart!*

WE KNOW HIM IN "THE BREAKING OF THE BREAD."

Even now, when our hearts are troubled "in the way," as we journey painfully along amid the pitfalls of the road, and the mists and darkness that beset our path, how we need that Thou shouldst "draw near and go with us!" that thou shouldst open our minds to understand the things of God and His ways! that Thou shouldst touch our hearts with one secret spark of the fire from above! We need that Thou shouldst tarry with us when the shadows lengthen on our path "toward evening," and our day is far spent." Ah, tarry with us, and let us, too, "know Thee in the breaking of Bread."

O Bread of Life, come down from heaven; how many have seen every cloud of doubt vanish as they sate at that Table with Thee, where Thou blessest, breakest, and givest Thy supersubstantial Bread;" and Thy gift is like fire from heaven laid on their

---
* St. Luke, xxiv, 30-40.

hearts to warm, to comfort, to strengthen, to inflame!

The two Disciples, when they had partaken of this Bread, and felt the sensible Presence withdrawn, at once followed the prompting of the divine charity which filled them. They return to impart to the eleven and the Disciples in Jerusalem the knowledge of His Resurrection, only to learn from them that Simon Peter had seen Him. And then they relate their own wonderful experience. But while the little band are thus rejoicing and talking about Him, lo! there He is in their midst!

Poor human nature! They are all burning with the desire to look upon His face; to hear the sounds of His loved voice; to fall at the feet so cruelly pierced for them on the cross; to feel the forgiving touch of these hands so often raised over themselves in blessing! And when He stands before them—not dazzling them with the glories of His risen body, but, as ever, veiling even the human majesty of His person—they think they "see a spirit," and are all trouble and fright!

Poor human nature! pitiable alike in its weakness and in its presumption! There are those among us who think that they could bear the sight of God's own native brightness and majesty, as He sees and knows Himself; and that their unaided power of intellect could contemplate, grasp and fathom "the multitude of His greatness;" measure from end to end the Infinite in every line of those manifold perfections, which, by their very nature, exclude all limit and measure; and yet they are frightened by the mere thought of seeing a poor human disembodied spirit—a ghost!

He has proved Himself to be very God by announcing beforehand to these same men that He would be put to death shamefully and rise the third day by His own divine power. This miracle of miracles is now accomplished. They behold Him in flesh and blood; and though Simon has thus seen Him and attested the fact to the other Apostles, and though the two Disciples who have just spoken attest a similar experience, they suppose that the risen Christ is only a spirit!

But that risen Body which He invites them to touch and feel is the pledge and prophecy of their own resurrection. The God-Man who, once freed from the grave, hastens to show Himself to them, to make them touch and feel these yawning wounds in hands and feet, is He in the light of whose countenance we shall see the essence of the Deity without cloud or veil in the life to come.

Then it is we shall understand what it must be to be *with Christ* when the infirmities of our present state shall have passed away, when we shall look upon His countenance on the throne of His kingdom without "trouble or fright," and when the glories of that face divine will prepare us for the Beatific Vision.

The best of us while "on the way," the most enlightened in human and divine knowledge, are not without uneasiness, doubt, and sinking of the heart when we look beyond the horizon of the present existence, and endeavor to penetrate beyond the dark and deep gulf which death opens beneath our feet. We need to take up the divine Book, to meditate His battle with suffering and agony, to read of His arising immortal from the grave, of the love which made Him hasten to reveal Himself to His own. We feel that it is to reassure us in our half-belief, in our hesitation between His remembered promises and the scoffing and skepticism of the anti-Christian world, that He stands all of a sudden in the midst of the Disciples, with the greeting: "*Peace be with you. It is I. Fear not!*"

CHAPTER III.

YEARNING TO BE "WITH CHRIST" AT THE END OF THE WAY.

II.

"*TO BE DISSOLVED AND BE WITH CHRIST.*"

> Dear Friend, far off, my lost desire,
>   So far, so near in woe and weal;
>   O loved the most, when most I feel
> There is a lower and a higher;
> Known and unknown, human, divine;
>   Sweet human hand and lip and eye;
>   Dear heavenly Friend, that canst not die,
> Mine, mine forever, ever mine!
> —*Tennyson.*

Paul was not, as we know, one of the eleven, or one even of the Disciples gathered "for fear of the Jews" in the upper chamber on that memorable evening of Christ's Resurrection. He was not privileged to be near the person of our Emmanuel either before His crucifixion or before His ascension. He was during the first stage of their apostolic preaching their bitter antagonist, the declared enemy of Christ.

And then came the miracle of his conversion—that extraordinary scene on the road to Damascus, when the Crucified appeared to him, when the light from His glorified countenance flashed upon the persecutor, overthrew him as with the suddenness of a thunderbolt, blinded him while opening up to the truth the eyes of his soul, and changed Saul into a chosen vessel of apostolic zeal.

TRANSFORMED BY MEETING CHRIST ON THE WAY.

How utterly the convert gave himself up to the Master as an instrument to be used by the divine Hand for any and every purpose we also know. The blood of Stephen, which he had shed by the hands of others, was like a voice crying out from the ground whithersoever he turned, urging him to superhuman toils in the service of the cause he had once blasphemed. He had heard Stephen's dying words: "Behold, I see the heavens opened, and the Son of Man standing on the right hand of God." *

It became Saul's privilege while yet in the flesh, and in the very midst of his apostolic labors, to be carried by the Spirit of God up to the very portals of that heavenly kingdom, to look upon its splendors, and hear the language of its inhabitants. Restored to earth and its labors, the Apostle ran his race as if his were the fire and strength and eloquence of a seraph.

THE SERAPHIC FIRE OF THE APOSTLE.

In his later epistles his love for our Lord, and for the Father who in Christ gave us all things desirable for time and eternity, is like a fire which has long been secretly growing, growing till the flames burst forth into a mighty conflagration. The super-

---
* Acts, vii, 55.

natural fire glows and burns in every page and line. When he speaks of that mystery of charity by which the Eternal Wisdom and Goodness planned our creation and redemption, our sanctification here below and deification in the life to come, the great Apostle is beside himself. The vision of this loving and fatherly Providence, compelling all things to conspire towards our good, overwhelms this ardent soul. His language is full of breaks and reticences, as if hand and pen could not keep up with the torrent of thought and feeling. Read the first chapter of the Epistle to the Ephesians to have some idea of the mighty forces which seemed to lift this Elias of the New Testament above the earth, and to be continually carrying him heavenward, as in a vehicle of flame.

OH! THE UNSEARCHABLE RICHES OF CHRIST.

"To me," he says, "the least of all the Saints, is given this grace to preach among the Gentiles the unsearchable riches of Christ, and to enlighten all men, that they may see what is the dispensation of the mystery which hath been hidden from eternity in God, who created all things; that the manifold wisdom of God may be made known to the principalities and powers in the heavenly places through the Church, according to the eternal purpose which He made in Christ Jesus our Lord—in whom we have boldness and access with confidence by the faith of Him.

"Wherefore, I pray you not to faint at my tribulations for you, which is your glory. For this cause I bow my knees to the Father of our Lord Jesus Christ, of whom all paternity in heaven and earth is named, that He would grant you, according to the riches of His glory, to be strengthened by His Spirit with might unto the inward man; that Christ may dwell by faith in your hearts; that, being rooted and founded in charity, you may be able to comprehend, with all the Saints, what is the breadth, and length, and height, and depth. . . . To know also the charity of Christ, which surpasseth all knowledge, that you may be filled unto all the fullness of God." *

WAITING AT THE GATES.

All this was written from his prison in Rome, with the near prospect of a martyr's death before his eyes. The same sentiments, the same exultant love for Christ, and overflowing tenderness for the spiritual children left behind in Greece, Macedonia and Asia Minor, are manifest in the Epistle to the Philippians, written at the same time and from the same prison. He yearns for that heavenly companionship with the Master, of which he had been vouchsafed a foretaste; he, too, would be at rest with that glorious company of the heavenly Jerusalem. But the ravening wolves were abroad among the flock he had gathered to Christ, and how could he forsake them in their danger, even with the prospect of the near felicity? "For to me, to live is Christ: and to die is gain. . . . I am straitened between two; *having a desire to be dissolved and to be with Christ*, a thing by far the better." †

The yearning to be plunged into that abyss of brightness, of which he had only had a glimpse at the gates of Paradise; the desire to be forever at rest at the feet of the Master on whose face he had

---
* Ephesians, iii, 8-19.　　† Philippians, i, 21-23.

looked, half-blinded by the glory; the attraction toward that blissful company of angels and Saints, who had hailed him in advance as one of their own; such were his preoccupations: how could he help preferring "to be dissolved, and to be with Christ?"

"SEEK THE THINGS THAT ARE ABOVE."

"If you be risen with Christ," he writes at the same time to the Christians of Colossae, "seek the things that are above, where Christ is sitting at the right hand of God: mind the things that are above, not the things that are upon the earth. For you are dead; and your life is hid with Christ in God." *

WHAT "DISSOLUTION" MEANS FOR THE CHRISTIAN.

We are, therefore, brought in spirit to consider, with infinite reverence and awe, what it is "to be dissolved and to be with Christ;" and thus to be "able to comprehend, with all the Saints, what is the breadth and length, and height and depth," of the glory and felicity which this everlasting companionship bestows.

"To be dissolved," to be separated temporarily from this body, from the manifold ties which bind even the lowliest to this present life and its associations, has no terrors for the soul who has lived, labored, and suffered for Christ, for whom God's will, in life and in death, has been the supreme law of love and duty. The perfect charity which makes the true Christian look up to the divine honor and glory as the aim of every deed and aspiration, to the divine pleasure as the source of every satisfaction and enjoyment, is only the preparation for that

---

*Colossians, iii, 1-3.

better, that perfect state, in which God is to fulfill to the utmost the purest aspirations, the holiest desires, of His faithful servant's will.

Death, then—the "dissolution" which fills the sinful, the worldly, the slave to self-will, with uncontrollable fear and agony—is bereft of all terrors for such as die in perfect charity with Christ; a charity which also implies the supernatural love of all mankind, and the ardent wish to satisfy all the claims of divine and human justice.

To the mind's eye of him who writes this page a twofold instance of this heaven-sent charity is now vividly present—the one taken from the lowliest walks of life, the other from the very highest.

HOW THE POOR OF CHRIST DIE.

It is July in Canada, in the memorable year 1847. We are at the Quarantine Station, some thirty miles below Quebec. On a little island ("Grosse Isle"), midway in the St. Lawrence, where it turns seaward and broadens out into the dimensions of a lake beneath the capes of the northern mountains, are several thousands of the fever-stricken exiles of Ireland, who have vainly fled from famine in their own native country, or been improvidently and cruelly heaped by the poor-house authorities in yonder emigrant ships. Of these, between twenty and thirty are riding at anchor on the fiery bosom of the broad brackish stream, with many thousands more of the dying, the sick, the famishing, and the vainly expectant, strong of limb and stout of heart. There is not hospital accommodation on the barren, uninhabited island for one-fifth of the diseased multitude. There is not a single spring of fresh and wholesome water there for the fevered wretches, who roam about among the rocks, with the thermometer above 90°, in quest of a cool, refreshing draught.

After a long day's labor, on ship and shore, the three priests who had come, in their turn, to minister to the sick and dying, had lain down for a few hours of needed repose, when the sound of voices beneath our window awakened one, at least, of the the three—the only one whom these poor exiles could claim for their countryman. Our servant was warmly expostulating with a woman who was as warmly pleading to see "the priest."

"Sure, I know it's half-dead they must be, the darlin' gintlemin, every one of thim. But my poor boy is tuk very sudden intirely, and he won't give me any pace till I bring him the priest. An' it's meself is not much better, God help me, with the faver, and the thurst, and the grief that is breaking my heart. For I have buried three of thim since we left Cork. And he is the only wan I have now, glory be to God."

And the voice sank into a low and pitiful wail. By this time the clergyman had come out into the sultry midnight air; and at his sight the poor mother poured forth a hymn of thanksgiving to God in that fervent, figurative, and eloquent language which wells so naturally from Irish lips up from the warm depths of the Irish heart. The woman was scarcely able to stand. The servant, who was himself a devoted man, and had come to the place from no mercenary motive, brought her out a refreshing and invigorating draught, together with some wholesome food wrapped in a paper.

She summoned all her remaining strength to guide the missionary to where she had left her dying son, still venting her gratitude in bursts of fervent thanksgiving to God and His minister. Happily, some of the hospital nurses who had directed the poor creature to the priest's house, met us as we blundered forward in the darkness, and half-supported, half-carried her to where her son was. He had found no place in tent or hospital when landed with his mother on the island during the afternoon, and, like hundreds of others, had dragged himself down to the beach, hoping to slake his intense thirst in the brackish waters. He had drunk copiously of them, and they had fearfully increased both the dysentery, from which he was suffering, and the malignant ship-fever, which had only half-declared itself at his landing.

Some of their fellow-immigrants, compassionating both mother and son, had found them a shady nook among the rocks, and beneath the shelter of some scrubby, overhanging firs. There, lying on a bundle of clothes, or bedding—the only remnant saved by the poor widow from the wreck of her home—lay a youth of twenty summers, a Tipperary boy, and no unworthy specimen of a noble race of men. The priest lost no time in doing his holy work with the dying man; for dying he was, with such fearful suddenness and rapidity did the malignant fever, complicated as it was with dysentery, the heat of the climate, and the absence of all proper dietary and medical treatment, carry off its victims. The boy was already half-delirious. But a draught from the cool and stimulating beverage brought by the clergyman restored the sufferer to momentary consciousness and vigor. He had been well brought up by parents who had known better fortunes; and all the piety of a pure soul and a generous nature burst forth at the sight of the priest and the near prospect of death. His only care in dying was about his poor, lonely, widowed mother. But when the priest promised him that she should not be friendless, all his thoughts were for God.

"I have seen so many die on ship-board, your Reverence," he said, "without priest or Sacraments, that I bless God from the bottom of my heart for having sent you to me." He had been to confession and Communion, as well as his mother, before setting sail. They had lived ever since in the near presence of death, of God, and of judgment, keeping their souls from sin. In the Viaticum given that night beneath the stars, with the tide-water of the great river beating on the rocks near at hand, and the guardian-angels of the Irish race kneeling invisibly around, He who was born in a cave by the wayside, and laid on the straw of a poor cold crib, came to be, to the young exile from far-away Tipperary, the pledge of the eternal possession.

Oh, never did the divine Sacraments and consolations of the Christian faith appear more sublime or more comforting than amid all the horrors and desolation of Grosse Isle!

GOING HOME!

"Sure, God has been good to us, acushla ma chree," she said, as she sate her down by her boy's side, when the last rite was ended, and the last blessing given, and had taken the weary, aching head on her lap. "Sure 'tis Himself has come for you, asthore, to take you to Himself. It's in His own blessed heaven you'll soon be, avourneen; and I'll not be long behind, plase God. For it's tired I am of this world, an' I'm longin' to be with God, an' with your father and the childher."

And she fondly kissed the face turned up to her in the faint light of our lantern.

The missionary, on his return to his cottage, sent back with one of the sick-nurses a warm shawl to protect the widow and her son from the heavy night dew, and some cooling drink for them. The next morning, as soon as he could, he hastened to the spot where he had left them, resolved to find them as speedily as possible a shelter from the burning sun. The boy was already dead, and some of the other able-bodied immigrants were with the disconsolate mother, offering whatever comfort and aid they could in their utter helplessness. She still sat with her back against the rock, as we had left her some six or seven hours previously, supporting the head of her son on her lap, and talking to him in a low, sweet voice, as if she beheld him in the better world.

When she became aware of the priest's presence, she looked up at him with hollow, tearless eyes, but with a rapt expression, and a countenance that seemed touched with a light from beyond the grave.

"Ah, then, ye're welcome, your Reverence," she said. "He's *at home* now, thank God. . . . Yes, asthore ma chree, it's at home you are at last; and the priest's blessing was on you when you were near the end," she went on, looking down fondly on the calm young face of him who seemed to sleep so sweetly on the maternal bosom.

"Och, then, it's better for you to be with God, alanna, than to be thryin' to build up a cabin for the ould mother among strangers, far away from your own and from blessed Ireland. God'll soon bring me to where you're all gone before me." And, as she spoke, the words fell from her lips one by one, wearily, almost inaudibly at the last.

The missionary, deeply moved, and trying to steel himself against emotions, which took away much of the strength he needed, spoke to the bereaved mother as tenderly as he could. But she heard him not. She had fainted. When she recovered consciousness, it was evident that the strength of maternal love, which had till then kept her up, was giving way to the terrible fever. The change from ship-board to the open air, and the fever-laden atmosphere of the island, with a day and night of exposure, had fearfully developed the germs of the disease in her system.

The missionary had her carried to the little chapel near his cottage; it had been changed into an hospital. He managed—the interior being already filled—to place a cot for the now delirious and unconscious mother on the shady side of the chapel, where kind hands would minister to her.

Why delay the reader? Before sunset that evening the dead body of her tall, handsome son was laid with those of more than a hundred other victims in one common grave, and the Church's *Requiem*, the sublime and beautiful prayers for eternal rest and the surpassing peace of that other world, was said above these remains with such a feeling of holy exultation as the priests in the catacombs laid to rest the bodies of the early martyrs. For he who writes these words attests before heaven and earth that the sufferers to whom he ministered on that island appeared to him confessors and martyrs of the faith, men and women whose supreme care was to keep their souls from sin in the perpetual expectation of death and judgment.

A day or two afterward, the poor widow from Tipperary breathed her last. In her own beautiful and most truthful language, she " went home "—to that home where every holy thought and aim, every holy word and deed, every pang of body and spirit borne for His love, who remembers all, has its unspeakably great reward. "Let my soul die the death of the just, and my last end be like to them!"*

SPAIN'S MOST GLORIOUS SON.

HOW CHRISTIAN KINGS DIE.

We have seen how, among a deeply-religious people, death is considered only to be the end of the road that leads to the everlasting home, the close of our earthly pilgrimage, the secure rest provided after faithful labor and long waiting at the feet, in the bosom, and in the house of our Father and Creator. The very expression, "going home," and the simple, heaven-sent faith underlying it, are familiar sentiments and language among a whole people long and much tried for their religion, and to whom that religion, with its promises, was the treasure supremely cherished.

---

* Numbers, xxiii, 10.

We have now to see how Christian kings know how to die the death of the Saints after having led a heroic and blameless life.

In the Alcazar of Seville, the most beautiful relic of the domestic architecture of the Moors left in Spain after the Alhambra of Granada, the royal officers in charge of the palace will show you through a succession of splendid courts and apartments, as well in the modern portion dating from the time of Ferdinand and Isabella as the more ancient mediæval portion repaired and rebuilt by Pedro I. (surnamed, wrongly, the Cruel). We were not insensible to the exquisite artistic beauties abounding everywhere, nor ignorant of the legends—authentic and otherwise—attaching to these glittering marble courts and the historic apartments. For we had studied in Seville itself the history of its kings and its palaces. But the guides only related to us the story of Don Pedro's terrible revenge or justice, or the anecdotes connecting Christopher Columbus with the modern portions of the pile. We remembered that the Alcazar had been the last dwelling place of the conqueror of Seville, St. Ferdinand, of Castile, and Leon, the twin-soul of his cousin, St. Louis, King of France, and one of the truest men and greatest Christians of all time.

We told the chief guide that the memory of St. Ferdinand was dearer far to us than the misdeeds of the Arabs and Moors who had preceded him in Seville, than the crimes—imputed or real—of the degenerate descendants of the warrior-saint. We besought him to show us the apartments occupied by St. Ferdinand. Touched to the heart, evidently by our unusual demand, and the earnestness with which we urged it, he at once led us to the rooms which the traditions of the place point out as those occupied by Ferdinand. "This," the man said, "was his bed-chamber, and here he received the last Sacraments and died." We had already been privileged to kneel at his tomb in the neighboring cathedral, and to look leisurely on that face which corruption has not touched. We now knelt reverently on the spot where he breathed his last, lying in sackcloth and ashes on the marble floor. The reverence thus paid to the memory of those who have been Christlike in life and death, is homage paid to Christ Himself, who "is wonderful in His Saints."

In the career of St. Ferdinand—from his boyhood so tenderly watched over and trained to all moral goodness and greatness by his heroic mother; from his early manhood, when she resigned in his favor, and placed on his head her own crown of Castile; all through his great undertakings and achievements for the redemption of Spain from the Moslem, and his fatherly enactments for the happiness of his people, to the conquest of Cordova, and Jaen, and Seville—there is enough of the real romance of war and chivalry, enough of the loftiest heroism in the deeds of the saintly king and his followers to furnish the matter of a dozen epic poems. The siege and fall of Seville alone surpasses in varied incident, and real grandeur of spirit and exploit, anything found in Homer or Virgil.

Ferdinand, sick almost to death from the beginning to the end of this successful crusade against the Moors, was still the light and life of the enterprise; the wise and skillful commander of a great, proud and mixed host; the ever-watchful and provident ruler of his own kingdoms. In all, his army and his people knew him to be not only wise in council, indefatigable, skillful, unconquered in the field, but the unwearied man of prayer in his own privacy—the man of God in all things.

Humane to the Mohammedans in their defeat, he respected their every right, save that of retaining possession of Spanish soil. Everything that a victorious prince could do to protect their property and persons, and to facilitate their passage to Africa or the neighboring Moslem States, St. Ferdinand did. For the peopling of the recovered principalities, and the regulation of their temporal and religious concerns, he took every measure that conscience and wisdom suggested.

So intent was he on securing the success of this mighty undertaking, that he refused to leave his post of command to comfort his dying mother, whom he had so many reasons for revering and worshiping as he did. When Seville fell, the progress of the terrible disease which preyed upon him did not prevent him for a single day from pushing his conquests further, and securing them against all enemies, and from discharging every duty of the sovereign, the legislator, the Christian, and the man.

No king, all through the Christian ages, ever beheld around him so many heroic knights and soldiers; so many men then and now reverenced as saints, as stood around Ferdinand III, of Castile, and Leon, on the day they returned thanks to the God of victories in the magnificent mosque of Seville, just consecrated as a Christian temple.

And when Seville heard that her saintly king was near his death, never was death-bed surrounded by a throng as illustrious, or marked by more touching circumstances—save only that of St. Louis, some years later, on the burning, plague-stricken shores of Northern Africa.

When they told Ferdinand that his last day had come, the man whose life had been one long act of devotion to the divine glory, and self-sacrifice to the good of Spain and her people, only trembled lest he had left unfulfilled any one of the many duties attached to his high station and responsible office. From his constant intercourse with God in prayer, and the light which purity of heart and life had drawn on his soul, he only derived a deeper sense of humility; of the distance which separates the creature from the Creator; the poor earthly servant from the infinite majesty of the heavenly Master; the sinner, conscious only of his failings, shortcomings, and guilt, from the most holy Judge and Rewarder of all human actions.

Eternity, with its unspeakable grandeur, its glory, and its bliss, seemed to the dying king, as the last waves of life brought him to the shore of God's empire, so far above all human merits, so out of proportion with our nature and our utmost needs and aspirations, that the thought of his own littleness, unworthiness, sinfulness, overwhelmed him. He commanded that they should clothe his tortured frame in sackcloth, and, with a cord round his neck, as one deserving of the worst punishment, to be laid prostrate on the ashes strewn on the floor. With his queen, his sons, nobles, his prelates, and followers in battle, around him, he confessed himself a sinner, deserving only of the divine wrath, and then poured out his soul in appeals for mercy, and tender protestations of his love for God, and his absolute submission to the divine Will.

While princes, prelates, nobles and warriors knelt and wept aloud—they who knew what a beautiful, a spotless, a glorious life was thus ending—they ministered to the king the last Sacraments and consolations of religion. The entire city, the whole of Christian Spain, watched, wept, prayed around that death-bed, around that palace.

To every one of the sublime and touching prayers of the Church, appointed to be said around the death-bed of the Christian, the warrior-king answered in a firm voice with the assistants—with a firmer voice, indeed; for the strongest there were moved beyond all power of self-control.

It was as if beyond the veil, the hosts of angels and Saints appeared with the Judge Himself, so earnestly did each supplication ascend for the soul just arrived on the confines of the world unseen.

"All ye holy Angels and Archangels!
 Pray for him!

"O, ye entire Choir of the Just,
 Pray for him!

"All ye Patriarchs and Prophets,
All ye Apostles and Evangelists,
All ye Disciples of the Lord,
All ye Innocents and Martyrs,
 Pray for him!

"We sinners, O God! beseech Thee to hear us!
That Thou do show him mercy,
 We beseech Thee to hear us!"

And then the startling injunction uttered by the Church, the Mother here below of Christ's children:

"Go forth from this world, O Christian soul, in the name of God, the Father Almighty, who created thee;

"In the name of Jesus Christ, the Son of the living God, who suffered for thee;

"In the name of the Holy Ghost, who was poured forth upon thee . . . . . .

"May thy place this day be in the everlasting peace;

"And thy dwelling in the Holy Sion!

"May Christ deliver thee from all pain, who did Himself endure the cross for thee!

"May Christ deliver thee from the eternal death, who did Himself die for thee!

"May Christ, the Son of the living God, bring thee to the ever-green fields of His Paradise;

"May that true Shepherd acknowledge thee there as one of His own flock;

"May He absolve thee from all thy sins, and give thee a place at His right hand among His own elect.

"May'st thou see thy Redeemer face to face, and, being ever by His side, mayest thou, with blissful eyes, contemplate the truth in its clearness.

"And thus, having become a member of the countless hosts of the blessed, mayest thou enjoy for ever and ever the sweetness of beholding the Godhead!"

So, at the gates of heaven, did the companions in arms of one who had all his life battled in the cause of Christ, plead to the Most Holy and Most Just for the departing soul of a Saint!

So mighty is the empire into which we pass through the vale of the shadow of death! So perfect is the purity without which none find entrance there! So great is the glory, so unspeakable the bliss, so vast and shining the hosts of blessed angels and blessed men reigning there with Christ!

And so, with the deepest humility, and the most loving trust in the God of his salvation, passed from this world the spirit of Ferdinand, of Castile, amid the tears and prayers of a nation, praised, blessed, and mourned by all Christendom.

Is he higher in heaven than the gentle, suffering, faithful and pure-minded mother whose death we related above? It were vain and presumptuous to inquire. Both are *with Christ in God*, inseparably, eternally.

What destiny can be compared to theirs?

Let us follow them in spirit beyond the Veil, and fathom leisurely the meaning of this great comforting truth—that *God* is the reward of the children of God.

CHAPTER IV.

WITH CHRIST.

AT THE FOUNT OF LIFE—THE REALIZATION.

> Lead, Kindly Light, amid the encircling gloom,
>   Lead Thou me on!
> The night is dark, and I am far from *home*!
>   Lead Thou me on!
> Keep Thou my feet; I do not ask to see
> The distant scene—one step enough for me.
>   —*Cardinal Newman.*

THE TWOFOLD KNOWLEDGE CONSTITUTING ETERNAL LIFE.

We can never meditate sufficiently the discourses and passing words of Him who, before the Incarnation, was "the true Light which enlighteneth every man that cometh into this world;"* and who, by His Incarnation, acquired, as it were, a new right to enlighten us, warm our souls into Godlike generosity, and lift our lives up to a divine level in all things.

---
* St. John, i, 8.

St. John, His own near kinsman according to the flesh, and the Disciple favored by His especial friendship, tells us in the same text* that "in Him [that is, in the divine Word from all eternity] was life, and the life was the light of men." At the end of His earthly labors, this heavenly Guide gave us, in His very last discourse, one truth among many, which discloses to us, when seriously pondered, understood, and taken to heart, the whole secret of heavenly bliss:

"This is eternal life: that they may know Thee, the only true God, and Jesus Christ, whom Thou hast sent." †

His passion was just about to begin, and every sentence and word here recorded of Him bears the stamp of a peculiar solemnity. There was a great fitness that He should forearm His Disciples—and through them forearm us—for the terrible struggle which the world wages against Christian truth and the Christian life. He, therefore, endeavors to fix their minds and hearts on the contemplation of the sublime end set before them. For nothing is so powerful to fire the souls of men, and animate them to the performance of the most heroic deeds, as the clear knowledge of a noble, a lofty, a most beneficial end to be reached.

Hence it is that He sets before them clearly the one great purpose for which He had become Man, and for which He was now going to endure a shameful death:

"This is life eternal: that they may know *Thee*, the only true God, and Jesus Christ, whom Thou hast sent."

---

* St. John, 1, 4. † Ibidem, xvii, 3.

This is the life which they must win for themselves by labors and a sacrifice like His own; this is the life for the attainment of which they must teach the whole human race to labor and to suffer, sacrificing everything else, if need be, and deeming every loss a gain, if only the possession of life eternal be secured thereby.

There is between this divine destiny set before the race, and Christ's last sacramental institution, a close and never-to-be-forgotten connection. The Paschal Supper was followed by that Mystic Banquet in which the Eucharistic Bread and Wine are substituted for the sacrificial lamb commemorative of the Passover and the redemption from Egyptian slavery. But this Bread, by a miracle of almighty love, contains the Body of the Lamb of God, who taketh away the sins of the world; and the Eucharistic Wine is the Blood about to be poured out on the cross in atonement of the sins of the entire human race.

REMINDER OF THE PRICE PAID AND THE INHERITANCE PURCHASED.

The Oblation of this Bread and Wine is to be to the end of time, among all peoples, in every clime, the rite recalling the price paid for the life eternal, with its infinite treasures of glory and bliss.

The banquet, in which this Bread is broken and this Wine partaken of daily all over the world, is to remind the believers in Christ and His promises that this supreme and abiding Gift of the God-Man to His own, and the divine Reality it contains, are the pledge of the eternal possession. It is "the mystery of faith" in which the believing soul grasps and holds beneath the sacramental veil Him whom we shall see face to face in the other life. The Bread here broken to us in God's house and at His table is the sign of the union by love and charity which binds together the souls of all God's true children on earth, and which will bind them everlastingly together in heaven. The Wine here poured forth is that blood which flows from the heart of Christ to the hearts of all His children— from the centre to the extremities of Christ's Body —warming us all into imitation of our Master, even as wine warms the strong man into attempting and executing superhuman deeds.

Thus do the divine institutions and sacraments of earth foreshadow the ineffable union and charity of heaven, where God is to be all in all. Therefore was it that He who is the Author and Finisher of our faith, when He had given to His Apostles the supreme pledge of His love, commanding and empowering them to perpetuate it among men, He lifted His voice in prayer to the Father, and with lips all aflame with the two-fold charity of the God and the Man, declared: "This is eternal life: that they may *know* Thee, *and Jesus Christ*, whom Thou hast sent."

COMMUNION OF SAINTS ON EARTH AND IN HEAVEN.

Let us ascend, therefore, from that earthly society of God's faithful servants, in which the sacramental Presence bequeathed to us as His last testament, is still the heart of the entire body, the centre and source of spiritual life, the sweet bond of communion between the living members; let us ascend to the glorious society of the City of God on high, where

Christ thrones everlastingly in the midst of His redeemed, and of the angelic hosts who are their brethren. There it is before us as St. Paul describes it:

"You are come to Mount Sion, and to the city of the living God, the heavenly Jerusalem, and to the company of many thousands of angels, and to the Church of the first-born, who are written in the heavens, and to God the Judge of all, and to the spirits of just men made perfect, and to *Jesus* the Mediator of the New Testament, and to the sprinkling of blood which speaketh better than that of Abel. See that you refuse Him not that speaketh."*

Our efforts toward understanding the supernatural knowledge of the *one true God*, and of the mystery of His Incarnate Son, Jesus Christ, as fully disclosed to the human intellect in the life to come, may be not unaptly likened to those of an infant who attempts to seize and hold a large globe of polished metal. Ravished at the sight of the splendid object, the child would fain possess himself of it; but every eager effort of the helpless little hands only seems to drive the shining mass farther from his reach.

In this life, and during the imperfection and immaturity of our highest powers, our mind must be satisfied with gazing from afar, and "through the glass darkly," at that Sun of the invisible heavens, whose face we shall behold one day undazzled, and "in whose light we shall see the Light."

---

* Hebrews, xii, 22-25.

WHEN WE HAVE THE FIRST GLIMPSE OF CHRIST'S FACE.

Ere Christians departing this life without stain of sin are admitted to the joys of Paradise, they have to undergo, as the Church teaches, what is termed in theology "the particular judgment," as distinguished from the universal judgment at the end of time. In both the one and the other Christ is the Judge, whose sentence decides the eternal destiny of the soul. On the place or the other circumstances of this particular judgment the Church has not pronounced.

Each one of us, therefore, has to come to *Him* on the confines of the two worlds in that brief interval which separates time from eternity, the present existence from the dread unknown and interminable future.

To His own faithful followers, passing out of the shadow of death, is not He, our *Jesus*, the first light that dawns upon the disembodied spirit? Tempering the radiance of His glory, as He did when He appeared in the midst of His own the evening of the Resurrection day, the gentle voice of the Redeemer will say: "Peace be to you! *It is I.* Fear not!"

AT THE END OF THE WAY.

Oh! the blissful transition, from the dark and fearful shadows of the valley of death to the golden shadow of that peace which is the very atmosphere surrounding Him who paid our ransom and wrought our deliverance! To the human souls just freed from all the snares and doubts of this life, half-unable to conceive the suddenness and the greatness of their coming bliss, and in their humility still troubled at the remembrance of past guilt, and trembling at the thought of the Judge's tremendous justice and unapproachable holiness, how aptly are the words of Scripture spoken: "Why are you troubled, and why do thoughts arise in your hearts? See My hands and feet, that it is I Myself." *

Now we can understand whence comes the light of judgment on all who believe in Christ and profess to follow Him: "See My hands and feet." There, in the wounds of *the Crucified*, are the shining characters in which divine love has written the story of its generosity. In their light human love has to judge its own return to Jesus Crucified.

But the scene in the upper chamber was one in which half-believing, half-doubting, troubled, and frightened men were the chief actors. At the meeting with the Judge at the very entrance to the land of the living, what a different meaning would the words of the Gospel have for spirits in whom already a mighty transformation has taken place!

THE INTRODUCTION TO THE FOUNT OF LIFE.

To look upon the human face of *Christ*, to fall at His feet and adore them, to feel the blessings which descend like streams of creating and elevating virtue from those pierced hands, to know that there, on the threshold of heaven, stands greeting us the Redeemer and Father of our souls! What an introduction to the everlasting kingdom! What a foretaste of that life, of that knowledge, that ecstatic joy, which are to follow on the Beatific Vision—the clear sight of

---

* St. Luke, xxiv, 38-39.

the essence of God, and the sense of possessing forever the very Fount of life and Author of all good!

So we may believe that the beginning of our beatitude in the life to come will be to look upon the face of our Saviour, our Model, our Judge, of Him who became Man to lift us up to the glory of children of God. In Him we know dwelleth incarnate the fullness of the Godhead. So on Him—"the first-begotten of the dead,"* "the first-born among many brethren"†—these brethren, at their first entrance into His kingdom, can rest the eyes of their soul, enraptured with the divine beauty and greatness of the Man-God, before being admitted to contemplate the unveiled glories of the divine Essence Itself.

Who that has tried to study Christ and the things of God earnestly while in the flesh, or has centered in the hope of that life eternal, spoken of above, all his deepest affections and aspirations, but could repeat truly, with all the voices of his heart, the words of the Parisian Hymn:

O videre Te, amare Te,
Perenniter laudare Te!

"Oh, to see Thee, to love Thee,
Eternally to praise Thee!"

And yet we have not approached, by mounting the first step in the mighty ladder of contemplation, that *Beatific Vision*, in which God, seen as He is in Himself, is to the blessed soul of man, as He is to the angels, as He is to Himself, the very Fount of life, the Well-spring of beatitude.

Here below, while we toil onward through temptations and pitfalls; while we try to rise above the

---
* Apocalypse, i, 5. † Romans, viii, 29.

delusions and fascinations of sense, and keep our eyes fixed on Him, who is "the day-spring from on high," let us sing in our heart of hearts:

> Lead, Kindly Light, amid the encircling gloom,
> Lead Thou me on!
> The night is dark, and I am far from *home!*
> Lead Thou me on!
> Keep Thou my feet; I do not ask to see
> The distant scene—one step enough for me.

But when, the pilgrimage over, we are at the gates of home, and its light, peace, security, and rest, fall on us with the fragrance of the everlasting hills, how sweetly He, the Shepherd of the flock, will lead us from light to light, from glory to glory, till we reach the centre and summit of all the hopes and aspirations of the human soul—the everlasting possession of God, perfectly known and loved as He is known; and with that possession, the added felicity of companionship with the blessed society of His angels and Saints.

As we pause on the threshold of that home, on the frontier of that empire, from which death, sin, suffering, fear, and doubt, are excluded by the Almighty Will, let us take this thought home to our hearts, that there God, in giving us Himself as our reward, gives us, with Himself, all that He has that is most precious—not merely that material world, His master-piece, created to be our home and kingdom, but the wealth of friendship, of love, of glory, enjoyed in the closest communion of our spirit with the spirits of all that is greatest, holiest, best and most perfect among angels and men.

This is a mere naked statement of the mighty fact whose manifold realities we are now about to explore.

THE FOUNT ITSELF.

God, then, perfectly known, securely and everlastingly possessed, is that Fount of Life for whose waters our souls are athirst. When we shall have arrived at some correct, though necessarily dim, conception of that God, infinitely great and good, infinitely to be admired, and praised, and loved, we shall be able to contemplate, with intelligence and rapture, that world of holy angels and holy men which forms God's crown in the heavens—and these heavens themselves the glorious abode of the King of kings and of the countless myriads of His happy subjects.

Our existence in that future state is to be life, true life, personal life, most perfect and most blissful life. The close and ineffable union between the soul and its Creator, between the supremely true and our intellect, between the supremely good, perfect, and lovely, and our heart, is to be a union between two persons who remain eternally distinct while being eternally united by mutual knowledge, esteem, praise and love.

Dear reader, in guiding you upwards along those dazzling and giddy heights, I am anxious not to advance one step without feeling that we have the lamp of Revelation to shed its steady radiance on our progress, that we are safely following whither the teaching of the Master leads us.

OUR BLISSFUL LIFE IN GOD NOT ABSORPTION IN GOD.

Our union with God in the land of the living is, therefore, not annihilation, nor absorption in God, but the elevation, the perfection, the deification—it is not too strong an expression—of the life begun here.

Do not weary, then, if I endeavor to account for and refute a few errors on this subject, and point out in the Old Testament writers the yearnings for this union with God, this clear sight of His Being, this secure possession of the Infinite Good. Some people are endeavoring, at the close of this nineteenth century of Christian civilization, to transplant hither the monstrous dogmas of Asiatic pantheism. Just compare their absurdity with the Gospel truth.

THE HEAVEN OF PANTHEISM AND THE CHRISTIAN HEAVEN.

The religions of India and the far East hold out to their hundreds of millions of followers the prospect of annihilation after death, or of the absorption of man's being into the Divinity, as the highest bliss to which human nature can aspire.

Far different is the destiny which revealed truth, the explicit and repeated declaration of Christ and His Apostles, and the consistent teaching of all Christian ages, propose to our belief. In the life to come man is to preserve his personal identity, his individual existence and consciousness, while enjoying the rewards due to his merits in this life, or undergoing the punishment meted out to evil deeds unrepented of to the end.

The glory and bliss of the good servant essentially depend on his being conscious of having labored to do the will of the Master. The misery of the wicked and unfaithful must equally flow from the voice of the individual conscience, recalling the trust betrayed, the opportunities lost, the graces abused, the dear ones ruined by neglect, or example, or positive teaching, and the companions scandalized and dragged down to the pit by the influence of a bad life.

Among the multitudes of the blessed in heaven there is not an angelic spirit or a human being that does not preserve his individuality, his personal identity, as well as the perfection of his own vital acts in the fruition of that life eternal, of whose glories we are going to speak in detail. In like manner, in the multitudes of the wicked—fallen angels and fallen men—who are everlastingly separated from God, there is not one whose conscience does not evermore tell him that the loss endured is the just retribution for past misdeeds.

The fatal fever dream of the East Indian, the Chinese, and the Japanese, that the soul is to be annihilated, or absorbed in the abyss of the Godhead, is only the perversion of the great truth revealed to man from the beginning—that the life after death, to which we are destined, consists in the closest union with Him who is the Fount of being and life.

REVEALED RELIGION TEACHES BLISSFUL UNION, NOT ABSORPTION.

No one among the great teachers of the Old Testament has more frequently or more beautifully expressed the belief in this supernatural destiny, with its inheritance of bliss and glory, than the Prophet-Poet David: "I have said to the Lord, Thou art my God, for Thou hast no need of my goods. . . . The Lord is the portion of my inheritance and of my cup: it is Thou that will restore my inheritance to me. . . I set the Lord always in my sight: for He is at my right hand, that I be not moved. Therefore my heart hath been glad, and my tongue hath rejoiced: moreover, my flesh also shall rest in hope. . . Thou hast made known to me the ways of life, Thou shalt fill me with joy with Thy countenance: at Thy right hand are delights even to the end."*

All through the songs of the "Sweet Singer of Israel" there runs, together with the literal meaning, expressive of the present needs of the warrior-king or the sentiments of the hour, a vein of prophetic inspiration, all pregnant with a higher meaning, and colored by the light of another sphere. The little theocratic community of the twelve tribes was but the forerunner of the Universal Church; David was the figure of Christ; and the passing events which awakened these songs preluded the future revolutions of humanity, the history of all time, and the everlasting years beyond time's remotest boundary. Hear the following strain:

"The Lord is my light and my salvation, whom shall I fear? . . . . One thing I have asked of The Lord, this will I seek after, that I may dwell in the house of the Lord all the days of my life: that I may see the delight of the Lord, and visit His temple. . . . My heart hath said to Thee: 'My face hath sought Thee: Thy face, O Lord, will I still seek.'" †

And again:

"Oh! how Thou hast multiplied Thy mercy, O God! But the children of men shall put their trust under the covert of Thy wings. They shall be inebriated with the plenty of Thy house: and Thou shalt make them drink of the torrent of Thy pleasure. For with Thee is the *fountain of life:* and in Thy light we shall see light." ‡

---

* Psalm XV, 2-11.   † Psalm XXVI, 1-8.   ‡ Psalm XXXV, 8-10.

Elsewhere David expresses, with the same definiteness, the longing of all created intelligences—a longing which is one of the vital forces of rational nature—to possess and enjoy the Supreme Good, and with It perfect and unalterable felicity:

"As the hart panteth after the fountain of water, so my soul panteth after Thee, O God! My soul hath thirsted after the strong living God: when shall I come and appear before the face of God?" *

Whatever doubt, ambiguity, or obscurity, may arise in the mind of scholars from the Hebrew expressions equivalent to "seeing the face of the Lord," in passages which speak, or seem to speak, of the clear sight of God in the life to come, no shadow of doubt or uncertainty can rest on the mind of the true Christian, after Christ's own explicit declarations on this matter, after the texts already quoted from His Apostles, re-echoing or explaining the Master's doctrine.

Again we repeat His dying declaration:

"Now this is eternal life: That they may know Thee, the only true God, and Jesus Christ, whom Thou hast sent." †

"This is the promise which He hath promised us: *life everlasting.* . . . We are now the sons of God; and it hath not yet appeared *what* we shall be. We know, that, when He shall appear, we shall be like to Him: because *we shall see Him as He is.*" ‡

Christ Himself, in another passage, ‖ speaks of showing Himself to His faithful disciples as the one Supreme Reward kept in store for love persevering to the end: "He that loveth Me, shall be loved by

---
* Psalm XLI, 2-3.　† St. John, xvii, 3.
‡ 1 St. John, ii, 25; iii, 2.　‖ St. John, xiv, 21.

My Father: and I will love Him, and will manifest Myself to Him."

And St. Paul: "We see now through a glass darkly: but then face to face. Now I know in part: but then I shall know even as I am known." *

Thus, steadily does the divine Book shed its light on our path upward. Now let the Church—"the ground and pillar of truth"—complete and explain the Book which she alone has compiled, sanctioned, and preserved for her children's instruction. Thus, between Him who died on the cross that we might have life and have it in its overflowing fullness, and her who is His spouse and the parent on earth of the children of God, we come to the Fountain of Life. We may kneel down in spirit, and reverently taste, so far as we may with lips that death has not yet touched nor the angel of the resurrection hallowed, the living waters as they flow from the very bosom of the Deity.

It was the Master who said: "Blessed are the pure of heart, for they shall see God!" May He purify heart and mind while we venture to approach the Holy of Holies!

THE BEATIFIC VISION.

In one of the most memorable assemblages ever held in Christendom, in the Council of Florence (1439-1442), the bishops of the East and West, under the presidency of the Sovereign Pontiff, and in the presence of the Greek emperor, decreed, in conformity with revealed truth, the constant traditions and universal belief in the Church, that "the

---

* 1 Cor., xiii, 12.

souls of those who, after receiving baptism, have incurred no stain of sin whatsoever, or who, after incurring such stain, have been purified in the body or out of the body . . . . are at once received into heaven, and *clearly see God Himself as He is*, in Three Persons and in one Substance, some, however, more perfectly than others, according to the diversity of their merits." *

Here, then, is the great dogmatic fact which is set up as a beacon light on the very portals of the unseen and eternal world, declaring to all the children of men not only the nature and source of the felicity there enjoyed, but also the conditions on which any human being can attain to it.

Those grafted on Christ by baptism, who have entirely preserved or recovered the innocence of their second birth in His Blood, "are at once received into heaven," when death's agony is over, "and clearly see God Himself as He is, in Three Persons and one Substance."

There is, consequently, no sleep of the soul after death and until the general resurrection. The soul, by its nature capable of knowing God with that perfect knowledge imparted by the clear sight of His essence and of His interior life, is, moreover, raised and fitted by the Creator for the new and supernatural conditions of its heavenly existence.

GOD SEEN AND KNOWN AS HE IS IN HIMSELF.

Such is the *reality* held out as a reward for the Christian's labors, sufferings, self-sacrifice, and divinest virtues; such is the "exceeding great reward" bestowed upon the deserving soul on its release from the body.

---
* In the "Decree of Union."

Like men who have been toiling, from the first peep of dawn till far into the afternoon, up the slopes of some mighty alp, we are glad to have reached the summit, and to rest awhile there above the clouds, with earth far away beneath us, and nothing between us and heaven. Yes, but there is this difference between us, dear reader, and the weary alpine climbers, that they cannot remain long on these icy summits, and that the prospect which rewards their toil only discloses a wider earthly horizon. Above them stretch the black, impenetrable abysses of the firmament.

As we pause on the height we have reached, we feel ourselves surrounded by the light and warmth of the Sun of Righteousness, while above us, around us, beneath us, are spread the immensities and glories of the heaven of heavens, and at its centre the abyss of life, of light, of joy, at which the exultant hosts of angels and Saints drink everlastingly.

Is this, then, what we believe in, what we hope for, long for, pray for? . . . . If so, we can afford, in the next chapter and the following, to satisfy the craving of our mind to know all about *Him* who is the Sun of these heavens, and the world after world of the blessed citizens among whom we are destined to live for evermore.

It is good for us to be here; for one day in these courts—though only spent there in spirit and contemplation—is worth years passed among the shadows, unrealities and deceptions of our own world of misery.

CHAPTER V.

WITHIN THE OCEAN DEPTHS OF LIGHT AND LIFE.

SEEING AND POSSESSING GOD.

So long Thy power hath blest me, sure it still
    Will lead me on
O'er moor and fen, o'er crag and torrent, till
    The night is gone;
And with the morn those angel faces smile
Which I have loved long since and lost awhile.
                              —*Newman.*

HARMONIES.

There is a supreme fitness between the nature of the reward kept in store for us by our Maker and Father, and the nature of the trial which His wisdom, in the beginning, decreed to impose both on angels and on men. They were to live by *faith* during their period of probation; the probation ended, they were to be rewarded by the *Beatific Vision.*

The Church has never given an authoritative interpretation of the text of St. Paul in the first chapter of the Epistle to the Hebrews:

"When He bringeth the First-Born into the world, He saith: 'And let all the angels of God adore Him!'" *

The bringing into the world of the Only-Begotten Son, as "the First-Born of the dead," or "the First-Born among many brethren," may surely be

* Hebrews, 1, 6.

interpreted as pointing to the first revelation of the whole design of the Incarnation made to the angelic world at the commencement of its period of probation, as well as the first revelation of the mystery of God's own interior life, in the fact that in God there was a plurality or trinity of persons.

St. Francis Xavier, in his catechetical instructions, says that such was the nature of the revelation made to the angels, and of the trial imposed on them.

There is a fitness, a harmony, in this. But, be that as it may, we are left in no doubt concerning the nature of our own trials in this mortal life.

All the duties enjoined by the divine law, all the virtues practiced in the fulfillment of our obligations toward God, the neighbor, and ourselves, repose on faith—on the fact that we believe in Him whom we see not, and whose commands we obey, trusting firmly in His solemn promise: that the happiness of the life to come shall amply compensate all the trials of the present, repair the injustices of our actual condition, and satisfy to the utmost the longings, aspirations and needs of our rational nature.

The greatest, the holiest, the most perfect, of the human race have toiled, suffered, lived, and died, looking forward with unflagging trust to the Author of their being, the Lawgiver and Judge of the whole earth, who has declared that to faith in Him, whom we love, obey, serve without seeing, shall succeed the clear knowledge, the undimmed sight of Himself in His glory; that to the undying hope which sustains us amidst present ills, shall succeed the possession of the Supreme Good, and the repose of His eternal kingdom; that all the charities practiced here below toward our fellow-men shall be rewarded by the unspeakable love of that most blissful society where charity reigns supreme in every bosom.

There is in the providence of God over those angels and men, who are capable of knowing, serving freely, and loving truly Him, the infinitely perfect, good, true, and lovable, a harmony most admirable to our intelligence. It is fitting that as faith in the unseen God, with His eternal world so far removed from our actual capacity, forms the very soul of our present life, so, in the life to come, we should have the veil of faith removed, and see Him whom we now believe in, find Him whom we now hope and long for, hold and possess perfectly, firmly, everlastingly, Him whom we now love, obey, serve, labor, live, and die for.

One of the greatest and holiest men, whose genius has adorned Christianity and become the most glorious patrimony of the race—St. Augustine—says, somewhere: "Thou hast made us for Thee, O Lord; and our heart knoweth no rest till it repose in Thee." The orange tree, if planted in a dark cellar, far away from the sunlight, may, indeed, take root in the soil and grow, and put forth sickly flowers, when the warm atmosphere of summer penetrates even the darksome cave around it. But the blossoms will fall, and no fruit will ever ripen on these branches. Even so, man's soul was created to bear perfect and immortal fruits of holiness and happiness, of which only the flowers can appear in this short life; flowers without either color or perfume when deprived of the atmosphere of supernatural faith; flowers which are only the promise of the fruit destined to ripen in the clear, full light of that Sun which illuminates the land of the living.

TENDENCIES AND ATTRACTIONS TO BE FULFILLED.

Our mind, in studying His works in earth and ocean, in sky and firmament, discovers everywhere the evidence of His power, His wisdom, His love. His Revealed Word tells us that all we see around us was created for us. But all these wonderful works of the infinitely good and great God, all these gifts of His liberality, only kindle within us an unquenchable desire to see Him as He is in Himself, to look upon His countenance, to hear His voice, to know Him perfectly, to praise Him to His face, to let our heart go out to Him without stint in thanksgiving, gratitude, and filial love.

This fair world resembles a vast and magnificent park belonging to a great prince, into which all men are admitted for the purposes of recreation, pleasure or study. Who can have enjoyed its shady walks, reposed by its running streams and gushing fountains, plucked the delicious fruits that hung overhead, and gone away from its varied scenes of solitude and restfulness without feeling and expressing the desire to see its liberal proprietor, to examine his dwelling-place, to form a personal acquaintance with him, if not to obtain the boon of his esteem or his friendship? God, we know, in creating us and placing us on this earth, beside bestowing on us the faculty of appreciating all that is beautiful in our present abode—in our place of pilgrimage, rather—has implanted in our souls a keen desire to know the Author of the Universe, to come to Him, to enter into personal relations with Him, to win His friendship and His love.

This aspiration of our nature, this irresistible tendency of the soul of man to know the Supreme

Truth, to love and possess the Infinitely Good and Fair, was intended as a mighty and ever-present impelling force, urging us toward *God* and the bliss of the other life. This yearning, innate in man, to know and see the Great Cause of all that exists, and in His light to possess the fullness of all knowledge, in His love to satisfy and rest forever the longing of his heart, must have its proper object in the life to come, else our present condition, with its beliefs, its hopes, and its efforts, would, in more than one respect, be a mockery.

HERE WE BELIEVE: THERE WE SHALL SEE AND KNOW.

Here, then, we *believe:* in the hereafter, we shall *see* clearly, and *know* the Author of our being and of all things, "even as we are known" of Him. Here we labor and suffer in the firm hope of a requital and a reward: there our expectation shall be surpassed by a recompense such as that no understanding, in this life, can grasp either its nature or its greatness.

Revealed truth, uttering for our comfort and encouragement the solemn promise of Him who is the Author and Finisher of our faith, says: "Blessed be the God and Father of our Lord Jesus Christ, who according to His great mercy hath regenerated us unto a lively hope, . . . unto an inheritance incorruptible, and undefiled, and that cannot fade, reserved in heaven for you. . . . Wherein you shall greatly rejoice, if now you must be for a little time made sorrowful in divers temptations: that the trial of your faith (much more precious than gold which is tried by the fire) may be found unto praise and glory and honor at the appearing of Jesus Christ, whom having not seen you love; in whom also now, though you see Him not, you believe; and believing shall rejoice with joy unspeakable and glorified, receiving the end of your faith, the salvation of your souls." *

Another of the three who beheld Christ transfigured on the Mount thus speaks of that end and consummation of the Christian's hope: "This is the promise which He hath promised us, *life everlasting.* . . . . We are now the sons of God: and it hath not yet appeared what *we* shall be. We know, that, when He shall appear, we shall be like to Him: because *we shall see Him as He is.*" †

THE TWOFOLD FOUNT OF HEAVENLY BLISS.

We are, therefore, brought, at the very outset, to examine the nature of that Beatific Vision—that bliss-bestowing, clear sight of the Godhead, which is the very inmost spring of the felicity of man and angel in that life of unending joy and unfading glory.

And let us at once hasten to say, that heavenly felicity arises from two sources—the Beatific Vision as the principal and essential, and the society of the blessed as the secondary and accidental. We shall endeavor to make clear to the reader the immense importance of both the one and the other.

SITTING NEAR THE FOUNT AND DISCOURSING ON IT.

If our intelligent, educated readers will pause a moment to think how this unclouded knowledge of the divine Essence can be to every created intelligence

---
* 1 St. Peter, I, 3-9.   † 1 St. John, II, 25; III, 2.

the cause of supreme and incomprehensible happiness, they can help themselves very much toward a perfect understanding of the present subject by recalling what is happening around them in the world of science, or by reflecting on their own personal experience.

THE JOY OF DISCOVERING THE UNKNOWN.

It is admitted that no pleasure, no satisfaction, is comparable to that experienced by the discovery of some truth hitherto unknown. Scientists will remember the rapture which took possession of Archimedes when an accident revealed to him the means of ascertaining the specific gravity of metals. Rushing out of the bath, where he found that his own body lost in the water a weight proportionate to the liquid volume it displaced, he exclaimed: "I have found it! I have found it!" This intellectual rapture, this delight of the rational soul, is shared, in a greater or less degree, by the discoverers, the inventors, the geniuses, of every age, whose labors enlarge the domain of knowledge. Think of the feelings of a man who, after years of laborious research, succeeds in analyzing a body which until then had resisted the action of every solvent, baffled the attempts of the most skillful chemists to fix the relative proportions of its component elements. Science reserves its highest honors, its most liberal emoluments, for men who achieve what their fellows never achieved before them—penetrated deeper into the mysteries of nature, annihilated space by the employment of steam locomotion, or laid a metallic cable beneath the ocean to enable continent to converse with continent.

THE JOY OF SEEING CLEARLY THE AUTHOR OF ALL THINGS.

What, then, must be the happiness of the man who is enabled to see clearly the divine Author of nature itself, to gaze down into the depths of that abysmal Being, in whom all is unlimited perfection and loveliness—infinite intelligence, infinite wisdom, infinite goodness, justice, mercy, liberality; who is the Life of our life, the Source and the End of our existence; our Maker and our Repairer; our Sovereign Lord, Lawgiver, and Judge; our Father and Rewarder—who, having made us for Himself, tries us by the labors and temptations of this life, only to make us worthy of Himself, only to bring us to Himself at the end of the trial, and to bestow on us, as our only fitting reward, *Himself and His own glory*. Aye, truly, no home is worthy of the children of God save God's own bosom.

The magnificence of this truth will dawn and grow upon us as we proceed to explore and to fathom, slowly and reverently, the shining abysses of truth disclosed by the study of what the Church means by the Beatific Vision.

SUPERNATURALNESS OF THIS CLEAR SIGHT OF THE GODHEAD.

The clear sight of God as He is in Himself is above the ken of bodily eye or created intellect. For there is no proportion between the capacity or natural powers of any finite understanding and the infinite God. Then the Beatific Vision implies not only an unclouded sight and clear knowledge of the Godhead, but a full insight into the mystery of His interior life. Now, such an insight, even among persons of the same nature and rank, is entirely beyond the conditions and requirements of ordinary social intercourse. It is a most merciful dispensation of Him who made man for the society of his fellow-men here below, that we are not gifted with the power of reading each other's mind and heart; of penetrating to the secret springs of our neighbor's life; of knowing his thoughts, his aims, his resolves. This power, and the knowledge it involves, would be destructive of both our liberty and our happiness. Hence it is that the Creator of the soul reserves to Himself this insight into the inmost depths of our moral nature.

SECRETS WHICH THE CREATOR OF SOULS RESERVES TO HIMSELF.

If we reflect a little on this head, we shall remember that, even in a family, children do not know the secrets of their parents, or parents those of their children, unless voluntarily disclosed to them. Between the nearest and dearest relatives, therefore, between the most intimate friends, there are, in the inmost lives of each, depths absolutely hidden from the other, and which must remain a secret forever, unless one choose freely to lift the veil mercifully woven over every conscience by the hand of Him who made the soul and will judge it.

We see, therefore, that even where we are best acquainted with our equals and neighbors, where we are most familiar and intimate with relatives and friends, we are content to know them, as they know us, by the qualities which appear on the surface, by the virtues which shine forth in a whole life of consistent uprightness, purity, and generosity. We cannot reach the heart from which good and evil flow, coloring the whole of our neighbor's conduct and our own.

The best and noblest—as we know by experience—find it one of the greatest delights of life, one of the rarest blessings vouchsafed by a kind Providence to His chosen servants, to be admitted to familiarity and intimacy with Godlike souls who, in the expansive intercourse of true friendship, open up to those they love the depths of their own inmost life and conscience. Most blessed and most blissful is the privilege of the man or woman who, having found a friend and companion in every way after God's heart and their own, enjoy, in the unreserved communion of thought and aim, of feeling and judgment, of taste and inclination, such heart-satisfaction, such congeniality of souls, as seems a foretaste of heaven.

Ah! these foretastes, these spiritual instincts, needs, yearnings, and satisfactions, are indeed, in this life, only the secret touches of His hand, who made our hearts for Himself, who will not give them rest or contentment till He brings us face to face with Himself.

THE NATURE OF SUBSTANCES UNKNOWN TO THE MOST LEARNED.

Even the impenetrable mystery which, to the eye of the scientist, as well as to that of the most unlettered peasant, envelopes not only the nature of the material substances around us, but still more, if possible, the origin and secret of the lowest and the highest forms of life, should teach man here below how far above the comprehension of the created intellect is the divine Nature—that Substance which transcends all substance; how unfathomable to the natural ken of man or angel is the secret of His life, with whom alone is the life-giving power as well as the knowledge of all life and all substance.

The geologist and the chemist may analyze the piece of granite broken from the oldest rocks, or the sand on the river bank or the shore of ocean, and determine the substances or elements that enter into their composition; or they may discuss, with more or less of uncertainty, the respective ages of the rocks they are thus comparing. But the substances themselves, and the laws which governed in the beginning the formation of these rocks, or which even now bind together the molecules of the grain of sand, or the atoms which form each molecule—what scientist has discovered or can disclose them?

To the most learned of mankind the sand on the seashore and the grass on the field offer impenetrable mysteries. What, then, must His nature, His substance, His interior life, who made the land and the sea, who made the earth and that wondrous universe, of which our telescopes only enable us to discover a little corner?

CONCLUSION: GOD IS, NATURALLY, THE MYSTERY OF MYSTERIES.

God is the mystery of mysteries. How could the intellect of man, for whom the substance of a grain of sand and the organism of a blade of grass are inexplicable mysteries, grasp the nature of the Infinite or fathom the secret of His life?

What, then, must be the joy of the created spirit, exalted and enabled by the Creator Himself to penetrate by clear knowledge this mystery of the divine

Nature, this secret of that most perfect, most blissful and bliss-bestowing life of Him who is called in Scripture the living God?

St. Paul contrasts the imperfect and unsatisfactory knowledge of God and divine things, to which even Christians can attain in this life, to the perfection of knowledge reserved to the life to come. "We know in part," he says, "and we prophesy in part. But when that which is perfect is come, that which is in part shall be done away. When I was a child, I spoke as a child, I understood as a child, I thought as a child. But when I became a man, I put away the things of a child. We see now through a glass in a dark manner: but then face to face. Now I know in part: but then I shall know even as I am known." *

This vision, as is, indeed, all that pertains to our adoption as children of God and to this eternal union with the divine Being by knowledge and love, is in itself supernatural. Hence, the power superadded in heaven to the human intellect, to enable it to see God as He is in Himself, is also supernatural. It is called by the schools of theology "the light of glory."

THE FIRST MOMENT OF THE BEATIFIC VISION.

How can we form ourselves or express to others what takes place immediately after death, when the sinless, stainless soul, passing beyond the veil which, during the present existence, hides from our view the world unseen, the world of eternal realities, is brought "face to face" with the Creator and Ruler of worlds, with Him who is the Source of being, of greatness, goodness, beauty, grandeur, light, and

---
* 1 Cor., xiii, 9-12.

life? He, the Almighty Father, has been preparing the faithful soul for this supreme moment. Every faculty is strengthened for the enjoyment of the new existence about to begin. We, in this life, can only strain our imagination to picture to ourselves the rapture of that first look on the unveiled face of the Sun of Righteousness. Do as we will, in meditating on the Beatific Vision, we fancy ourselves gazing on some transcendently beautiful and glorious form, like that of the most Godlike we have met with, conversed with, worshiped and loved, during our earthly pilgrimage. But the Godhead has no bodily form, no human semblance. And we may, to help our mind toward some conception of the truth, try to recall what we felt when we were admitted to the intimacy of some holy and beautiful soul—like St. Philip Neri, or St. Francis of Sales, or St. Francis Xavier; a soul all aglow with the divine fire, like Moses after his communion with God on the Mount, and bearing about with it on the bodily features a reflection of the divine splendors resembling the heavenly tints on a mountain peak after sunset. In conversation with such beings one feels that there is a something divine. One forgets the bodily form, which is only a transparent veil behind which the beautiful spirit is visible to our spirit. There is sweetness, there is light, there is strength, and there is peace unspeakable, in this close communion here below with men or women, from whom the sweet odor of Christ goes sensibly forth, in whose speech and form the Spirit of God makes Himself felt, as an unearthly virtue lifting us above ourselves.

Was it not so with our Lord while He still walked the earth, teaching, healing, comforting, and saving?

What, then, will it be when, arrived at the portals of the everlasting home, we shall behold *the Father*, and all the desires and yearnings of our human spirit are gratified, as in Him the living God appears, and the eyes of the soul take in that uncreated beauty, while the abyss of Love Eternal opens out, like the arms of a mighty ocean, to take the pilgrim into Its bosom? when Truth Itself will say: "Well done, thou good and faithful servant?"

We read and we speak of the living God: do we ever bring home the thought to ourselves that it is He—Father most loving, true, and just—into whose embrace we expect to come one day, and that soon?

ILLUSTRATIONS.

A child, taken away from the parental arms and long, long absent from that dear presence which is upon earth the image of God's fatherly tenderness and care, yearns with all the force of filial affection for the day of re-union. Oh! the bliss of the hour which gives son or daughter to a father's arms or a mother's heart! Human nature, the experience of the noblest and most heroic, attests that, once restored to the incomparable sweetness of parental love, one has no thought but to be forever in those arms and on that heart. And this deep, deep draught of purest love and happiness is in proportion to the long days of separation.

Can these experiences of what is most holy and touching in human life enable us to conceive somewhat of the rapture, the blissful repose, the utter and unspeakable satisfaction of every power and faculty, in this first embrace given to the long-tried exile in this life, by Him who created the father's heart and the mother's unfathomable depths of tenderness? What is created goodness compared with the Uncreated? What are human love and tenderness, in their widest reach and their divinest intensity, in comparison with His, who created us because He loved us, who gave His Only-Begotten Son to death for us, who will have His adopted children receive no other reward than *Himself* and a share in His own most blissful life throughout all the endless cycles of eternity?

We try to approach these awful depths of the Love, infinite and incomprehensible, of that Father who is in heaven. Thinking, writing, speaking, upon this sublime subject, one is like a babe in arms, gifted with an exquisite sense of harmony, ravished by the sounds of a heavenly music, but incapable of expressing by one syllable of articulate language what passes in its soul, or of executing on the simplest instrument one melody or one note of all those that are still charming and enchaining its sense.

CHAPTER VI.

STILL AMONG THE DEPTHS.

A little longer, and thy heart, beloved,
  Shall beat forever with a love divine;
And joy so pure, so mighty, so eternal,
  No creature knows and lives, will then be thine.

THE POSSESSION OF GOD AND OF ALL THAT GOD HAS.

Such are the sublimity and magnificence of the perspectives opened out before us by the Church's doctrine on the life to come, and the nature of the beatitude enjoyed there, that the thought of it, in cool and calm reflection, comes back upon the mind, and causes a fear and sinking of the heart. We feel like one suddenly elevated from debasement and poverty to regal rank, pomp and splendor. We look around on palaces, domains, and crowds of courtiers and attendants, and ask ourselves: "Can all this be real? really mine?"

If we have not quoted in vain the very words of Christ Himself, and the solemn utterances of His Apostles, the Sacred Scriptures must have given us a solid and immovable ground on which to rest our faith in this doctrine, as defined by the Council of Florence and believed by all the children of the Church. But it may still more strengthen our faith to listen to the testimony of the early Christian ages on this very doctrine of the Beatific Vision as we have been expounding it.

WITHIN HIS BOSOM WHO IS THE LIGHT AND THE LIFE.

St. Irenæus, martyr, and Bishop of Lyons, who lived in the century immediately following that of the Apostles, who was, moreover, both a disciple of St. Polycarp and Papias—themselves disciples of St. John the Evangelist—speaks on the nature of heavenly bliss with no uncertain or hesitating voice:

"Eternal life," he says, "becomes the possession of each one by the fact of his seeing God. . . . For, just as those who see the light are within the light and receive its radiance, even so those who see God are within God—the recipients of His brightness. And this radiance gives them life. Wherefore those who see God are the recipients of life. By this means He, who is beyond our comprehension, makes Himself visible and comprehensible to man, in order that He may impart life to such as perceive and see Him. For, as He is unsearchable in His greatness, so is He unspeakable in His goodness, which impels Him to give life to those who see Him.

"Inasmuch as one cannot be a living being without having life; and as our continuance in life comes from God's allowing us to partake of it; and as the partaking of God consists in seeing Him and enjoying His goodness; hence it follows that man shall see God and shall live by thus seeing Him, being thereby rendered immortal and lifted up to God's own height." *

Of course, at the very beginning of Christianity, and when persecution decimated the rising Christian societies in the East and the West, theology had not become the carefully and clearly formulated science it was in the thirteenth century. Its terms had not been settled once and forever. Nevertheless, the thought of the great Martyr-Bishop of Lyons is manifest:

"To see God is to possess eternal life. The light proceeding from His substance, which creates in the soul the power and fact of vision, or clear sight, brings us within the light itself, renders His being, of itself, incapable of being seen by created faculty, visible to our ken, and places the goodness, which is also unspeakable because infinite, within the grasp of our affection. And this clear sight and this possession constitute the life eternal. The very substance of this life is to be made to partake of God—that is, to see Him and enjoy His goodness."

---
* Irenæus, "Advers. Hœroscs," L. IV, xxxvii.

AT "THE FOUNTAIN ITSELF OF TRUTH AND GOOD."

Coming down from the second to the fourth century, we hear the great St. Gregory Nazianzen affirming that the contemplation of the Sovereign Good is the reward of our labors, and the end held forth to us by the Christian religion:

"May we be able," he exclaims, "to come hereafter to the Fountain Itself, and to behold the pure truth with pure minds, receiving there the reward of the labor endured in the pursuit of virtue, in that we shall there more fully enjoy the Sovereign Good and Its contemplation. Such is the aim which souls in love with the study of divine things hold forth as the end toward which our present religious trials are directed." *

RECEIVED INTO THE LIGHT OF THE HOLY TRINITY.

In another discourse, speaking of the blessed in heaven, he says: "A light which no words can describe will receive them, together with the sight of the holy and royal Trinity shining with a purer and brighter radiance, and permeating with Its whole substance every part of the soul. And this contemplation of itself I judge to be what is principal in the kingdom of heaven." †

"TO SEE" IS "TO POSSESS" GOD AND ALL GOOD WITH HIM.

Listen, now, to what this great archbishop's devoted friend, St. Gregory of Nyssa, wrote. He is explaining the text, "Blessed are the pure of heart, for they shall see God:"

---

* "Oratio in laudem Cæsarii;" now marked "Oratio XIV."
† Ibidem.

"The promise is such a mighty one that it exceeds the extreme limit of bliss. What could any one desire after such a blessing as this, since we possess all things in Him whom it is given us to see? For the wonted Scriptural meaning of 'to see' is 'to possess;' as in the passage, 'that thou mayest see the good things of Jerusalem' (Psalm CXXVII, 5,) 'to see' means that 'thou mayest find;' and again (Isaias, xxvi, 10,) 'he shall not see the glory of the Lord,' the Prophet declaring that the not-seeing will be the not-partaking of. So, then, he who sees God, hath obtained all good in Him whom he seeth, life without end, without interruption, life eternal, bliss unfailing, boundless dominion, unmixed joy, the true light, glory above all change, perpetual exultation—all good, in one word." *

"THE REWARD OF THE JUST IS TO BEHOLD THE UNVEILED FACE OF GOD."

From that same fourth century other voices reach us. St. Ambrose declares: "This is the reward of the just, that they see the face of God, and that light which enlighteneth every man coming into this world. . . . Then, the veil being taken away from the face of God, we shall be allowed to contemplate His glory." †

St. John Chrysostom: "Those who are there [in heaven] continually behold God, their King, inasmuch as they see Him not only present before them, but beautifying the entire heavenly abode by the splendor of His glory." ‡

---

* "De Beatitudinibus." † "De Bono Mortis," xi, 49.
‡ "Orat. Panegyrica in S. Phil."

"THE CLEAR SIGHT OF GOD IS THE FULFILLMENT OF THE PROMISE."

Lastly, thus speaks St. Augustine, the great spiritual son of Ambrose: "In the clear sight of God is the fulfillment of the promise held out to our delight and desire. . . . Christ will then hand over to God, His Father, the kingdom, when He will have brought the believers to the contemplation of God, in which is the aim of all our good deeds, as well as eternal rest, and the joy that can never be taken from us." *

And from near Jerusalem comes this voice: "Those who will have done good deeds shall shine like the Sun among the angels of God throughout the life without end, and in company with our Lord Jesus Christ, always seeing Him and by Him seen, flooded with perpetual joy flowing from Him." †

These are only a few testimonies from among a host of saintly authorities. Let us here recall what was said in a preceding chapter—not only that each of the Saints who enjoy the bliss of heaven preserves there the consciousness of being the very same human being who believed, hoped, labored on earth to fulfill the divine Will, but that the acts of knowledge, love, praise, and thanksgiving, elicited in heaven, are the vital acts of the human soul itself. This is to caution the reader against the plausible errors of those who would have the divine Essence so fill, permeate and overflow the beings of the blessed in the Beatific Vision, and the blissful life of which it is the principle, that the action of God in them supersedes, annihilates or absorbs all proper vital action of the soul itself.

---
* "De Trinit.," L. I, ix-x.
† St. John Damascene, "De Fide Orthodoxa," L. IV, in fine.

Having thus stated the doctrinal fact of the Beatific Vision, or the clear sight of God as He is in Himself, let us endeavor to arrive at some clear conception of the transformation divinely wrought in the soul and its faculties to enable it to see God as He is in Himself, and in this supernal light to know all things as He knows and sees them.

Had we been destined to live a thousand or two thousand years even on earth, and were we to devote to the attentive study and contemplation of divine things the principal part of our lives, our time would never suffice to obtain a very superficial notion of the various spheres of knowledge that come within the scope of the blessed in heaven.

The very thought of the Beatific Vision and of the fact that it opens up to the eye of the soul in the life to come the divine Essence, the being and life of the Triune Godhead, is apt to produce, even on the serious-minded, something like the effect produced on the nerves and the brain by the sudden approach to a precipice of incalculable depth, beneath which stretches out, from horizon to horizon, the most glorious of prospects. One recoils, dizzy and almost terror-stricken, from the verge, even though beyond and beneath lie the magnificences of a world unexplored and unsuspected.

Oh! the worlds upon worlds of being, of grandeur, of beauty, and loveliness, which are to be disclosed to the eye of our mind—aye, and to the eye of our glorified body as well—in that eternal life where all shall be a new, a divine existence!

THE LIGHT OF GLORY.

It behooves us, then, to examine and understand, to the best of our ability, everything connected with it. Let us, then, return to some of the questions already considered too briefly.

What is that "light of glory," of which Christian theology speaks as a divine help bestowed on the created intellect for the express purpose of enabling it to behold the Godhead in His own native splendor? We are to make use of the analogies of the natural order as a means toward understanding the truths and facts of the supernatural and heavenly. Just, then, as the soundest and strongest human eye, during this mortal life, needs, to enable it to see, the light which makes all objects visible—even so, in the life to come, both our interior and exterior sense need, in order to see the sublime objects of the supernatural world, a light in harmony with that world, supernatural and divine.

Understand this well before proceeding further. The bodily organ may be as powerful and piercing as that of the eagle, yet nothing would or could be visible to it if no light whatever existed to bring external objects within the scope of vision. With the aid of light, on the contrary, spread over earth and sky, the organ of vision embraces, in a manner, the universe. Now, while we are in this body of flesh, God and the entire spiritual world are shrouded in mist or darkness impenetrable.

When the soul is freed from the body, and no moral obstacle interferes with her enjoyment of the rewards of the perfect life, the Creator, to prepare her for that clear knowledge of Himself, which is the reward of faith, perfects all her powers. The supernatural element which He adds to the faculties He has Himself created, is most aptly called, both by the schools of theology and by the councils, "the light of glory." It produces in the soul a manifold effect. It elevates the mind to a divine state of existence and vital action, enabling it to see the divine Essence as It is in Itself, expanding its capacity so as to embrace, so far as a finite being can, the divine immensity. It makes the divine Being, in every line of Its infinite perfection, beauty, and loveliness, visible to the mind, intelligible to the understanding. So that this glorious Essence, this infinitely perfect Being, becomes united to the intellect, just as when, of a sudden, to absolute darkness here below on earth succeeds light, flooding the whole of creation—not only the light itself pours into the open eye, but it brings with it the image of the external world, thus suddenly revealed.

ELEVATION AND EXPANSION OF OUR FACULTIES.

In like manner—but in a manner more wonderful and more perfect far than this analogy conveys—the "light of glory," and with it the revealed Essence of the Godhead, floods the soul, elevating, expanding, filling it, standing, within it and without, one visible, intelligible, clearly-discerned ocean of being, perfection, beauty, and loveliness, seen in its height and depth, its length and breadth—a glorious and ecstatic vision.

And with the divine light of glory thus elevating and enlarging the mind, or intellectual powers of man, in the Beatific Vision, is inseparably and simultaneously given that energy and capacity to the will (or affections), which enables it to hold, possess, enjoy, that Sovereign Good, for which the soul has been yearning in exile. Thereby the divine Object, which the mind apprehends with such marvelous distinctness, is given to the heart to love with like intensity. The elevation and enlargement of the two faculties are made harmoniously.

Our purpose now, however, is more with the operation of the intellect in the Beatific Vision, bearing in mind that the degree of love, and, therefore, of bliss, is proportionate to the degree of knowledge.

ANALOGIES FROM NATURAL SCIENCE.

There are many considerations which can assist the mind in arriving at a dim, but not incorrect, conception of the scope of that Beatific Vision; of the immense variety of objects which the "light of glory" brings within the field of the mind's clear and perfect knowledge. The attentive study of this single point, with the aid of Christian theology, of that true philosophy which investigates these heights and depths with the lamp of faith, lifts up a serious soul above itself, and fills with a divine ardor the most advanced scholar as well as the simple-minded believer.

We know from daily experience that the light diffused throughout all space renders the most distant worlds from which it travels visible to the inhabitants of this little earth of ours. The most powerful instruments devised by science help the naked eye to discern such as its unaided power could not perceive, and to form probable conjectures about the arrangement and movements of these mysterious masses of suns and systems placed by the Almighty Hand at such enormous distances from us and from each other. The spectroscope has wonderfully aided science toward a knowledge of their physical constitution; and other kindred instruments, by measuring the action of the waves of light, afford elements for calculating the distance of these far-off provinces of creation which we shall thoroughly know and clearly see one day.

AIDS THUS AFFORDED TO OUR FACULTIES FOR ACQUIRING KNOWLEDGE.

The advance of astronomical and physical discovery, the progress made in perfecting scientific instruments of every kind, do but help to enlarge our view of the universe, to bring new cosmic systems within the field of study, and to enable the human mind, by careful and conscientious observation, to form more exact notions about material substances, their constitution, and the laws which govern them.

Even our puny globe affords to the intellect of man a field of study, investigation, and discovery, which will test to the utmost the patience and science of unborn generations. Men bestow the highest fame and the richest rewards on the successful labors in this field—on such as enlarge the boundaries of human knowledge, or help, by their inventions, to subject the material world and the great elemental forces of nature to the uses of human life and the progress of industry. In this field, narrow as it really is in comparison with the boundless universe outside of our globe, men find a noble exercise for their intellectual faculties and no mean source of contentment and comparative happiness.

IN THE BEATIFIC VISION ALL IS INTUITION, NOT INDUCTION.

Now, take this consideration, based on the safest and most honorable experience, for a starting point to enable you to estimate the infinite field opened up to clear and full knowledge—no longer to timid investigation and a slow and patient observing and chronicling of facts and conclusions, but to a divine knowledge, second only to the infinite and connatural knowledge of God Himself. . . . As if some angel, by the divine command, took us all of a sudden up to these eternal heights, and touched mind and heart with that light and flame of the Beatific Vision, let us gaze awhile on all that it discloses to the ravished soul.

WHAT IS SEEN AMID THIS OCEAN OF LIGHT AND LIFE.

"Who beholds on earth the greatest and wisest of men," says one who was both wise and great as well as holy, "only sees the external seeming; the internal beauty and perfection of the soul he cannot see with the eye. But whoso enjoys the clear sight of God sees the perfections and the wealth of the divine Being, both interior and exterior. The blessed see the Fount of Life, the Fount of Light and Wisdom, the Fount of Goodness and Truth, of Beauty and Sweetness, of Joy and Bliss. They see the infinity of His essence, the immensity of His greatness, the length of His eternity, the sublime height of His majesty, and the unchangeable firmness of His throne.

"They see that almighty Power which made all things, the Wisdom which designed and executed this universal frame, the Goodness which gives to all things their perfection and binds all things to Itself. They see the Mercy which forgives guilt, and the Justice which punishes what has not been forgiven.

"They see, finally, the divine Persons, and the eternal and most perfect way that they proceed from each other; how the Son is begotten of the Father as His Word and Wisdom, abiding eternally in Him; how the Holy Spirit proceeds from both as Their love and abides in both; how these Three are distinguished from each other by Their proper personal characteristics, so that They are Three Persons really subsisting, and that all the while Theirs is one Essence, one indivisible Divinity, one Power, one Wisdom, one Goodness, one Majesty, one Light, one Immensity, one Eternity.

"All who see God, see all these things with clear, unclouded eye, firmly, unchangeably, and distinctly; not as we conceive of them, under diverse notions and mental visions, but with one simple and most luminous vision of the mind." *

TAKE UP AND SPELL THIS SYLLABLE BY SYLLABLE.

This comprehensive glance at the divine Being, as we conceive It to be unveiled in the Beatific Vision to the souls of the blessed, may not strike the person who reads the foregoing as at all affording a clue to the interior glory of that Ocean of perfection, goodness, loveliness—to the incomprehensible felicity of the Three divine Persons whose mutual knowledge and love of each other and of that Essence which overflows and flowers into this living Trinity. Yet, by taking up the pregnant passage just quoted, and by spelling it to one's self, sentence by sentence, and thought after thought, the subject grows on the mind; one horizon opens out into a wider, and that only leads to a wider still, the depths of that divine perfection and loveliness deepening and widening as we advance; and one infinite perfection connecting with another, and filling the soul

---
* Lessius, "De Summo Bono," L. I^o, c. viii.

of the beholder with ever-increasing rapture, as light begets light within these abysses, as glory leads up to glory, as one mighty well-spring of life and truth, of knowledge and love, of grandeur and beauty, calls out to the soul to pause and drink; and then another and another gushes forth within the bosom of that Spirit whose varied riches not all the cycles of eternity can exhaust for the intellect which contemplates or the heart that enjoys.

Then we are to consider that the clear sight of the Godhead; the intimate knowledge of His life, His being, His perfections; the unveiling to our eyes of the secret of that divine Mind, which conceived the plan of the universe, and of that Free Will which called it into being, is not the only effect of the "light of glory."

THE DIVINE MYSTERIES UNVEILED.

The Mysteries which form the object of the Christian's faith in this life, and in which he believes because God has revealed them, stand manifest and intelligible in the light of the other world. The union, in our own persons, of the soul with the body, of a purely spiritual substance with material organism, does, indeed, pave the way toward conceiving the Incarnation as possible. But in the light of the eternal day we shall understand clearly how our spiritual soul was created and marvelously fitted for the twofold purpose of rational and animal life; and how God became very Man, uniting, really and physically, the divine nature with the human in the Person of the Son, without ceasing to be God, or suffering, in His divinity, loss, or change, or eclipse of splendor.

HEAVEN AND ITS TWOFOLD EMPIRE SEEN AS ONE SEES A HALL.

In this divine light are also clearly seen all the wonders of that heaven—God's glorious dwelling-place and the home of angelic servants and human children. Holy Writ calls the place by various names. It is not only heaven, and the heaven of heavens, but the kingdom or empire of God—His house, His city, His temple, and the land of the living. We shall see, as we explain what relates to the place, its inhabitants, and their occupations, the fitness of all these names. Suffice it now to say that, together with His own Being in all its perfection, God will enable the blessed soul to see the magnificence and glory of that heavenly city, that immense and everlasting empire, which is the home and the possession of His elect. It is but just and reasonable that each new citizen of heaven should thus at once become perfectly acquainted with his abode for everlasting; with every one of those who dwell therein; with the hierarchies and orders of angels; with those of his own kind—men and women of every degree of merit, virtue, and heroic sanctity—God's most perfect creation in the moral world, all and each standing out distinctly revealed in their respective degrees of excellence and glory.

Then, as the sight of that glorious society bursts upon the soul, it also clearly discerns God's wonderful providence over His own elect, and the whole scheme of that Wisdom which "reacheth from end to end mightily, and ordereth all things sweetly."* It will be made manifest how the material world was created and ordered for the purposes of the rational

* Wisdom, viii, 1.

and spiritual, and how all things were intended to glorify the common Creator.

GOD'S GOVERNMENT UNDERSTOOD.

We who are tempted to murmur at the apparent triumph of wickedness over innocence, of evil over good, and error over truth, will then see the hidden reason of God's grand design. The whole course of His government, when the reign of His justice in heaven is taken into account, will appear like one magnificent and eternal harmony, in which the few discordant notes are made to enhance the general effect.

In that supernal light, which not only imparts to the intellect a grasp and a penetration almost divine, but gives* to the eye of the glorified human body a power commensurate with that of the intellect, the entire frame of creation will be seen and known perfectly in its dependence on the Creator.

THE UNIVERSE SEEN AND UNDERSTOOD.

The universe itself, from its centre to its furthest circumference, is intelligible to the mind, visible to the bodily sense. Even in our present condition, with the limited scope of our faculties, and the various obstacles which add to the difficulties of far-reaching bodily vision, the naked eye can see as far as the rays of light enable it to perceive objects— to the enormous distances where shine the stellar masses of the Milky Way, or the isolated suns around either pole. In the life to come, and the perfected or almost deiform condition of the soul,

---

* Besides the glorified Body of our Lord, that of His Blessed Mother, according to the Eastern and Western Churches, enjoys the bliss of heaven.

no such obstacles will interfere to prevent the fullness of knowledge, the unlimited range of the intellectual and the bodily vision. "The immeasurable circuit of the universe," says Lessius, "is to them only what a basilica or a hall would be, because of their gift of celerity." So, the spirit-like independence of distances is added to their supernatural gift of vision and knowledge.

THE NATURE OF ALL THINGS PENETRATED.

Not only that, but their knowledge embraces the nature, constitution and properties of all created things—spiritual as well as material. The mind, the eye of the blessed, may thus be said to render them present to all that exists. For their contemplation and knowledge of all and each are those of one who sees a thing as if he were present and looking into its very substance. Thus does God communicate to His friends in the other life His own attributes of omniscience and omnipresence, in so far as finite beings are susceptible of them.*

And so we may rest both mind and heart for the moment from the contemplation of all that glory.

Ah! Father, whose greatness is above all praise, whose love exceeds all thought of ours, it were enough, in order to make heaven the paradise of all delight and joy, to be evermore near Thee, to feel that Thou art our possession, all our own, and that nothing can separate us from Thee!

---

* It is clear that, no matter to what height the faculties of angel or man are raised by "the light of glory," or how vastly the sphere of their knowledge is enlarged, the angelic as well as the human intellect must ever remain finite in its nature and limited in its grasp. Clearly and fully as they see the divine Essence, their vision and knowledge of the same cannot be, like that of the divine Intellect, infinite and "comprehensive." Even so, as God cannot exhaust His creative power by producing a work or a single being in any sense *infinite*, the intellect of the blessed, outside of the Beatific Vision, can be exercised only on a finite and limited object.

CHAPTER VII.

THE SOCIETY ENJOYED IN GOD'S HEAVENLY EMPIRE.

I.

CHRIST AND HIS HUMAN KINGDOM.

"Then shall the just shine as the sun, in the kingdom of their Father."—*St. Matthew*, xiii, 43.

THE IMMENSE FIELDS OPENED OUT FOR ACTIVITY IN HEAVEN.

The most prevalent notions about the bliss of the life to come would have it to consist in perpetual repose and contemplation. It is true, that the *divine Object* so clearly seen there never departs from the mind. Even now the angels of every order and degree, who are employed in ministering on earth to the various needs of the human race, or whom the Ruler of the Universe sends to govern in His place the worlds which float around in immensity, never lose that Beatific Vision. The clear sight of the Godhead follows these mighty spirits at the remotest point of creation, and fills them with the same rapture as if they stood by the throne of Christ in that particular portion of the heavens where He reigns with His elect, and where the sacred Trinity manifest Their glory more fully to the angelic hosts and the multitude of the blessed. The clear sight of God is never withdrawn from those to whom it has once been vouchsafed. When we come to speak in detail of the angelic world, this truth shall be explained more fully.

THE BEATIFIC VISION ENJOYED THROUGHOUT THE HEAVENLY WORLDS.

We mention here what reason enlightened by faith can readily perceive and understand, that whether Saints or angels stand ministering around the throne of God and His Christ in heaven, or are sent to the uttermost limits of the universe on some special mission, that divine countenance follows them everywhere, and they gaze upon it continually while most actively busied in fulfilling their ministry toward mankind or regulating the inferior world.

The highest, the primal and essential source of heavenly beatitude is the clear sight of the Godhead, the rapture and joy which it begets. But, as we have already hinted more than once, the secondary source of bliss consists in the knowledge, love and companionship of the glorious society of heaven, of Christ and His Saints, and the angelic world who, with the Saints, form one Church Triumphant under Christ, their Head.

Here, again, comes to our mind the pregnant meaning of the oft-quoted words of the Lord:

"This is eternal life, that they may know Thee, ... and *Jesus Christ*, whom Thou hast sent."

It is not merely the clear knowledge conveyed to the soul by the Beatific Vision of the Mystery of the Incarnation, and of the entire order of God's providence in connection therewith, that is such a source of deep joy; it is also, and more than that, the personal friendship of that same Christ Jesus, His companionship and conversation, as well as the mutual friendship, companionship and intercourse of the glorious human and angelic worlds who, in heaven, unite to call Him King and Lord.

THE GLORIOUS SOCIETY OF THIS EMPIRE A SOURCE OF SECONDARY BLISS.

Can we realize in thought what it is to enjoy that unspeakably blissful and bliss-bestowing society of the heavenly kingdom? Everything in the study of this sublime and fertile subject reminds one of the fruitless attempts made by hardy adventurers to scale the loftiest summits of such mountain chains as the Himalayas. One, after traveling thousands of miles from the seashore, and traversing the ever-ascending upland plains which lead to the foothills of the great mountain masses, is confronted with majestic, snow-clad summits, surpassing Mont Blanc in elevation; and these great heights overcome, others stand out distinctly against the dark blue sky which seem as high again. Vainly have the boldest and most experienced attempted to assail these unapproachable heights. Human strength and endurance give way long ere the shining crests, lost in the cloudless air, have been reached.

So is it with these heavenly subjects. One has only reached up midway along some one of those giddy heights, when, lo! beyond it and above, rising, shining, rank upon rank, ascend the glorious objects of one's research and contemplation!

And yet we must not be disheartened by our failure to reach our aim. It is God's work we are endeavoring to accomplish for the good of souls and our own instruction. So, humbly trusting to His Holy Spirit for light and strength, we can contemplate from afar the sublimities inaccessible to man while cumbered with this body of death.

Let us divide, the better to aid our infirmity, the objects of our present study. Christ reigning with His elect naturally attracts our human sympathies. They form the first part of that blessed society, which is Christ's special kingdom. How vast, how wonderful in excellence, in holiness, in power, and in glory, are those uncounted millions who claim Him as their First Born of the dead, as their elder Brother and Saviour, we shall see presently. This is truly the human world of the heavens—magnificent world! The angelic world, wider still, with its incomparably superior numbers, composed of beings nearer to God in knowledge and power, will next engage our attention.

CHRIST AND HIS ELECT.

No language can convey even a dim notion of this assemblage of all that has ever existed on earth of most perfect and most holy men and women, with spotless and generous youth, and childhood transplanted in its first flower of innocence and loveliness to the land of the living. St. John, in the Apocalypse, affords us but a confused and disconnected description of the society of "the just made perfect." The truth, however, will grow on us, as we advance, calmly considering and weighing every authority we find in Scripture and theology.

THE PERSON OF CHRIST.

We could only describe, in speaking of our Lord's dealing with men during His stay upon earth, how the Godhead concealed Itself in Him, manifesting Its power only by the miracles performed for the poor and suffering, or at the entreaty of those who had laid Him under some obligation of gratitude. But the human side of His character was continually displayed by a thousand acts of sweetest charity, compassion, mercy, and kindliness.

In heaven, on the contrary, where all the grandeur and loveliness of both the divine and the human nature united in His Person shines forth revealed and is known thoroughly, the study of Christ must be to highest seraph and to highest Saint, to the Mother who bore Him as well as to the innocent children martyred at His birth in hatred of Him, a source of endless rapture. He is the crown of our nature, which, in Him, is deified and exalted to the throne of heaven. He is the most perfect of men as well as very God. He is our glory. As Man, He is the Master-piece of creation; as the Eternal Word and Son, He is the Power which made all things, and the Wisdom which governs them.

CHRIST'S BEAUTIFUL EARTHLY CHARACTER.

But what renders Him most dear to us are the human virtues which He practiced, the human qualities which made Him the most lovable and the most admirable of men. Who that has deeply studied the life of Christ from Nazareth and Bethlehem to the cross of Calvary and the rock on Mount Olivet, where a loving tradition still worships the very last foot-prints He left on our earth, but has been lost in wonder and gratitude for all the divinely human virtues, deeds, benefactions and teachings which have marked His pathway among men? Even now, after nearly nineteen hundred years, the high and the lowly, the learned and the simple, continually flock from every shore to that Holy Land in which He was born and died. They lovingly trace every scene of recorded suffering, miracle, sermon, parable, and missionary labor, from Bethlehem to the sources of the Jordan, and from the Lake of Genesareth to the seashore of Chanaan. Everywhere they "worship where His feet have stood," they gather and treasure up in their heart of hearts the "sweet odor" He has left behind in city, and hamlet, and country-side; on the mountain-top which beheld His night-long vigils and prayers; on the banks of Jordan, where He was baptized; on the waves of Galilee which His blessed feet have pressed; until the eyes of their love-lit souls almost think they see Him—the gentle, "the meek and humble of heart," the divinely compassionate and patient, the unwearied Shepherd of souls—once more lighting up the wilderness with His visible presence. Even the fourfold narrative of the Gospels only affords a colorless and imperfect outline of that character, whose grandeur, like that of the highest peak of the Himalaya, grows upon the devout student, till human strength fails long before he has had a far-off glimpse of the shining summit aloft in the heavens. Nevertheless, it is not the sublime displays of His power, nor the divine wisdom of His teaching, that move our souls so deeply and draw us to Him with such irresistible force, as the sweet human sympathies which betray the Son of the Virgin Mary, the Man born in a rocky cave by the road-side, hunted, while yet a babe in arms, like a wild beast, through the mountains of Judea into Egypt, and compelled to hide, in the carpenter's shop at Nazareth, His quality, His mission, and His growth in all the lovely virtues of boyhood and youth. It is when we behold Him, touched by the utter bereavement of the widow of Naim, raising her only son to life, or weeping at the grave of that other only son and brother, Lazarus, or shedding tears of patriotic grief and bitter human sorrow over the near prospect of Jerusalem destroyed and His own nation almost annihilated, that one admires and adores the infinite mercy of the Godhead, compassionating, in human form, with the truest and deepest human tenderness, the ills which befall our humanity. We know, then, that He is, in truth, God brought very near to us—our Emmanuel, our Saviour and Consoler.

HOW WE SHALL KNOW HIM IN HEAVEN.

Much, in every way, is the knowledge we obtain and the spiritual profit we gather from this study of the life of our Lord, as imperfectly described in the Gospels; much is the light, the comfort, that reward our following, in spirit, His footsteps all over the theatre of His earthly labors. But what can that knowledge be, or what that consolation, compared to the light and bliss which flood the soul admitted to His close and eternal companionship in the life to come?

The three chosen Disciples, who were privileged to witness His Transfiguration on the Mount, were dazzled overpowered and prostrated by the glory which burst from His bodily frame, like intolerable light from a tropical sun at its rising. And yet He had not fought, single-handed, the dread battle with the humiliation and death of the cross; and His sacred Body had not put on the glory won by the agony in the Garden, the buffeting, the scourging, the crowning with thorns, and the Crucifixion. . . . Who can fathom these depths of shame and suffering, can estimate the glory of His Resurrection, and the splendor with which the Crucified shines on the throne of the heavens?

THE FLOWER AND CROWN OF OUR HUMANITY.

He is, as Man, exalted to the right hand of God, the crown and boast of our humanity, the divine flower into which the root of Jesse blossomed. If Peter, on the Mount, and gazing upward at His transformed appearance and at the ecstatic worship of Moses and Elias, could only murmur, in the excess of his bliss, "Lord, it is good for us to be here," let us also believe that it is good, even looking up from the plain and amid the bustle of the hurrying crowd, for us to dwell a while on these magnificences of Christian truth. Christ as Man, as well as Christ in His Godhead, is for angels and Saints a subject of ecstatic rapture, of never-ending gratitude and adoration. Of Him who, for our salvation, ran such a race of abasement and suffering, the Saints in Paradise, like their brethren in exile upon earth, may well sing, as they meditate on what they owe Him and what He is in Himself:

> O videre Te! amare Te!
> Perenniter laudare Te!

> "O to see Thee, to love Thee!
> Everlastingly to praise Thee!"

One of the most glorious disciples formed by the Seraphic Francis of Assisi—St. Bonaventure, called by the middle ages the "Seraphic Doctor"—thus vents his love for Christ Crucified:

"Transpierce, O sweet Lord Jesus, the marrow and vitals of my soul with the delightful and most salutary wound of Thy love, with the flame of a true, steady, and holy apostolic charity; so that my soul shall faint and melt away with the mere unceasing love and desire of Thee. Make me yearn and pine for Thy courts; make me wish to be dissolved, and to be with Thee!

"Grant that my soul shall hunger for Thee, O Bread of Angels, O Food of Saintly Souls—for Thee, our daily Bread above all substance, possessing all sweetness and savor, and all that can delight the taste. Thou on whom the angels ever seek to gaze, let my heart still hunger after Thee and feed upon Thee. Let all the depths of my being be filled with Thy sweetness.

"Oh, let me ever thirst for Thee, Fount of Life, Fount of Wisdom and Knowledge, Fount of Light Eternal, Torrent of Rapturous Bliss, overflowing Abundance of the House of God.

"Be Thou the object of my ambition; let me seek Thee and find Thee; ever tend toward Thee, and at length come to Thee. Let me study Thee, speak of Thee, and do all my actions in praise and honor of Thy Name, with humility and prudence, with tender love and deep delight, with promptness and affection, and with perseverance to the end.

"And thus be Thou alone evermore my hope, my sole trust, my wealth, my happiness, my pleasure, my joy, my repose and rest, my peace, my only delight, my fragrance, my savor, my food, my refreshment, my refuge, my helper, my wisdom, my portion, my possession, my treasure, on which my mind and my heart shall be firmly set and immovably rooted forever."

CHRIST ON EARTH AND IN HEAVEN INSEPARABLE FROM HIS PARENTS.

In contemplating on the throne of heaven Him who is the Father of our souls and their Saviour, can we forget her who is His Mother, and who, as God's creature and a human being, is, after her Son, the most exalted and perfect of her kind? Protestantism has too long refused, in its blind, un-Christian, and unreasonable prejudice, to render the Mother of the Redeemer the honor, reverence, and homage due to her quality, apart from the gratitude due to the noble Mother and the "strong woman" who consented to bring forth and rear her Babe in such hardship, privation, and peril, and to follow Him, unflinching, to the bitter agony and humiliation of the cross.

But, even among Protestants, there are those who unite with the ancient Churches of the East and West in acknowledging the claims which Mary, the Mother of Christ, has to the filial love, respect and gratitude of the entire human race. To them, as to us, Jesus and His Mother Mary stand in heaven, side by side, as the Parents of us all—she, the Mother of the New Life, being the highest of His worshipers, the first to voice the praise and adoration of His elect, the first to plead for the manifold necessities of Christ's family on earth.

> Soul, is it faith, or love, or hope,
> That lets me see her standing up
> Where the light of the throne is bright?
> Unto the left, unto the right,
> The cherubim arrayed, conjoint,
> Float inward to a golden point,
> And from between the seraphim
> The glory issues for a hymn.

These two, and the royal Joseph, who watched over them on earth, as over God's choicest treasures, were, assuredly, gentle, true and most delightful companions and friends to all who sought to know, to study, and to follow the Word Incarnate; most compassionate to all who, for body or spirit, stood in need of the divine Physician. We cannot separate these three while following Christ during the most attractive period of His mortal life—His infancy, boyhood, and youth. It is no idolatry, no injury to the God who gave them to our love and veneration, to pay them the homage of our grateful reverence, when we approach in spirit the cave in Bethlehem, their journeyings to Egypt and back, and the carpenter's shop at Nazareth. Shall we separate those who were called on earth, and are denominated in the Gospel, "the parents of Jesus," from Him who disdained not to be called their Son? Did not holy Anna and the no less holy Simeon, when Mary and Joseph brought Him for the first time to the Temple, pour forth their souls in rapturous thanksgiving, when the contact with the Incarnate God gave light to their minds to know Him, and fired their hearts with His love?

Who among us but would, at death's approach especially, not give worlds for the privilege of receiving, from the arms of that Most Blessed Mother, the divine Babe, the Light of the Gentiles and the Glory of Israel? How gladly, like Simeon, would we depart from this world, with the assured hope of salvation in the next, repeating in our turn this hymn of the predestined:

> "Now Thou dost dismiss Thy servant, O Lord,
> According to Thy word, in peace!
> Because my eyes have seen Thy salvation,
> Which Thou hast prepared
> Before the face of all peoples:
> A light to the revelation of the Gentiles,
> And the glory of Thy people, Israel." *

It is from that Mother the world ever receives Him who is the Light and the Life. What mother, what woman, can compare with her?

CHAPTER VIII.

AMONG THE MULTITUDES OF THE BLESSED IN CHRIST'S HUMAN KINGDOM.

"According to Thy Highness, Thou hast multiplied the children of men."—*Psalm XI*, 9.
"Heaven and the heavens of heavens do not contain Thee."—2 *Paralip.*, vi, 18.

II.

Although we have only bestowed a timid and hasty glance on His excellence, majesty, and loveli-

---
* St. Luke, II, 29-32.

ness, who is "flesh of our flesh" as Man, and the life of our life as God, we can now turn our eyes to the radiant multitudes who fill the courts of our King—the First-Born from among the dead. Let us, if we can, count the millions there who, descended from Adam, can truly call Christ their Brother. Contemplate their ranks in spirit. There is not one there—not one—on whom rests the stain of moral guilt. Nothing undefiled can pass beyond the frontiers of that land of the living, or enter that Presence, or enjoy the Vision, in which essential holiness is possessed by the holy, or join that society of "the spirits of the just made perfect."

THE COMPANY OF THE TRUEST AND THE BEST.

Picture to yourself a company of all the men and women most distinguished in all the earth for their well-proven goodness, generosity, heroism of life, excellence in learning, as well as in the services rendered to their fellow-men; all persons the most admirable, the most lovable, the most ready to render to every quality of every one of their brethren a just and willing tribute of praise; a company from which jealousy, envy, pride, and self-love are banished, and where the thoughts and efforts of all are directed to secure the honor, comfort, and felicity of each. It would be such a happiness, such a reward, to spend one day in the week, or even one hour in the day, in communion of heart and mind with such a select and glorious society. Yes, one day occasionally spent in breathing the air they breathe, and in filling one's soul with a draught of goodness from their speech and their example, would lift one above the miseries of this life.

What, then, must it be to be one, and forever, of the most blessed company who surround the throne of the living God—to be united to every member of this immense and most glorious society by the ties of a friendship which is eternal and founded on the knowledge of merits crowned by God's own praise? No torture is more terrible to the noble of soul and pure of heart than to be condemned, by some freak of fortune, to associate with an assemblage of the low-lived, the criminal, the degraded. This companionship with the fallen, the wicked, the vile, is one of the worst punishments inflicted in hell.

THE FRIENDSHIP OF THE BEST AND TRUEST A PART OF HEAVENLY FELICITY.

On the other hand, the companionship and lifelong and everlasting friendship of the noblest, the purest, the best, must be a part of the felicity of heaven. In order, however, to have a just idea of the real greatness of the honor and happiness derived from this intercourse with the citizens of the heavenly kingdom, both men and angels, we ought to examine more closely to what a supreme degree of moral excellence all spirits are raised on entering upon the life eternal. For it is manifest that the happiness derived from all friendship depends upon the acknowledged goodness and greatness of the persons united by this sacred bond; so that the most perfect friendship is between persons in every way exempt from selfishness and all vice, and, at the same time, endowed with the most exalted qualities of mind and heart—persons who, in loving each other, consider that all they have belong to their friends.

THE SUPREME PERFECTION OF MORAL NATURE—WHENCE DERIVED.

But what is this special perfection, this supreme excellence of both their intellectual and moral nature, to which man and angel necessarily attain in that life where all trial ends, where all merit is rewarded, all labor is succeeded by repose, and all the aspirations of the soul by perfect fulfillment?

Religion teaches, and the light of reason in Christian philosophy acquiesces in the teaching, that eternal life means final perfection for all created beings admitted to its enjoyment.

It is a cardinal doctrine of Christian theology, that man only attains in the life to come the full perfection of his nature, both in body and in soul; for the human personality is not the mere spiritual element, but the material organization as well, which forms a part of his being in this life—labors, suffers, and enjoys with him—and must, to constitute his perfect felicity and the completeness of his being, be united to the soul in the future existence.

Of course, the resurrection of the body, of which we shall treat fully before the end of this volume, is a supernatural fact expressly revealed by Christ. His Resurrection is the type and the pledge of ours. The felicity and the glory which He, as Man, enjoys in heaven are to be shared by every child of Adam admitted into the life eternal. We shall differ from Him only in degree, and in the essential distinction which His union with the Divinity establishes, and the wide gulf it opens between the Man-God and the most exalted and perfect of creatures.

TRANSFORMATION OF THE JUST AFTER DEATH.

We can help ourselves toward some conception of the mighty change which takes place in the whole nature of man after death, and when raised to the height of the Beatific Vision. For the moment and the purpose of our argument, we speak of the blessed as they will be after the resurrection.

ILLUSTRATIONS FROM THE TREES OF THE FOREST.

Look at the mightiest trees in the forest. There are some to which, on a careful examination of their structure, and from a thorough knowledge of the laws which regulate their growth, naturalists grant a thousand or even twelve hundred years of existence. But even the mightiest of these giants of the vegetable world, which have outlived empires and peoples, are developed from a tiny fruit or germ. From the acorn springs the oak; from a seedling one-fifth the size of an acorn proceeds the pine, the yew tree, the prodigious trunks of the Californian Wellingtonia. If one were gifted with an angelic intellect, able to pierce the organic envelope of the tree germ, even before the blossom on the branch opens to the sun, and what is to be the future tree—the pride of hillside or Alpine valley—begins its life of one thousand or two thousand years, doubtless one might discern there the principles of that long life and sturdy strength unfolding themselves. The flower is transformed into the fruit—into the acorn; and this, cast on the earth, in due time, aided by the vital warmth and moisture furnished by the elements, will burst its woody shell, and send its tender roots into the ground, and put forth its first seed leaves toward the sun. It is but a tiny, helpless thing, which the foot of the passer-by or the ravages of a little insect may destroy in this first stage of its growth. Come back after a few summers and you will find a sappling; and the sappling slowly shoots up into the tree capable of battling with and defying all the force of the storm.

ILLUSTRATED BY THE STAGES OF HUMAN EXISTENCE ITSELF.

It is a marvelously instructive study. But how much more so is that of human existence in its three stages: Before birth; through all the dangers, trials, and battles of infancy, childhood, youth, and perfect manhood, till death closes the extremest period of old age; and then beyond the grave. The dark, blind, helpless, vegetative period before birth bears, to that which follows between birth and the grave, the same proportion, in the development of all the energies and aspirations of rational life, as this second stage itself bears to the eternal future. It is the cry, the complaint, of the *élite* of our race, that even the longest human life is too short for the acquisition of knowledge, or the accomplishment of the generous labors which the good and the great have begun for the benefit of their kind. We can bring no great work to perfection within the brief span of our present existence. Small is the sum of science which the most long-lived student can acquire, since, as he grows older, he only perceives more clearly how little he has learned, and to him the horizons of knowledge stretch out into infinity. So is it with those who have toiled to reach the heights of sanctity. A life of self-sacrifice and devotion to others only discloses heights of moral perfection far above their ken, toward which their soul aspires, and vast regions upon earth where peoples who know not God cry out in darkness and from the depths of moral misery for the voice and hand of an Apostle.

THIS LIFE ALL TOO SHORT FOR THE EARNEST WORKER.

We say it ourselves every day, that life is all too short for the zeal of the earnest, the serious-minded, the true-hearted. And yet we all have aspirations, yearnings, hopes, tendencies, and a thirst for the infinite and everlasting, which suppose that there is in the unknown future a period of perfection, fulfillment, satiety, and complete satisfaction for all that is divinest in the sentiments and conceptions of man.

Let us believe it, then: "God, who commanded the light to shine out of darkness, hath shined in our hearts to give the light of the knowledge of the glory of God in the face of Christ Jesus. . . We are cast down, but we perish not: always bearing about in our body the mortification of Jesus, that the life also of Jesus may be made manifest in our mortal flesh. . . Knowing that He who raised up Jesus will raise up us also with Jesus, and place us with you. . . For which cause we faint not: but though our outward man is corrupted [*i. e.*, decayed]: yet the inward man is renewed day by day. For that which is at present momentary and light of our tribulation worketh for us above measure exceedingly an eternal weight of glory. While we look not at the things which are seen, but at the things which are not seen. For the things which are seen are temporal: but the things which are not seen are eternal. For we know, if our earthly house of this habitation be dissolved, that we have a building of God, a house not made with hands, eternal in the heavens. For in this also we groan, desiring to be clothed upon with our habitation that is from heaven. . . . Now He, that maketh us for this very thing, is *God*, who hath given us the pledge of the Spirit." *

WHAT WE ARE MADE FOR.

Such are the thoughts, desires, anticipations, with which the Christian soul is moved as life advances and the end draws near. They are the merciful touches of that Creator-Spirit who "maketh us for this very thing," this "eternal weight of glory," this incorruption and immortality with which we, the predestined heirs to all this glory, yearn unceasingly. The converted Corinthians, to whom St. Paul taught so sublime and elevating a doctrine, needed its lessons, and the promises they held forth, to rise superior to the frightful corruption that surrounded them; to worship the God of holiness with pure hearts and life unblemished amid the sensual idolatry of that infamous land; and to resist the persecutions let loose against the new faith. What cared they for "the momentary and light tribulation," which was the lot of the Christian, when they looked forward to the fruit of tribulation, that "eternal weight of glory," exceeding all measure of human suffering and present merit?

---

* 2 Cor., iv, 6-18; v, 1-5.

THIS TRANSFORMATION, OR GROWTH, IS VITAL AND FROM WITHIN.

We must not, however, consider that this transformation of the present embryo or infant-like state of man into that truly Godlike excellence, perfection, and grandeur of the eternal beatitude, is a something merely external to the soul itself. A child may be allowed to disport itself in the loveliest of gardens, reveling in its delights, while still remaining a child in mind, and stature, and disposition. Or it may be taken into the most magnificent of courts, and behold all the splendor of the apartments, and varied greatness of king and courtiers; and, on returning to its home, all that it has seen will be only a memory, leaving the child what it was before.

Such is not the change wrought in the blessed by the Holy Spirit when they enter into the joy of their Lord. Between the highest knowledge and the highest sanctity reached by the soul before death, and the perfection of mind and heart wrought by the clear sight of God in glory and the fruition of that most blissful Presence, there is an infinite distance. How can we measure or understand it?

HOW WE CAN ESTIMATE THIS MIGHTY GROWTH.

We who have lived long enough have known men and women to grow from dull and uninteresting childhood to the highest degree of mental culture, of social distinction, of moral greatness, and loveliness. It was the development of the obscure, invisible germ of excellence to its bright flower in springtide and its glorious fruit in the autumn of life. But, in very truth, the ripest knowledge here below and the rarest goodness and holiness of life are but the flower and the promise of that supernal excellence seen and possessed only in the land of the living.

St. Paul, who was running himself the race of suffering, with his cruel death ever in view, needed to keep his own eyes steadily fixed on the glories of that everlasting kingdom. Fourteen years before he wrote the words we quoted several paragraphs back, he had been "rapt even to the third heaven—caught up into paradise." The words that he had heard there he dared not to utter to mortal ear. But the rapturous vision disclosed to him illuminates his Epistles with the light descending from beyond sun and stars. "You are our epistle," he says to these Corinthians, most of them, probably, of Hebrew parentage,—"you are our epistle, written in our hearts, . . known and read by all men. . . . You are the epistle of Christ, ministered by us, and written not with ink, but with the Spirit of the living God."* And comparing the conduct of the Israelites of old, who forced Moses to veil his countenance, with these fervent disciples, who only sought to know and to imitate Christ, he uses these wonderful words: "Now, the Lord is a Spirit: and where the Spirit of the Lord is, there is liberty. But we all beholding the glory of the Lord with open face, are transformed into the same image from glory to glory, as by the Spirit of the Lord." †

As if the study of the Gospel truth, and the fervent following in the footsteps of the Master, wrought such fruit in the lives and souls of these men and women that it seemed the Spirit of God

---

* 2 Cor., iii. 2-3.   † Ibidem, iii, 17-18.

carried them forward from height to height of perfection, effecting here below in them a lively image of the transformation wrought in heaven by the Beatific Vision.

COMMUNITIES ON EARTH THE IMAGES OF THE HEAVENLY.

There are on earth, at the end of this nineteenth century, communities of men and women among whom one seems to breathe the air of paradise; where somewhat of its light rests upon every face; where the chance wayfarer comes of a sudden into the shadow of the peace that is not of earth; where the language one hears belongs to another sphere; and a something goes out from the dwellers therein which pierces the soul, as with a ray of light, or with that dart of fire the angel sent through the kindred heart of Stanislaus Kostka.

What, then, must it be to be with Christ and His Saints in glory? With Christ and His Saints!

CHAPTER IX.

LOST AMONG THE HUMAN WORLD OF HEAVEN.

"O Israel, how great is the house of God, and how vast is the place of His possession! It is great, and hath no end: it is high and immense!"—*Baruch*, iii, 24-25.
"Behold how good and how pleasant it is for brethren to dwell together in unity."—*Psalm CXXXII*, 1.

"LORD, IT IS GOOD FOR US TO BE HERE!"

St. Peter, speaking in the name of his two companions amid the glories of the Mount of Transfiguration, could only express the rapture they felt by the simple words, "Lord, it is good for us to be here!" And yet only two of the great figures of the Old Testament, Moses and Elias, formed the company of the Redeemer. Nevertheless, such was the overwhelming sense of blissfulness caused by Christ's allowing the light of His concealed divinity to burst forth for a moment, flooding His own person and those of His two great servants, that the place became heaven to the three favored Apostles. "Lord," Peter goes on to say, "let us make here three tents—one for Thee, and one for Moses, and one for Elias." St. Mark adds, in relating the words of Peter: "He knew not what he said," being beside himself from mingled happiness and awe. What, then, must be the intoxicating effect of beholding, no longer with the weak eyes of their mortal flesh, but with the eyes of our transfigured body, those shining multitudes of the blessed, whose head is Christ, mixed up with the myriads of angels, all forming around the enthroned Incarnate Son a living world so glorious and so vast that it requires the transformed senses of the other life to seize both the intensity of their glory and the incredible extent of their numbers! O kingdom of the living God, who can by thought or imagination reach thy frontiers round about, or conceive of thy splendors, or tell of thy riches and of the numbers and felicity of thine inhabitants!

THE FRIENDS WE SHALL HAVE IN HEAVEN.

We call them most happy here below who, possessed of vast domains and boundless wealth, surround themselves with the friends of their choice in endless succession, entertaining them with all the pleasures that money can purchase and human ingenuity devise. Their felicity is, amid their own broad lands and in their princely abodes, to dispense unlimited hospitality, and hear their own praises sounded by the men and women on whom they lavish magnificent entertainments.

But in heaven, the least portion of the happiness of God's friends is the assurance that this kingdom, with its riches and glory, is all their own; that theirs is the sweet society of that infinite multitude of sainted men and women and glorified spirits; but that God Himself is all their own. To the man who has, for a great portion of his life, been condemned to wander homeless over the earth, to depend for his subsistence on his own labor, and for his happiness on the uncertain favor of strangers and the inconstancy of fortune, there is unspeakable joy to find himself suddenly in possession of broad acres he can call his property, with a mansion worthy to be his home, and wealth sufficient to banish all fears of future need.

BECOME POOR TO GAIN HEAVEN.

How many souls, since Christ was born, lived, and died in voluntary poverty, have forsaken broad lands, wealth, home, friends, and country itself, to cast their lot with Christ—to become one of those of whom He said: "Blessed are the poor in spirit, for theirs is the kingdom of heaven!" How paltry these right royal souls deem the price they pay for that kingdom, when they first set their foot on the land of the living, and feel that it is their own, all their own, in its length and its breadth, with its wealth and its glory, its loving hosts of true friends, and the God who made it as their crowning possession so long as eternity endures!

THE BLISSFUL INTERCOURSE OF THAT KINGDOM.

What are the pleasures of a passing acquaintance, with the noblest, most cultivated, and most virtuous society in marble halls, enchanted gardens, or grounds resembling Eden in its bloom, compared with the honor, the joy, the felicity, of mixing evermore with the company of Christ and His friends, where the minds of one and all are so elevated, illumined, and enlarged, that they take in, by intuition, all the divine perfections, all the natural and supernatural excellences of Saints and angels, and all the marvels of God's wondrous works throughout creation? Drinking evermore full draughts of knowledge and love at the fount of the divine Essence, each spirit there pours out its love and admiration on all the members of that blessed company, whom God has made so good and great, and in loving whom it loves the Giver of all good gifts.

THE SWEET AND HOLY TIES OF EARTH NOT DISSOLVED IN HEAVEN.

Nor must we forget for a moment that, once we join that heavenly society, the ties which on earth bound us to kindred, friends, and neighbors, are not dissolved forever, so that among the citizens of that kingdom we only meet new faces, or find no happiness from association with our own. There is not a tie formed by nature here below between our souls and the souls of others that will not subsist, strengthened, hallowed, and perpetuated in eternity, provided that we shall have respected these ties ourselves in this life, and hallowed them by making of them means of benefiting or sanctifying the dear ones thus connected with us.

THOSE WHO THERE SHINE LIKE STARS.

It will repay us well to pause awhile on this truth, as on a rich mine of instruction and comfort. Certain it is, that persons who, on earth, have been to those of their own household, by word and example, a cause of edification—who have exhorted and encouraged children and servants to be, like themselves, true children of God—shall, in heaven, have children and servants around them, as so many jewels in their crown of merit.

THE MARTYR-MOTHER OF THE MACHABEES.

Who can imagine that the mother of the Machabees is separated, amid the great army of martyrs on high, from the seven heroic sons whom she beheld most cruelly tortured in Antioch, suffering in her inmost soul every pang inflicted on her boys, till the youngest had won his palm, and then her own turn came to be tortured and to triumph? What praise must everlastingly be hers as she moves with her glorious offspring through these crowned battalions of God's witnesses! And Mathathias, the priest, with his Godlike progeny, the champions of faith and country, of religious freedom and political independence, who made the name of Machabee as glorious in Judea as that mother and her offspring had made it in the Syrian capital—do they not triumph together with God in heaven, as they fought together for God in the land of their fathers?

NOE THE JUST, OUR SECOND PARENT.

Looking farther back in the ages, I remember that other parent of our race, Noe, and remember how he and his were true to the living God among the gigantic vices and crimes of a lost world. They alone were saved from the universal destruction. What, though one son and his progeny may have proved unworthy of such a parent, shall Noe not behold around him in the land of the living myriads to whom he transmitted the promise and the undying faith in its fulfillment? Is not the promised One descended from that blessed seed saved in the Ark? Did not Abraham and Sarah inherit Noe's faith with his blood? And what a galaxy of holy, heroic souls surround every one of these sublime patriarchs, who kept the faith in spite of the incredible seductions of an idolatry of which we of the nineteenth Christian century can only form a very dim notion; who preserved their souls and their lives from the stain of the frightful moral corruption of Chaldea, and Canaan, and Egypt!

THE FAITHFUL GENERATIONS BEFORE CHRIST.

Recall to mind, both before and after Christ, the generations of heroic believers, among whom "Women received their dead raised to life again: but others were racked, not accepting deliverance, that they might expect a better resurrection; and others had trial of mockeries and stripes, moreover also of bonds and prisons: they were stoned, they were cut asunder, they were tempted, they were put to death by the sword, they wandered about in sheep-skins, in goat-skins, being in want, distressed, afflicted: of whom the world was not worthy:

wandering in deserts, in mountains, and in dens, and in caves of the earth."*

THE CHRISTIAN HEBREWS, PARENTS OF CHRISTENDOM.

St. Paul wrote this of the ancient Hebrews. How many in his own days sealed with their blood their testimony to Jesus Christ! How many more—a fact we ungratefully overlook—labored successfully to bear His name to the remotest corners of the then known world! Remember the holy households Paul, and Peter, and their fellow-apostles met with everywhere, to whom they brought the light of the faith, and who spread it so zealously on every shore. The Acts and Epistles of the Apostles mention many—a few only, however, of the multitude—of these blessed families, whose men and women, sons and daughters, were among the glorious parents of the early Church—the parents, in truth, of our Christendom! Shall none of those whom they were instrumental in giving to God, and in making worthy of Him, surround their benefactors in heaven? All through the history of God's revealed religion we read of fathers and mothers rearing their offspring in the fear of the Lord, and walking before them in the paths of generous and heroic performance of the service due to the divine Majesty. When Christendom counted within its pale all the nations of the civilized world, every Christian people possessed saintly homes innumerable. To the education and the examples given there, to the heroic blood thus inherited, we owe it that, amid the wreck of former institutions, there subsist in the most

---

* Hebrews, xi, 35-38.

afflicted lands the traditional Christian virtues which are the seed of a future more glorious than the world has yet seen.

Writing these lines in the land most tried of any for religion's sake—among a people to whom, during centuries, the words just quoted from St. Paul could be spoken of every generation; a people beaten and ground in the mortar, exterminated, exiled, despoiled; the sad remnant oppressed by a tyranny so fearful that it seems inconceivable to any not born on the soil, and their home-life broken up by enforced emigration—yet the heroic faith and sublime endurance of fathers and mothers have fostered the germs of life; and these germs are, to-day, under God and for His Church, the hope of the world.

MODERN PEOPLES WHO HAVE KEPT THE FAITH.

Shall such fathers and mothers have no special glory from the company, the praise, the love, of their faithful children in the land of the living?

How many such families and such noble parents do we not all know? How many fathers to whose lives we can apply literally the words of the Apostle: "By faith he abode in the land; for he looked for a city that hath foundations: whose builder and maker is God." And again: "All these died according to faith, not having received the promises, but beholding them, afar off, and saluting them, and confessing that they are pilgrims and strangers on the earth. For they that say these things, do signify that they seek a country. . . . But now they desire a better, that is to say, a heavenly country. Therefore God is not ashamed to be called their God: for He hath prepared for them a city." *

---
* Hebrews, xi, 9-16.

They possess now that country, and that God-built city, where their "Women received their dead raised to life again."

HONOR PAID IN HEAVEN TO THE PARENTS OF THE SAINTS.

It is related in authentic history that when the tidings reached Portugal, in 1693, that the heroic John de Britto had been—like his namesake, John the Baptist—beheaded by the King of Marava, because he would not sanction an adulterous connection contrary to the holy laws of matrimony, the martyr's mother, who was then at the Portuguese court, was forced by the queen to be seated on the royal throne, and, during three days in succession, to receive the homage of the royal family and the nobles of the kingdom. Such is the honor Christian sentiment pays to the mothers of Christ's glorious servants. Do we not perceive that, had the noble lady been in heaven, the entire "army of martyrs" and all the Saints of God would have congratulated and blessed her for having reared such a son?

THE RELATIONS OF HOME AND COUNTRY IN THE LAND OF THE LIVING.

The sweet relations of home and country are not ignored in the life to come; the holy affections of home and kindred are not buried with us in the grave. Purified from all earthly dross, exalted, and perfected, conjugal, parental and filial love forms no small element of the happiness enjoyed by the Saints. But in all the new relations into which the soul enters on becoming a member of the heavenly city, as in all that constitutes its life, the divine

Will so regulates all others, the union of all human hearts there is so close with that of Christ, their Model and the Fountain of all Grace, that the perfect and ecstatic love of God only fills every citizen there with a more ardent and holy love for everybody and everything dear to God.

STILL LOST AMONG THE MULTITUDES OF THE BLESSED.

THE NUMBERS OF CHRIST'S REDEEMED.

As we proceed with our great subject, it will be more and more apparent that we need not restrain our imagination while picturing to ourselves the various features of greatness, vastness, and magnificence which are proper to that city of God—the masterpiece of the divine Love and Power. The felicity enjoyed there, the social condition of that everlasting kingdom, the fact that the Author of all things there bestows *Himself*, known in His essence and possessed in His infinite loveliness, as the reward of His faithful servants, as the crowning glory of all His works—all this argues that everything, spiritual and material, in that final order shall be on a scale of perfection and immensity corresponding to the completion of God's designs.

We have spoken coldly of Christ reigning in glory, surrounded by His redeemed. What is, at present—what shall be, when the last child of Adam and Eve is added to them—their real numbers?

ESTIMATE OF THE NUMBER OF THE TRULY FAITHFUL.

We can only form conjectures. It is computed that the human race, as it is to-day, counts some one thousand millions of individuals. This number is renewed at least twice in a century. Of these millions, those alone, according to Catholic doctrine, have a right to the supernatural beatitude, won for the race by the Blood of Jesus Christ, who have become, by baptism, members of His mystic body, the Church; and of the members of the Church none can make good their right but such as die in the charity of Christ, unstained by mortal guilt.

"THE NARROW GATE."

He, our own loving and merciful Redeemer, speaks of the road which leads to that supernatural heaven as "the narrow road," and of those who follow it to the end as "few indeed" comparatively. As we, His professed disciples, look around us, remembering how high is the standard of virtue set up by the Gospel, we are continually saddened by the contradiction we behold among Christians, between their profession and their practice. How many, even among those who are the guides, and should be the models, of the multitude fall beneath the level of natural generosity in aim and deed, not to speak of that supernatural ideal which shines forth in the life of Christ, and which His Saints, in every age, made the object of their fervent imitation! To all professed Christians who disgrace their faith by their practice, who nurse themselves into the hope that all shall be well with them in the end, or that aims, words, and deeds, and a whole life beneath the standard of good pagan morality, shall be crowned by the reward of a supernatural heaven, we recommend the calm and serious perusal of Christ's words in St. Luke, xiii, 22-30.

"BLESSED ARE THE POOR!"

Still, among the faithful of the poor and labering classes, in countries we need not name, how much of heroic piety and Godlike virtue one may find without searching far? We repeat, though for another purpose, what we said above: In the ancient land, where we are writing, the very atmosphere is impregnated with the fragrance of the Christian virtues exhaled from the homes and lives of these toiling, suffering, oppressed masses. It is like a lonely Alpine valley in full springtide, when meadows and hill-slopes are all aglow with the glory of innumerable flowers of the field, when swarms of bees are reveling in their sweets, and the very air is loaded with their mingled perfumes. And how many households are there of the middle and upper classes in every land, in which the lives of parents and children are in strictest conformity to the dictates of conscience! We have known so many, so many who, true to the light given them, seemed incapable in practice of doing what they deemed to be wrong! And knowing this, we remember with fear and trembling the words of the Master: "Whosoever doth not carry his cross and come after Me, cannot be My disciple." Or again: "Strive to enter by the narrow gate: for many, I say to you, shall seek to enter, and shall not be able. But when the Master of the house shall be gone in, and shall shut to the door, you shall begin to stand without, and knock at the door, saying: 'Lord, open to us!' And He, answering, shall say to you: 'I know you not whence you are.' Then you shall begin to say: 'We have eaten and drunk in Thy presence, and Thou hast taught in our streets.'

And He shall say to you: 'I know you not. . . . Depart from Me all ye workers of iniquity!'"*

DID NOT CHRIST SPEAK LITERALLY OF THE JEWS IN HIS DAY?

It is a terrible lesson. But it is the retribution which awaits the neglect to profit by the golden opportunities of the present life, and thereby purchase the eternal reward we have been foreshadowing. It is the just punishment of the perverse use of God's best gifts, of the frustration of His most merciful designs, of His most fatherly and loving providence over us.

At the end of the same chapter the great heart of the Redeemer gives vent to the bitter grief that fills it at the prospect of the desolation of His native land, the extermination of its people, and the ruin of that beautiful capital. "Jerusalem, Jerusalem, that killest the prophets, and stonest them that are sent to thee, how often would I have gathered thy children, as the bird doth her brood under her wings, and thou wouldest not!"

Oh! the mystery and the wonder of that Infinite Love which, ever since that day, has been seeking to gather the children of the Church and all the race of mankind through the Church under Its wings in that secure and everlasting peace of the heavenly city!

While the sword of Titus was drinking the blood of more than a million of Hebrews, and the City of the Great Sacrifice was razed to its foundations, thousands of that chosen race were spreading the religion of Christ throughout the Roman Empire, and laying the solid foundations of that Church

---

* St. Luke, xiii. 24-27.

which is on earth the nursery of saints for heaven. How many millions of her children has this spouse of Christ sent to join Him in heaven during the nineteen centuries, well nigh, of her existence? No one has revealed to us. But suppose their number to be equal to that of the inhabitants of the earth at this day—*one thousand millions*—and then allow your imagination to range over the glorious ranks of this immense multitude.

MAY WE COMPUTE THE SAINTS IN HEAVEN TO-DAY AT ONE THOUSAND MILLIONS?

We are only endeavoring, with the light of faith, and beneath the eye of God, to attain to some approximation to the sublime reality. One thousand millions of sainted human spirits forming around Christ, the Man-God, the Saviour, a living crown of glory in His kingdom! Let us suppose that all the nations of the earth, at the present moment, were civilized and at peace with each other; that steam and electricity had made traveling by sea and land incomparably more safe and easy than it is at present, and that telegraphy enabled thought to travel with the speed of light from people to people and man to man. Suppose, moreover, that Christianity was at the beginning of that era long hoped for, when the errors and follies of materialism, socialism, and a false science, had had their reign and passed away, and the whole race of man were prepared for the reception of the Gospel truth, how enthusiastically would the young, the wealthy, the learned, and the religious-minded, undertake to visit every land, and study and benefit every tribe of earth! Even for the mere purposes of science or recreation a voyage among these one thousand millions of our fellow-men, undertaken and accomplished under the circumstances described, would nobly fill up a life-time.

THE FELICITY OF SOCIAL INTERCOURSE WITH SUCH A WORLD.

What, then, shall we say of that world beyond the stars, which the Almighty Creator has made for His elect, and where He has gathered under the wings of His love, amid the most perfect of all His works, the most saintly, the most noble of the race of man.

There each citizen of God's own kingdom delights to visit, honored and honoring, blessed and praised, praising and blessing in return, all these happy subjects of the eternal King. Time exists no longer in that land of the living, and distance is annihilated there; and the charity which there reigns supreme enables all its inhabitants to revel in their sweet and blissful intercourse with each other from the centre, where Christ sits enthroned, to the utmost limit of its circumference.

These are only germs of thought—imperfect helps toward meditation on the subject which is of all the most momentous and the most interesting. And it is to this company of their departed brethren that our dead go "who die in the Lord."

ECHOES OF A SAINTLY VOICE.

Do not weary in pursuing our inquiry. We have only glanced, as yet, at one class of the citizens of the heavenly kingdom, and this by far the less numerous and less elevated. We have been with the Saints a few moments. Ere we pass to the company of the angels, let us listen for a moment to another voice.

A beautiful page from a saintly writer may well conclude our meditation on this subject:

"Love makes all things sweet, and, as it is torturing pain to be separated from the object of true affection, so is it bliss to be with the loved one. Hence it is that, as the blessed love God even more than themselves, they are unspeakably happy in the enjoyment of His Presence and in the company of those who are most dear to them. A poor mother will take more delight in looking at her own child's inferior beauty, because he is her own, than at her noble neighbor's more handsome boy. The mutual love of the blessed is far above the natural love of mothers for their offspring; every one of their holy company is most perfect and worthy of affection, being transformed by the Beatific Vision, and fired by the charity which all conceive for the living God: how delightful then must their mutual intercourse and conversation be! Seneca says that the possession of no good, how great soever, could satisfy unless it were shared by another. The possession, therefore, of the Supreme Good is rendered still more delightful in that it is shared by so exalted a company. What pleasure could a man without a single companion find in the lordliest of palaces? It would soon become to him a dreary wilderness.

"The city of God, on the contrary, is filled with the noblest citizens—all partakers of the same divine life, the same beatitude. What, then, must the conversation of such wise and holy personages be? And how much their spiritual joy must be increased by their exchange of thoughts and sentiments?

For, if one of the greatest discomforts of human life be, to have to bear with the ill-temper, the follies, and the impertinences of rude and ill-bred people—and if one of its greatest pleasures is derived from conversing with gentle, pious and learned friends, we can fancy what will be the heavenly sweetness of that intercourse between the blessed, where no vulgarity, no rudeness, no impiety is possible, but all is peace, piety, love, and sweetness. Hence St. Augustine says: 'Every one shall there rejoice as much in the felicity of another as in his own ineffable joy, and shall have a source of new joy in every one of his companions. In that place are all things that are needful or delightful—all riches, ease, and comfort. Where God is, one can want nothing. All there know God without error, behold Him without interruption, praise Him without weariness, love Him without satiety, and find in this love a rest overflowing with God.' *

" Besides all this, the security which the soul feels, that this possession of supreme bliss is unalterable and eternal, is in itself a source of joy unspeakable. In this life the fear of losing the goods that we enjoy embitters the cup of our sweetest pleasures. Pleasures lose all relish in presence of danger. The felicity of heaven being everlasting, can neither change nor diminish: their eternity is the crowning joy of the Saints." †

---

* "Libro de Spiritu et Anima."
† Nieremberg, "Temporal and Eternal," iv, 5."

CHAPTER X.

AN HOUR IN HEAVEN WITH THE ANGELS.

CHRIST'S GLORIOUS ANGELIC EMPIRE.

1. Another attempt to estimate the number of Christ's redeemed.
2. The nine concentric and subordinate angelic worlds.

WE CAN ONLY SEE A LITTLE CORNER OF THE GLORIOUS IMMENSITY.

The best painters of the ages when Christian art had not degenerated from its divine ideal were content, in treating such subjects as heaven, to give us only a small number either of Saints or of angels; and to these they gave a beauty all celestial. Travelers who have visited the Royal Museum, in Florence,* will remember Fra Angelico's exquisite "Last Judgment," and the bands of the elect conducted upward along the slopes of the everlasting hills toward the shining gates of the heavenly Jerusalem. As they ascend, and approach the portals, the light from within gradually transforms every countenance.

Where did Angelico behold that light and that unearthly beauty? His Saints and his angels are but few; but they are types of the countless hosts of their happy brethren. So must we rest satisfied with gazing on one corner only of that twofold world on high. Let us dwell a little longer on the population of Christ's human kingdom before we mix among the multitudes of His angels.

---

* This museum is near San Marco, and is quite distinct from the museums in the Uffizi and the Pitti Palace.

A FURTHER ESTIMATE OF THE NUMBERS OF CHRIST'S ELECT.

Everything in the life to come partakes of the Infinite. All our notions of greatness, of time, and space, and numbers, must be laid aside, or much modified, when we come to measure the things which pertain to eternity. In estimating the number of those happy souls who, through grace and the saving merits of Christ, have succeeded in reaching heaven, we may have startled the unwary reader by summing them up at one thousand millions. A careful statistician, by merely ascertaining the probable Christian population of the globe four times in each century of the Christian era, and reckoning the number of Christian infants dying before the age when they could sin, would come to a figure probably little short of a thousand millions. A generous interpretation of what is said in the Gospel about the small number of the elect, and a large-hearted view of God's mercy toward adult Christians, would swell this figure to limits that we must leave to others to define with more precision. Certain it is that, in the mediæval times, as in the early ages of the Church, as even now in more than one country we could name, men and women set their hearts on dying well and making their peace with God thoroughly and sincerely, no matter how tepidly or sinfully they had lived. Nor was it the voice of the Church or her ministers which had, directly or indirectly, encouraged the belief, that one could, at one's will, and through mere outward repentance, without change of heart and effectual reparation to God and man, merit on a death-bed the glory of God's everlasting kingdom, or compensate at the last hour for all the evil done in a long mis-spent life. But these ages were ages of deep and living faith, when men had a vivid and abiding sense of God's judgments and of the meaning of heaven and hell. No matter, therefore, how conscience had slept or its voice had been disregarded while health and strength lasted, at the approach of death it asserted its full power. Men trembled to appear guilt-stained, unrepentant, and unassoiled before the judgment seat.

CHRIST'S GRACE CAN CREATE A CLEAN AND CONTRITE HEART IN A MOMENT.

Then, again, men, in recalling Christ's death and suffering for sinners, could not forget that He had promised the bliss of Paradise to the repentant robber crucified at His side. It was, therefore, one of the most solemn and comforting facts in the history of man's redemption, that the Redeemer from His cross took the dying sorrow of His guilty companion in suffering and the cry of the dying sinner's heart as sufficient ground for forgiveness. And, not only that, but there are the never-to-be-forgotten words: "Amen, I say to thee, this day thou shalt be with Me in Paradise." Here is a criminal reconciled to God in his last hour, and absolved by the Judge Himself. And that very day the soul of the repentant thief, prepared by love and grief and trust in the Saviour's mercy, purified by suffering willingly endured in such companionship, washed in the redeeming Blood, is associated in bliss with Christ Himself—with his blessed soul freed from the body, but enjoying, even before the Resurrection, as before his death, the ecstatic joys of the Beatific Vision.

Here is one fact in answer to the heresy, that the souls of the departed, even of the just, are cast, somewhere and somehow, into a sleep which lasts from their separation from the body until the sound of the last trump. If He bestowed Paradise and the Beatific Vision on the penitent thief, did He withhold them from Noe, Abraham, Moses, and David?

In the ages of living, practical faith, even the powerful, violent, lawless feudal nobles trembled when death was near, and, looking for mercy to Christ Crucified, remembered that He had pardoned the repentant thief. Who will dare to say that their sorrow was unavailing, or their appeal to the Redeemer and Father of souls unheard? Who will presume to stand between Infinite Mercy and the dying sinner?

WERE THE MASSES OF THE LABORING POOR LOST IN THE CHRISTIAN AGES?

And, then, there were, in these ages, the oppressed, the suffering, the believing multitudes—the poor whose lot on earth was so pitiable, and to whom Christ promised for inheritance the kingdom of heaven. He who writes these lines has long ministered to them, read their brave, honest hearts in life and health, and held their hand in his when they were entering the dread shadows of the valley of death. He does not believe that of them only the few are saved while the majority perish forever. Nor, going back, age after age, to the apostolic times, does he deem the notion tolerable, that the great mass of those who sincerely believe in Christ, and seek Him in life and in death, are lost to His kingdom.

You can, therefore, dear reader, double the one thousand millions, and even treble them, and still be far on this side of exaggeration or improbability.

CHRIST'S EMPIRE COUNTS AT LEAST THREE THOUSAND MILLIONS OF MEN.

Three thousand millions of human beings enjoying the possession of Christ's everlasting kingdom, admitted to the joys of the Beatific Vision, reigning on high eternally with God and His angels—what a magnificent result of Christ's labors hitherto, and of the apostolic mission continued after Him by the Church! And then add to that number the increase due to the labors of the Church through the thousands of years she still has to live.

Oh! the glorious kingdom where our humanity has its true home, its perfection, its beatitude!

But we have not yet allowed our thought to dwell on the most exalted, and incomparably the most numerous, portion of its inhabitants—the angelic hosts.

If, by allowing our mind thus calmly to think over the numbers of those whom the eternal Shepherd of souls has gathered into His fold—and to which such mighty accessions are sure to come in future ages—we are filled with gratitude toward Him, with great hope and great love, let us confirm and increase still more the spiritual exultation we feel by contemplating the multitudes of these sublime spirits, the first-born among created things—the nearest in their natural attributes and excellence to the Divinity Itself.

WITH THE ANGELS AT LAST.

Let us begin with an estimate of their numbers. The Scriptures give us a few *data;* the teaching of the great Christian schools and the writings of the Holy Fathers and Doctors of the Church will furnish a further supply of knowledge on this point.

And, at the outset, let us bear in mind that in heaven the angels are our fellow-citizens, our brethren, our dearly loved and honored benefactors and friends, whose labors, ever since the world began, aimed at seconding God's designs over the human race. Most familiar, most loving, most delightful, is the intercourse of these mighty beings with the Saints, with every member of Christ's human family reigning with Him in glory. Incredible, then, as are the numbers of these angelic spirits, great as is the excellence of their nature, surpassing as is their glory, they are all—*all* our brethren and devoted friends.

The great number of one's true and powerful friends on earth is a chief source of happiness, as it is reckoned to be a principal element in one's greatness. The lowliest and least among the human inhabitants of the celestial kingdom count as many friends as there are Saints and angels together; for God Himself, being there our Friend, inspires all His subjects with the same sentiments of esteem and affection.

ESTIMATES OF THEIR NUMBER.

St. Paul, in the passage quoted above from the Epistle to the Hebrews, speaks of "many thousands of angels" as forming a part of that "cloud of witnesses" surrounding Christ in the heavenly city.

Daniel says that "thousands of thousands ministered to Him, and ten thousand times a hundred thousand stood before Him." * And Baldad, in the

---
* Daniel, vii, 10.

Book of Job, asks: "Is there any numbering of His soldiers?" *

But the mighty hosts beheld in these passing prophetic visions as ministering immediately to the divine Majesty are only a fraction of the angelic armies, the remainder, and probably by far the greater part, being employed in governing the countless worlds throughout the realms of space. Such is the sentiment of some of the holiest and most learned Christian men of all time.

We repeat it: in approaching in thought the things of the invisible and eternal world, we must divest ourselves of our narrow notions, our limited views, of the petty standards by which we measure all things. We know that our own globe, immense as it appears to us, is, in reality, but a grain of sand lost in the infinitude of the great universe. And if all our measure prove too short and utterly fail us—even if "the scientific imagination" itself is overwhelmed in estimating mere material spaces, magnitudes, distances, as well as duration, which approaches nearer to what is spiritual—shall we not allow the mind, enlightened by Christian truth, to spread its wings, and soar beyond the uttermost limits of the starry world, and enter into that other world where time is not, where all is eternal, and where the Infinite God imparts to man and angel as much as they can bear of His infinitude, as much of His divine attributes as is compatible with a created nature?

MODERN SCIOLISTS AND MEDIÆVAL SCHOLARS.

Our modern sciolists, or self-constituted arbiters of knowledge and science, are wont to laugh at these

---
* Job, xxv, 3.

great Christian scholars, whose genius created modern civilization. We, who are not carried away by materialistic theories or anti-Christian prejudices, can well appreciate the wonderful depth and breadth of view with which these mediæval scholastics approached the mighty problems presented by the unseen and spiritual world. The ancient ecclesiastical writer known as Dionysius the Areopagite wrote an exhaustive treatise on the angels and their hierarchies, or orders. It was a timely accession to Christian literature; for it refuted the Eastern heretical doctrines about angelic spirits, as summed up in Gnosticism, and it completed the dimly-outlined doctrines and traditions of the Jewish Church upon the same subject.

THE ANGELIC DOCTOR.

St. Thomas Aquinas, who resumes in his own teaching all that is to be found in the Scriptures and the Holy Fathers, after stating with admirable clearness and precision the doctrine of the Church on these angelic spirits, enters upon speculations regarding their nature, powers, numbers, and officers, which are worthy of reverential study, every position of his being founded either on the authority of Scripture and tradition or on some deep law of nature.

One measured utterance of his on this subject is the following: "The proper order of the universe seems to demand that what is most noble among existing things should surpass either in quantity or in number the beings which are less noble; for the less noble seem only to exist for the more noble: whence it is needful that the more noble, existing as it were for themselves, should be multiplied to the fullest extent possible." *

Some writers have concluded from this and other passages in the writings of the "Angelic" Doctor—so-called because he wrote learnedly and magnificently about the angels—that the number of these exalted beings, who are nearest to God in natural excellence, exceeds that of all the beings of the inferior creation taken together. But St. Thomas is careful to qualify his assertion. The order of the universe and the proper gradation of all things therein could, according to him, be as well secured by the "quantity" or amount of perfection in one or a limited number of superior beings, as by a great number of individuals enjoying each an inferior "quantity" or amount of perfection. Nevertheless, as these pure spirits, whose constitution renders them independent of matter, and are, like God Himself, all intellect and will, find their ultimate felicity in the contemplation and love of His infinite perfections, and in the enjoyment of their own blissful society, it would seem most worthy of the Creator's magnificence to have multiplied their number beyond that of all the beings of the inferior creation.

WHY GOD SHOULD HAVE CREATED SO MANY ANGELS.

There is no man, how good and great soever we may fancy him, but would surround himself with rational beings of his own kind rather than with dumb animals with whom there could be no intellectual intercourse. God is known, and loved, and

---

* Ordo univers; exigere videtur ut id quod est in rebus nobilius excedat quantitate vel numero ignobiliora; ignobiliora enim videntur esse propter nobiliora; unde oportet quod nobiliora quasi propter se existentia multiplicentur quantum possibile est.—*St. Thomas*, "Summa Contra Gentes," L. II, 92.

praised by every angelic spirit; whereas the material world, though perfectly and wonderfully ordered, and resplendent with its own infinite beauty and variety, can lift no voice to praise its Author, and has no heart to love Him.

In man, whose spiritual soul links him with the angelic world above him, while his body links him with all the descending ranks of being in the inferior world down to inorganic matter, God finds the mind to know Himself, and the heart to love and praise Himself in the name of all these beings of an inferior nature. Man is thus, between the Creator and the irrational creation, and with the inorganic world of matter, the great high priest who praises, worships, and glorifies God in their name.

We have, in the light of reason and of faith, been endeavoring to form an estimate of the number of men who, true to God in their mortal lives, are judged worthy to reign with Him eternally. What the final number of the elect will be, He alone knoweth who has reserved to Himself the knowledge of that great last day which is to close the period of human existence upon this globe of ours.

But to what magnificent proportions soever revealed truth and the sentiment of the Church permit us to swell the multitudes composing the human element in the Church Triumphant, we are safe in ascribing to the angelic hosts proportions incomparably more magnificent.

WHO WILL LIMIT THEIR NUMBERS?

Who will set limits to the power and the goodness of our great God? And what an idea of both this greatness and goodness is derived from an attentive consideration of the almost infinite multitudes who form the population of His heavenly kingdom!

Let us not fear, therefore, to allow our minds to dwell with admiration, love, and awe on that most glorious people—the uncounted myriads of angels with whom God has destined us to be hereafter united. St. John, rapt like St. Paul to the gates of the everlasting city, finds no language sufficient to express what he has beheld there. His mind is chiefly taken up with the vision of the great people of Saints, human like himself, and most of them, like himself, children of Abraham. This vision was both to the Apostle and to his fellow-Christians of Hebrew descent a source of the greatest consolation. The book was written while the nation were being exterminated and their miserable remnants dispersed over the empire, and while the Romans were driving a ploughshare over the site of Jerusalem.

St. John lifts their minds and hearts to the contemplation of the heavenly Jerusalem and the indestructible kingdom on high, in which, around Christ, the blessed race of Sem and Abraham held so conspicuous a place. "I saw a great multitude," the Apostle says, "which no man could number, of all nations, and tribes, and peoples, and tongues, standing before the throne, and in sight of the Lamb, clothed in white robes, and palms in their hands." * In the preceding chapter he says: "I beheld, and I heard the voice of many angels round about the throne, and the living creatures and the ancients: and the number of them was ten thousand times ten thousand, and thousands of thousands." † The

---

* Apoc., vii, 9.   † Ibidem, v, 11.

favored friend, the beloved disciple of Him who is hymned and adored there as the Lamb, is overwhelmed by the sublimity of the spectacle opened up before him. Words fail him to describe what he beholds. Even then, before the close of the first century of the Christian era, "no man could number" the blessed men and women gathered up in heaven as Christ's harvest. And as to the angels, no unit occurs to him as a first element of his enumeration: millions "and thousands of thousands," stretching away into the vastness of the heavenly city, make up the glorious object which dazzles and bewilders the sense of one who has not yet put off his mortal flesh.

Were some one of these angelic spirits even now to come down and describe to us these mighty hosts, how could we take in and retain details, every one of which implies immensity? We may rest satisfied of this—that the numbers, the glory, the happiness, and the joy of that twofold united world of men and angels are worthy of Him whose goodness, love, and magnificence are mirrored forth in this His heavenly creation—the end and perfection of all His works.

THE HIERARCHIES AND ORDERS OF ANGELS.

Theologians, following certain indications in the text of Scripture, adopt the ideas of the writer known from early mediæval times as Dionysius the Areopagite. From him St. Gregory the Great adopted the now common division of the angels into three hierarchies, each of which includes three orders. Thus, there are altogether nine degrees of subordination, or excellence, in that seemingly boundless world of pure and blessed angelic spirits, with whose eternal destinies ours are inseparably associated.

Each of these degrees comprises uncounted millions of members, whose varied individual excellence furnishes to their own intelligence, and to that of their human fellow-citizens, a subject of delightful study and contemplation—a theme for rapturous praise of the divine Author of all things.

We have often heard even well-educated people ask, If the occupation of the soul in heaven and throughout all eternity would not be monotonous, irksome, wearisome, in the perpetual contemplation of the Godhead, or the continual joining with the choirs of angels and Saints in praise of the divine Greatness, Goodness, and Mercy?

Our clogged intellectual faculties here below find such difficulty in apprehending, though never so faintly and confusedly, the abysmal perfections and loveliness of the Infinite God, and the all but infinite extent, perfection, loveliness, magnificence, and variety of His works—all revealed in a new, clear, and wonderful light to the mind of the blessed in the life to come. What an endless source of delight and joy must be the study and contemplation of the angelic world in its marvelous extent, its unimaginable grandeur and variety in the greatness, beauty, and loveliness of the beings who fill its shining ranks! Only try to ascend in thought from those who minister at our sides, unseen to all our needs here below, up, up, up to those sublime spirits who stand nearest to God, in the perfection of their being, and in their offices toward His divine Majesty and the inferior creation!

SURSUM CORDA!

To the man who closes his eyes to the distracting glare and glitter of this world of sense, and shuts his ears against the noise of the street and the voices of the rushing multitude, and who invokes the Spirit of God to his aid, light will come to make him understand how incomprehensibly beautiful, magnificent, and immense must be that world where these nine orders of angels rise one sublime sphere above the other, leading the human mind and heart upward to the very essence and bosom of the Creator of all.

WHY NOT LOVE TO EXPLORE THE PROVINCES OF GOD'S EMPIRE.

The wealthy, the educated, who have leisure to travel, find endless delight in visiting different countries, peoples, and cities; in contemplating the great architectural monuments—the masterpieces of art left by past genarations; in studying the institutions, manners, and customs of peoples civilized and uncivilized. Others, in love with nature, explore the mountainous regions of both hemispheres, and take a pride in leaving their foot-prints on the highest and most inaccessible summits; and others again are enthusiastic in studying the marvels of the vegetable or animal kingdoms beneath the tropics. The Brazilian forests, the East Indian Archipelago—wonderful fragments of a submerged continent—the mysterious depths of the African or Asiatic continents, offer to generation after generation of the learned and the adventurous a fertile field in which to win fame. And, in spite of the labors and enterprise of so many centuries, the surface of this little globe of ours is only very partially known; its natural treasures are still a mine almost untouched.

If it be so for a little speck of earth with its contents, what must it be for the boundless universe?

What, in particular, will it be for us in that vast and glorious world beyond the stars, where the God of Spirits reveals Himself to His own, and where shine displayed these spiritual empires to whose greatness, extent, and glory nothing here below that man's eye can see or his mind divine can afford the remotest clue?

IF WE COULD ONLY SPEND ONE HOUR THERE!

An hour with the angels in heaven! Could we be privileged to spend it, as an encouragement to undergo further sufferings or face any amount of labor, the hour might seem an eternity of delight; and after such enjoyment all suffering would be sweet, and all labor of no account. O peoples composed of beings most like to God—O most blessed spirits, who are His most devoted servants and our most loving friends, a thousand and a thousand years would not suffice to survey your universe, to take note of what God has made you, of all that He has given you, to sound your love for Him, to measure the greatness and variety of your natures, to receive the expression of your brotherly charity for your human brothers! But you who now, while we are still on the way to our heavenly home, guide our path and sustain our feeble efforts, give light to our minds and whisper comforting words to our faint hearts,—you will introduce us one day—O blessed day!—into that world where we shall see you, know you, hear you, live with you eternally, and, by loving you and praising your excellence, love and praise in you the Almighty Giver of all being and perfection. "They that hope in the Lord shall renew their strength; they shall take wings as eagles; they shall run and not be weary; they shall walk and not faint."* So shall it be in that other life, when God Himself shall be as a river of strength, and light, and gladness, on whose bosom we shall be borne from realm to realm, from the centre to the circumference of that angelic empire, and round about its frontiers. Who can think of all this now, and believe all this, and not feel his soul lifted up almost to the everlasting gates, and a ray of light from the splendors within falling on his brow and kindling his soul to new sacrifices and heroic service for Him who rewards us with such fellowship?

CHAPTER XI.

THE PLACE ITSELF.

EXPLORING THE LAND OF THE LIVING.

O Israel, how great is the house of God,
And how vast is the place of His possession!
It is great, and hath no end: it is high and immense.
—*Baruch*, iii, 24-25.

Hitherto we have allowed our mind to dwell on the blessedness of being eternally with God, of enjoying the bliss-bestowing sight of His Essence, of being taken into the secrets and intimacy of that life in which the Three divine Persons form a society, so united by perfect mutual love and mutual knowledge that their union is the type of all social life and love. We allowed ourselves then to rest our eyes on Christ, the Eternal Word and Son of God made Man for us men, and reigning in heaven

---
* Isaias, xl, 31.

both as Man and as God together with the glorious multitude of His redeemed. And we have just spent an hour gazing from afar at the resplendent armies of angels, who form with the redeemed the subjects of God's everlasting kingdom, the happy citizens of that heavenly Jerusalem—the abode of the peace eternal and unspeakable.

We have now to speak of that particular place beyond the limits of this ever-moving, ever-changing, perishable universe, where He who called all creation into being has framed a perfect world to be the country, the *home*, in which He, the Father of all, is to dispense bliss unmeasured to the children worthy of His love; the home into which He gathers from exile and trial all who have believed in Him without seeing Him, hoped in Him and loved Him through all the storms of adversity and the long Arctic cold and darkness of an unbelieving and scoffing world; the glorious kingdom, in which His reign consists in doing the will of the faithful servants who have here below made His will their law and life, and in intoxicating them with draughts from the fountain of divinest knowledge and most ecstatic bliss.

Who can attempt to describe to those who are still struggling on over a road bordered by the crowded graves of past generations, with death ever hovering above their path, ready to snatch away his victims at any moment, that *land of the living*, at whose frontiers death's power expires? O empire, of which nothing on earth or in the worlds one beholds floating around it can give an image—empire of eternity, everlasting reign of peace, of truth, of charity, if I could only speak of thee aright!

BARUCH'S SUBLIME CONCEPTION OF THE PLACE.

There is in one of the prophetic books, written during the Babylonian captivity, a chapter of surpassing eloquence, all aglow with the divine fire of inspiration, and abounding in utterances that verily seem to come from one who has seen the glories of heaven and speaks to his exiled and despairing brethren from within the splendors of the other life. "How happeneth it, O Israel, that thou art in thy enemies' land? Thou art grown old in a strange country; thou art defiled with the dead; thou art counted with them that go down into hell. Thou hast forsaken the Fountain of Wisdom; for if thou hadst walked in the way of God thou hadst surely dwelt in peace forever. Learn where is wisdom, where is strength, where is understanding: that thou mayst know also where is length of days and life, where is the light of the eyes and *peace*. . . . . O Israel, how great is the house of God, and how vast is the place of His possession! It is great, and hath no end: it is high and immense."*

OPINIONS CONCERNING THE SITUATION OF THE PLACE.

The Hebrew doctors and commentators commonly taught that there were seven heavens, or divisions of the universe, outside of our globe, the highest or remotest of which was the abode of the blessed. St. Paul speaks of having been "caught up into the the third heaven," and then "caught up into paradise," as if the third heaven were only a resting place on the upward journey to paradise. But St. Paul, like the Hebrew teachers from whom he had

---
* Baruch, III, 10-25.

learned cosmography, did not presume to give a precise and formally revealed notion of the supernal paradise and its location in space. Both he and they spoke in accordance with the science of their respective ages and the traditional notions inherited from the past. St. Thomas Aquinas maintains that there are three heavens: the sidereal or starry heaven, the crystalline, and the empyrean—this last being the place where God has created the home of His elect, the kingdom and empire reserved to His faithful servants—angels and men.

MEASURING BY GOD'S INFINITE MAGNIFICENCE.

In this division modern science can find nothing to object to. The space reserved to such visible and invisible solar systems as we can discover with our telescopes may extend to a distance for the measurement of which the orbit of the Planet Neptune might be assumed as any fraction of a unit, or a full unit, at our will. Beyond this belt of suns, systems, and nebular or cosmic masses, the "scientific imagination" can fancy that second or far wider belt, or hollow sphere, called the "crystalline heaven." Remotest of all would be that most wonderful, perfect, and magnificent world—the empyrean space of the scholastics, the heaven of heavens, the abode of the blessed. It were worse than blind, unreasoning folly, where one admits the existence of a God, of an infinitely perfect, powerful, and wise personal Being, who is the Creator and the Ruler of all that exists, to get appalled or confused by the immensities of space, the plurality, magnitude or magnificence of worlds called into existence, embellished and regulated by Him whose power, whose wisdom, and whose riches no creative act can exhaust. Jews and Christians believe in such a God. Christians, moreover, believe in the Incarnation accomplished; in the existence of a future life in which the Incarnate Son of God is to reign over angels and men; of a kingdom, a heaven, a paradise, in which God's glory is to shine forth with a splendor that nothing here below can foreshadow.

Clearly He, whom we believe to have made our earth and made our sun in the firmament, and created all that we see in space around us, can, without any stretch of His omnipotence, make something better than the sun, something even more infinite in vastness, grandeur, and magnificence, than yonder Milky Way.

We are now considering the supreme display of His power, love and wisdom, in the creation of that true country in which He purposed from the beginning to gather His exiles—the home which He has prepared for His own. We shall, therefore, believe that the grander, the more immense, the more magnificent under every one of its aspects, that heavenly world or empire can be, the more worthy it is of our Father and our God.

HEAVEN'S IMMENSITY JUDGED BY CATHOLIC THEOLOGY.

The divine book of Scripture, from beginning to end, clearly teaches that heaven is outside of our earth. Beyond this the Church has defined nothing; and we are left free, guided always by the united lights of reason and faith, to speculate on the matter, without presuming to dogmatize, or give for positive and revealed truth what is only the reverent opinion of the most enlightened and the most pious.

A great and saintly writer of the sixteenth century, discussing, in his green old age, this mighty topic of the life to come, resumes all that is most consoling in the doctrine of the Church and the belief of the Christian ages in the following words:

"The dwelling-place is called the *kingdom of heaven*, and that for many reasons. The first is, that it is a region of the vastest extent—vaster, indeed, than the limits of human thought can conceive. The earthly globe which, compared with the highest heaven (*supremum cœlum*), is a mere speck, nevertheless embraces many great kingdoms—so many that we can scarcely count them. How immense, then, must be that *kingdom* which is alone of its kind, and which comprises the entire extent of the heaven of heavens, with its immeasurable spaces?" *

The present accepted systems of astronomy and cosmography had only begun to be seriously discussed in the age of Bellarmine. Nevertheless, his conception of that "immeasurable region placed beyond the highest visible heaven—*super cœlestis regio*," is consonant alike with the reality, with the researches of science, and with the teaching of the greatest Christian intellects. Bellarmine, of course, affirms that God's empire extends over all created space. But of this wide domain he claims the highest rank for that special province, kingdom, or country, in which God's most exalted creatures, His princes and sons, dwell everlastingly.

---

* Bellarminus, "De Æterna Felicitate Sanctorum," L. I, c. 1: Habitatio Sanctorum multis de causis Regnum cœlorum dicitur. Primum quia regio est amplissima, et multo amplior quam humanæ cogitationis augustiæ capere possint. Orbis terræ, qui velut punctum est, si comparetur ad supremum cœlum, multa et magna Regna complectitur, ut vix numerari queant: quantum igitur erit Regnum illud, quod est unicum, et par totam cœli cœlorum latitudinum spratiaque diffunditur!

"That sublime habitation," he goes on to say, " is called the kingdom of heaven for this further reason, that it contains such a multitude and diversity of inhabitants as no abode or city could contain, such, indeed, as belongs only to the vastest monarchies." *

RAPTURE CAUSED BY THE THOUGHT OF THAT WORLD.

Of course, both the Saints in glory and their fellow-citizens, the angels, will find, throughout all the cycles of eternity, an infinite variety of bliss in viewing not only the immense extent of their own immediate country, but also the different worlds throughout space, in which the Almighty Father manifests His power and His wisdom. The Beatific Vision follows them everywhere. All places, all occupations, the contemplation of His magnificence in His works, ever bring His face and the loveliness of His Being more vividly before them. Remember—to compare earthly things with the heavenly—that great-souled and holy man, who, being forbidden by his physician to think so constantly of God and divine things, endeavored to distract his thoughts by wandering among the flower-beds in the garden. His love for the God of his soul wasted his bodily frame; the sweet tears that flowed so plentifully and continuously threatened the loss of his eye-sight. They thought the air of the open fields would revive him, that the sight of the flowers would distract his mind and repose the weakened eyes. And, as he went from flower-bed to flower-bed, bending low to examine the beautiful things, their wonderful colors, and delightful fragrance, in every one of them he

* Ibidem.

saw the hand of God; in all this varied beauty and sweetness, a foretaste of the clear sight of the divine Loveliness threw his spirit into rapture, and the tears flowed anew; for it was in vain to endeavor to lock up in that pure and much-chastened soul the fountain of love and gratitude. Excluded from the garden, he would retire to the top of the house, to be far away from the noises of the street, and to enjoy a wider view of the starry heavens in the cloudless sky of Rome. But the spectacle of all these worlds only lifted his soul upward toward their Creator—up to that kingdom where He stands revealed to the eyes of His own. And then all the magnificence of that everlasting kingdom seemed disclosed to the pilgrim, now near the end of his road, and his heart became aflame with the desire to lay aside this mortal coil, and to be present with Christ at the eternal source of life and joy. And when his own sought for him and would lead him away from this consuming contemplation, he would exclaim: "O earth, how little, how insignificant art thou when we think of heaven!"

Aye, what is it all in comparison with the kingdom of God, the land of the living?

SURSUM CORDA!

Our faith, therefore, bids us not only to open wide our hearts when we come to think of that broad empire where Infinite Love reigns supreme, but also to enlarge our minds, and give our thoughts wings to bear them over all these immensities. Do we, in the midst of this sensual, sceptical nineteenth century, need as much as the converted Corinthians of St. Paul, that he, come down from paradise, should repeat to us the words of Isaias: "Eye hath not seen, nor ear heard, neither hath it entered into the heart of man, what things God hath prepared for them that love Him." It is worth while to glance at the text of Isaias itself: "From the beginning of the world they have not heard, nor perceived with the ears: the eye hath not seen, O God, besides Thee, what things Thou hast prepared for them that wait for Thee."

We did not dare to fathom the bliss bestowed by the Beatific Vision, nor to dwell long on Christ's glorified humanity, enthroned at the right hand of God and communicating to the countless millions of His redeemed the immortality, the glory, the supernal bliss of body and soul, which are the fruit of His own victory over suffering and death; and we only glanced at the intolerable splendors of those mighty hosts of angelic spirits—our companions, friends, and brethren in heaven for all eternity.

Truly, "from the beginning of the world they have not heard nor perceived with the ears" what is meant by that kingdom; that land where men live eternally; that glorious country of the blessed; that home of which it is truly said: "The eye hath not seen, O God, beside Thee, what things Thou hast prepared for them that wait for Thee."

Remember, that in that *land* the elect of our race are to live, after the resurrection, in body and soul, their heavenly existence being in every way like to that of Christ risen from the dead.* Their bodies will be endowed with the same spirit-like qualities which appeared in His while He conversed with His Apostles and Disciples during the forty days

---

* We shall treat of their qualities when we have described the general resurrection.

before the Ascension. This shall be treated of at length in another chapter. We only mention it here to enable you to understand with what infinite ease the gift of "agility," bestowed on the bodies of the Saints, and described so minutely and from sound Scriptural data, will enable them to pass from one province to the other of their heavenly domain.

HOW THE BLESSED ENJOY THEIR IMMENSE DOMAIN.

Just as the divine power, added by the Light of Glory to both the intellectual vision and the bodily sight, makes the most distant objects in the remotest parts of the universe visible and almost present to the sense; even so will the glorified children of God be enabled to pass with such incredible rapidity from the centre to the extremities of their heavenly abode, that they may be said to be, practically, present to every part of it.

ANTICIPATING THE RESURRECTION.

We may borrow from the science of our day a familiar illustration of our meaning. The electro-magnetic fluid travels, like light, with such inconceivable rapidity that both the one and the other make the circuit of our globe in an instant of time. Thus, one using the telegraph at the remotest shore of the Pacific Ocean could communicate, if the telegraph wires were continuous, with his family or friends not only at the opposite extremity of that world of waters, but at the very antipodes, in a very brief space of time. Electricity thus enables men at the opposite poles of the earth to speak to each other, to be in a way present to each other, thereby annihilating distance. The gradual improvement of the electric telephone already permits instantaneous communication by speech to persons situated in the opposite extremities of a great city and its suburbs. Nay, the electric wires already convey sound distinctly from one city to another. Nor is it possible to say how far these means of social intercourse may be perfected in the near future. Moreover, light, which travels faster even than electricity, is already beginning to be made use of in telegraphy. Man is only discovering slowly, age after age, the wonderful secrets and agencies of the material world. And by the use of these he becomes, in a certain and real manner, present at will to the remotest portions of his earthly habitation, to the most distant tribes of his fellow-men.

But these material fluids or agencies, which thus enable man to speak with his fellow-men at the ends of the earth, and this wonderful substance called ether, which science supposes to exist through all space, are only the dim images of the true spiritual substances—of God, angels, and human souls. The capacities of ether pervading the universe, and bearing from one end to the other of creation on its particles the images of things, and flashing their knowledge on the wings of light, should teach us to anticipate and divine the far mightier capacities of the glorious and living spiritual substances for whose use this world was made.

If human thought expressed by human speech can travel round the globe on a metallic thread with almost incalculable speed, what must be the power of those pure and mighty spiritual beings whom we call angels, and who come nearest to the Infinite

Creator? And what also shall be, in their glorified condition in the other life, the power of human spirits and of their spiritualized bodies endowed by that same Creator with qualities rendering them in every way able to second the desires and movements of the animating soul?

We can, with the aid of such considerations as these, perceive the perfect truth of what was said in a preceding chapter, that to each of the inhabitants of God's celestial empire, the uttermost extent of its boundaries, in its length and breadth, its height and depth, would only be what to a sound eye would be the interior of a hall or basilica.

And yet, the power of thus passing, with the rapidity of thought, round and round the immeasurable spaces of that magnificent and privileged universe will detract nothing from the intense spiritual enjoyment of contemplating the perfect beauty and infinite variety which the Creator has imparted to His work.

THE HEAVENLY COUNTRY OR CITY THE HOME OF THE BRIDE.

We have seen how the inspired writers in the Bible speak of this everlasting empire and its glories, in a strain which approaches mental intoxication, although it is quite clear that they have been only vouchsafed a shadowy and most imperfect glimpse at the reality. St. John, in the Apocalypse, or Revelations, conveys the most appropriate and satisfactory notion both of the place and its inhabitants, by representing them both as a bride prepared and decked for her nuptials with the Bridegroom, God's own Eternal Son made Man, and to be united in perfect and everlasting felicity with His spiritual body, the elect of blessed angels and blessed men.

What the most powerful, the most perfect, and most devoted of men would do for the woman chosen to be his bride from among all womankind, that, to an infinitely superior degree, and in the divine order, will Christ and His Father and the Holy Spirit do for the body of the elect—the heavenly spouse. The wealth and labor expended in earthly bridals, on preparing a palace, costly raiment, and rarest jewels, banquets and festivities, can only suggest to the enlightened and spiritual-minded what the Almighty, in His wisdom and love, has done to create and adorn a home worthy of Himself and the friends whom He gathers there to share the bliss of His own intimate society, His own life for evermore.

THE BRIDAL FEAST.

We have endeavored to describe both the immensity and glory of that happy multitude, and the vastness and magnificence of the abode prepared for them. These bridals are to last forever; no decay can ever touch the stones of that house of the Lamb, no dimness can fall on the dazzling lustre of its gold, or the sheen and sparkle of its gems. The flowers which crown the guests at that bridal feast shall never fall or fade. The joys which fill every bosom there shall never cease to be renewed, even when the suns we behold shall have long lost their light, and not one drop shall be left in the bosom of the Pacific and Atlantic Oceans.

THE MAGNIFICENT HOME PREPARED FOR US BY OUR FATHER.

The other names bestowed in Scripture on the everlasting abode of the Saints—those of city, house, and paradise, or garden of delights—will scarcely help us to arrive at a fuller and more satisfactory conception of the mere physical heaven than what has already been said. When, here below on our earth, a parent, whose sole aim is to provide a home for his offspring, bestows both his means and his utmost labor not only on erecting for himself and them a dwelling that shall last for ages, but also on creating near it a garden and plantation which shall minister to their delight, we have an image of what fatherly love and forethought are ever prompted to do. But this instinctive and provident love of the human parent is intended to guide our thoughts toward the perfect creations, in our behalf, of the almighty love of the Father in heaven.

The endeavors and labors of parental devotion in this life to secure the independence and happiness of those most dear should prepare our understanding to conceive what that Fatherly Love is doing in the better world, where infinite power is at Its command to build up a home and plant a paradise which may fill with rapture the angelic spirits as well as those of their human brethren. Men and women who have a keen sense of the beauties of nature take great delight in embellishing their home with the most beautiful works of art, and in surrounding it with gardens and parks filled with the most exquisite flowers, the rarest plants, the stateliest trees—all, in a word, that is most magnificent in the vegetable world.

In the heavenly paradise, or garden of delights, there lacks in Him, who planned it for His own, neither the power nor the will to make everything in nature minister to their sense of the beautiful, everything sing a hymn to the glory of the Creator.

But what is all the varied beauty, all the undreamed-of magnificence of the physical world, compared to the spectacle offered to God and to each of His Saints by the spiritual beauty of their own radiant multitudes? "Thy Saints, O Lord, shall bloom forth like the lily: and as the odor of balsam shall they be before Thee." Hence Dante, in his descriptions of paradise, likens the shining ranks of the blessed to an immense flowering expanse, over whose blooming and dazzling surface the angels, like bees of living fire, were continually darting hither and thither, as if intoxicated with the sweets they sipped from all this infinite loveliness and fragrance.

Hence, too, the burning words of the Psalmist: "Sing ye to the Lord a new canticle: let His praise be in the church [assembly] of the Saints. . . . Let them praise His name in choir: let them sing to Him with the timbrel and the psaltery. . . . The Saints shall rejoice in glory: they shall be joyful in their beds." *

Like guests at the banquets of the ancients, the blessed are represented as reclining each on a bed around the festive board. We know now on what they feed, and how full and intoxicating is their cup. What wonder that "The high praises of God shall be in their mouth" evermore! "In that eternal home," says St. Gregory the Great, "while the mind of the just rapturously bursts forth into high praise, their voice is raised in a song of thanksgiving." †
More than that says St. Augustine: "Their sole labor is endless praise of God, without ceasing, without wearying. Oh! happy should I be, and everlastingly happy, if, after laying down this wretched

---

* Psalm CXLIX, 1-5.   † "Moralium," L. VIII, c. 39.

body, I could deserve to hear the strains of that heavenly melody sung in praise of the eternal King by the citizens of that supernal country and the hosts of the blessed spirits. Most fortunate and happy beyond measure shall I be if I may deserve to sing these strains myself, and to stand thus before my King, my God, my Chief, and to behold Him in His glory!"*

CHAPTER XII.

THE PLACE ITSELF—ITS PHYSICAL CONDITIONS.

You will ask, But what are the physical conditions of that land of the living, the eternal abode of the children of God? The question is a natural one, and comes in opportunely here. Let your own reason calmly weigh every consideration that is about to be presented in answer to this query. It is wonderful how much reason, when it apply its own power undisturbedly, and beneath the eye of God, to investigate these lofty subjects, discovers of mines of hidden truth.

THE MOST PERFECT OF WORLDS FOR THE MOST PERFECT OF BEINGS.

As both angels and men, in their state of final perfection in heaven, are assigned a dwelling-place worthy of the almighty power, wisdom, and love of their Master and Parent; so is it in accordance with the invariable laws of His providence that all

---

* St. Augustine, "Meditations," c. 25.

the physical conditions of the world, created and disposed especially for their uses, should be in perfect harmony with their supreme bliss, with the condition of their own physical nature, and the requirements of their moral and physical existence.

Now, if we consider on the surface of our own little planet how nature—or, rather, He who is the Author, Lawgiver, and Ruler of nature—has fitted every living thing in the vegetable and animal world to its surroundings, and has adapted these surroundings themselves to the living things they are destined to feed and sustain, we shall find little, if any, difficulty in conceiving how the Almighty Hand has framed and disposed all things in the heavenly empire in conformity with the life of its blessed inhabitants.

VARIED CONDITIONS OF LIFE ON OUR PLANET.

Travelers and naturalists who have ventured nearest to the Arctic and Antarctic poles have found life on the land as well as in the waters of these desolate, snow-clad, and ice-bound regions. Beneath what would seem the everlasting snows of the highest latitudes, heaths and mosses live. This the scanty herds of reindeer which roam over the interior of Greenland know perfectly well. For their instinct, or intelligence, leads them to seek the sunniest plains and slopes, where the snow lies least thick, and this they scrape away with their feet, or help to thaw with their breath, till they get at the underlying heaths and mosses. But how do these manage not to perish beneath their thick covering of snow and ice?

Our boldest explorers and most intelligent observers remarked that such heaths as the *Andromeda*, by their vital heat and respiration—for all organic substances respire—form a veritable ice-coated dome in the overlying snow, and this protects them from the intense cold of the atmosphere. They found the lovely little heath, with its buds all formed in their sheaths, ready for the return of spring. Even so the polar bear and the seal form for themselves, or seek in the thick snow and ice, caves in which the former sleeps away a part of the long Arctic night, and to which the latter retires for rest and security near the water that affords it abundant food. Nor must you fancy that the Arctic seas themselves, even around the pole, and loaded with their enormous burthen of ice, are bereft of all living things. It is quite otherwise. God, who balances our globe upon its axis, and imparts to it the double movement of diurnal revolution and yearly translation round the sun, sends the warm currents of the equatorial and tropical waters, all teeming with life, to warm and vivify the polar seas, while the icy currents from these are ever flowing toward the equator, there to be heated anew and return to whence they had come. Thus does life, with heat, circulate in the very waters all over the earth—a study for the deepest philosophy, but not the result of man's contrivance.

So in every zone of climate all over the earth does the all-wise Ruler and Maker suit to every living thing the soil and atmosphere of its birthplace, and cause plant, and beast, and bird, as well as the reptile in the grass and the insect on the wing, to be born and to thrive amid a nature in every way adapted to their various wants and capacities.

The Creator of man, in preparing and disposing this globe for his temporary dwelling-place, evidently intended him to live rather amid the fertile and genial regions of the two temperate zones than in the dark, icy, awful solitudes around either pole, or in the sandy and sunburnt deserts of the tropics, or even among the teeming and unhealthy forests beneath the equator. Still, even there, as we know, Providence by degrees adapts the physical frame of man to the excessive heat and the equally excessive moisture.

If we pass from the present conditions of human life on this earth to that other and final stage of human existence, we can apply these analogies to the physical conditions of the heavenly country. We must consider that God destines it to be the abode of man not merely during the period before the resurrection, while the soul is separated from the body; but also during the endless cycles of that blissful existence, when the souls of the just being reunited to immortal bodies, man shall live in body and soul as long as God in the heavens.

Whether the blessed society of men and angels in the life eternal shall be united on one mighty sphere, as superior to the sun in extent as the sun itself surpasses this little globe of ours, or whether their home shall be a world composed of innumerable suns with their satellites, all governed by this law, that they shall contribute in every way to the perfect felicity of their inhabitants, it were idle here to inquire.

We know for certain—for it is a matter of faith, expressly revealed in the New Testament—that the bodies of the Saints shall be like that of Christ Himself, divinely raised above the present needs, and dangers, and infirmities. We shall feel there neither hunger nor thirst; shall suffer from neither heat nor cold; we shall fear neither pain, nor illness, nor decay, nor old age. The institutions divinely appointed here below for the growth of the race, and its social welfare, shall have there no reason for existing. Men will not be born in that kingdom, or grow from infancy to adult age, or need to be protected against the approach of sickness and death. They will be perfect in every faculty of soul, and perfect also in every bodily sense and power needed for the purposes and enjoyment of that most holy and perfect life.

PERFECT FITNESS—THE LAW OF THE PHYSICAL WORLD IN HEAVEN.

Whatever, therefore, there is in the bodily senses which is intended and adapted by the Creator to contribute to the perfection and felicity of the spirit in the life to come, that will have its proper object and sphere of enjoyment there. For the human soul is endowed with a twofold excellence; it is both rational and sensitive. The rational faculties in heaven have their peculiar bliss in the clear sight of God and the manifold and most perfect knowledge accompanying it; the bodily senses have also their satisfaction and happiness in the perception of the many most noble and beautiful objects suited to their exercise.

EVERYTHING IN HEAVEN THE PERFECTION OF PHYSICAL BEAUTY.

The very names bestowed in Scripture on the heavenly abode, and the very descriptions given of it under these various designations, indicate extraordinary perfection and loveliness in the physical conditions of the place. If it is painted to us as a city, its structures are of the rarest, most precious, and most magnificent materials known to the human mind, or even expressed in human language. The dwelling-place of the elect is "a new heaven and a new earth." The holy city—the "New Jerusalem" —is seen "coming down out of heaven, from God, prepared as a bride adorned for her husband." This is "the tabernacle of God with man," where "He will dwell with them. And they shall be His people: and He shall be their God." It has "the glory of God: and the light thereof is like to a precious stone, as to the jasper-stone, even as crystal. . . . And the building of the wall thereof was of jasper-stone: but the city itself pure gold, like to clear glass. And the foundations of the wall of the city were adorned with all manner of precious stones. . . . The twelve gates are twelve pearls. . . . And the street of the city was pure gold, as it were transparent glass. . . . And the city hath no need of the sun, nor of the moon, to shine in it; for the glory of God hath enlightened it, and the *Lamb* is the lamp thereof. And the nations shall walk in the light of it: and the kings of the earth shall bring their glory and honor into it. . . . There shall be no night there."*

If we divest this description of the high coloring so natural to the Oriental imagination, and of the figurative forms given to the language of all Eastern peoples, the simple substance and obvious meaning of the Apostle-Prophet will suffice to prove that in the land of the living, in the city of God on high, the divine magnificence will display itself by surrounding the happy denizens with all the objects

---
* Apoc., xxi, 1-25.

which can charm the purified and exalted bodily sense, and impart to the entire physical world there the dispositions most in accord with the high spiritual nature of its inhabitants, and their state of everlasting peace, continual contemplation of the divine Essence, and all the wondrous works of the Godhead, with their blissful intercourse with the Three divine Persons, and their companionship with each other and with the angelic hosts.

St. John, to convey to those who still live upon earth and take their estimates of what is most beautiful and precious from the usual standards prevalent even in our own day, speaks of the land of the living as "a bride adorned for her husband." This suggests the utmost display of ornament. And, when we recollect that the society of the blessed is elsewhere called "the bride of the Lamb," and that He, the divine Bridegroom, bestows his utmost power and care in preparing and decking out the abode of His bride, we must conclude that heaven is, even in its physical constitution and outward charms, as far above the earthly Paradise, in which Adam and his newly created companion were placed, as the perfect life of eternity and the exalted state of those who enjoy it are above earth as it is, and what experience tells of its pleasures and its grandeurs.

THE BLESSED IN HEAVEN BETTER ABLE TO APPRECIATE GOD'S WORKS.

Seeing God clearly as He is in Himself, the light of divine knowledge, which elevates and expands the powers of the mind and those even of the bodily vision, enables each blessed soul to know and appreciate thoroughly all the glorious works of God.

The most glorious, undoubtedly, is that church of the heavens, that bride of the Lamb, that society of men and angels whose Head is Christ the Son of God made Man; and what a world for study, for contemplation, for rapturous admiration and ecstatic love is that society in which Christ is Head and Lord! And next to that spiritual and moral world is the heaven of heavens, the magnificent universe created, regulated, and adorned for the abode and the happiness of the glorified children and servants of God.

The great early Christian scholars and teachers, whom we call the Fathers of the Church, were wont to give their cotemporaries some idea of the physical aspect of the heavenly paradise by describing the earthly one, thus enabling hearer or reader to conclude how incomparably superior the former must be to the latter. Thus, for instance, does St. Basil the Great speak of Eden:

"There the winds lose their violence; the seasons their extremes of heat and cold; there is neither hail, nor lightning, nor whirlwinds; there is neither the frost of winter nor the rains of spring, neither the heat of summer nor the withering dryness of autumn. All the seasons conspire to maintain a moderate and harmonious temperature. The seasons themselves seem to circulate with joyous dance around that happy realm. All the pleasures of spring-tide blend there with the fecundity of summer, the joys of autumn, and the repose of winter. The streams are narrow and clear, delighting the eye by their brightness—sources of greater usefulness even than pleasure. God made the place on purpose to be a nursery for all His plants and flowers.

With time sprang up trees of every kind, most beautiful to look upon, most delightful to the eye, and bearing all manner of delicious fruit."*

But the words of even St. Basil are colorless and fail to bring forth in relief a single outline of the divine picture afforded by the reality. The highest sanctity and the sublimest genius, while cumbered with this body of flesh, vainly strive to think out what the land of the living should be and is, and, more vainly still, attempt to express these feeble imaginings.

"What could the race of man (in the state of innocence) have to do with fear or grief," asks St. Augustine, "amidst the affluence of all things that were best? There was no fear of death, no danger of ill health; they lacked nothing of all that a righteous will could obtain. Nor had man, living in bliss, any internal element that could wound either mind or body. Their love for God was one that nothing troubled, and so was that which linked husband to wife in faithful and pure intercourse. And from this twofold love sprang deep joy. . . . There was a quiet avoidance of sin, which, so long as it lasted, no evil from without could trouble or sadden."

BELLARMINE'S ESTIMATE OF THE HEAVENLY PARADISE.

"But," exclaimed Bellarmine, "even had the earthly paradise been free from all ills and abounded in the greatest good of every kind, how much more exalted must be our conception of the heavenly paradise, which must be all the more happy that it

---

* S. Basil, "Libro de Paradiso," quoted by Bellarmine.

is the more sublime, all the better in every way that it was created for so much better beings? The heaven of the blessed must infinitely surpass in sublime elevation the Garden of Adam. The blessed in heaven, for whom sin is impossible, as well as death, are infinitely better than the inhabitants of Eden who were liable to sin and to die. We may, therefore, conclude that the heavenly paradise is not only free from all evil, but abounds with all good things, and that these are incomparably superior both in number and quality to such as were plentifully vouchsafed to the earthly Paradise." *

It must suffice, so long as we are in this mortal body, that we recall to mind the pregnant words of St. John, that this glorious empire, destined to be man's true and everlasting home, has been created, ordered, and adorned by the hand of the Infinite Love "like a bride for the bridegroom." Yes, throughout its length and breadth, the land of the living is the masterpiece of the divine magnificence; throughout its length and breadth it is the home of that society which is the mystic body of Christ Himself, purchased by His Blood, and made happy by every contrivance of His power.

Within its vast limits range the myriads of those bright angelic spirits, whose companionship alone would constitute such bliss as no human experience may enable us to judge, and, just as they evermore serve and contemplate God, arranged in their nine mighty divisions, or shining innumerable armies, even so shall it be with the children of men. "The nations shall walk in the light of it," [the splendor of the Lamb.] "And there shall be no curse any

---

* "De Æterna Felicitate Sanctorum," L. IV, c. x.

more: but the throne of God and of the Lamb shall be in it, and His servants shall serve Him. . . . And they shall reign for ever and ever." *

Can all this lift up our thoughts above earth and its attachments, and fix our affections and hopes on the heavenly country?

OUR LIFE ON EARTH THAT OF TRAVELERS IN THE DESERT.

Whatever claim we may have to native land, or to any little scrap of earth inherited from our ancestors, or acquired by our own industry, we can enjoy its possession for only a few years. We are but travelers and pilgrims here below. Our road leads, in God's design, toward another, a happier, a greater, and a more lasting country.

He who created the earth for man would have man while dwelling on it consider it to be only like a tent put up by the Arab in the sandy wilderness. It is a shelter from the heavy night-dews, a place of repose after the heat and fatigue of the preceding day, but it is to be struck ere the dawn, and the travelers have to pursue their journey.

Do not fancy for a moment that there is exaggeration in the metaphor of this earth's being a tent in the wilderness. The more the Christian mind reflects on the reality of things, and takes in by slow degrees the unspeakable greatness of the other world, the more the littleness, the nothingness almost, of the things of this life—possessions, pleasures, poverty, privations, and sufferings, heroic deeds of charity, and self-sacrifice—force themselves upon the mind, and appear in the light of that eternity, and

---

* Apoc., xxii, 3-5.

are measured by the scale of that infinitude, of which everything partakes in the land of the living.

"The heaven of heavens is the Lord's: but the earth He has given to the children of men."* Yes, He has assigned this little globe, this speck amid the immensity of creation for man's temporary abode, while his trial lasts, and time is given him as the purchase-money with which to gain the "heaven of heavens." And here, in the plan of that Creator and Father of us all, comes in aptly the saying of St. Augustine already quoted: "Thou hast made us for Thyself, O Lord: and our heart knoweth no rest till it reposes in Thee." † He has destined us for the glory and bliss of the divine adoption and the Beatific Vision; and, like water let down from its source on the eternal hills, we are impelled by all the forces of the moral world to seek and find our divine level.

HEAVENWARD IMPULSES.

This instinctive impulse of the human soul found expression in the words of the Psalmist: "As the hart panteth after the fountains of waters: so my soul panteth after Thee, O God. My soul hath thirsted after the strong living God: when shall I come and appear before the face of God? . . . Why art thou sad, O my soul, and why dost thou trouble me? Hope in God, for I will still give praise to Him: the salvation of my countenance and my God." ‡ Was not this, also, the cry of St. Paul, in the wonderful passage of his Second Epistle to the Corinthians?—"In this also we groan, desiring to be

---

* Psalm CXIII, 16.
† "Lib. Confessionum," c. 1: Fecisti nos, Domine, ad Te: et inquietum est cor nostrum donec requiescat in Te.
‡ Psalm XLI, 1-6.

clothed upon with our habitation that is from heaven. . . . . For we who are in this tabernacle do groan, being burthened: because we would not be unclothed, but clothed upon, that that which is mortal should be swallowed up by life. Now He, that maketh us for this very thing, is God, who hath given us the pledge of the Spirit. Therefore, having always confidence, knowing that while we are in the body, we are absent from the Lord (for we walk by faith and not by sight). We are confident and have a good will to be absent rather from the body, and to be present with the Lord."*

The practical fruit to be gathered from all these divine impulses toward the blessedness of the life to come is contained in the words by which the great Apostle concludes this passage: "And, therefore, we labor, whether absent or present, *to please Him.* For we must all be manifested before the judgment seat of Christ, that every one may receive the proper things of the body, according as he hath done, whether it be good or evil."

To be sure, when we have passed beyond the veil, we shall find no difficulty in doing the divine will: "Turn, O my soul, into thy rest: for the Lord hath been bountiful to thee. He hath delivered my soul from death, my eyes from tears, my feet from falling. I will please the Lord in the land of the living."† The difficulty lies in our showing a generous will to please Him now.

Let us be generous indeed! For who can begin to take the measure of His generosity when the time for repaying us comes?

---

* 2 Cor., v, 2-8. † Psalm CXIV, 7-9.

It is well, however, to stimulate our generosity both of deed and of purpose by comparing all that is most magnificent in this life with the grandeurs and glories of that eternal empire destined to us.

THE WISEST OF MEN FORGETTING HEAVEN FOR EARTH.

We have, in the experience of King Solomon, a memorable example to warn us of the littleness and vanity of even widespread earthly dominion, of all the riches and pleasures of this life, and of the highest learning and wisdom undirected by the Spirit of God. Hear his own words:

"I said in my heart: 'I will go and abound with delights, and enjoy good things.' And I saw that this also was vanity. Laughter I counted error: and to mirth I said: 'Why art thou vainly deceived?' I thought in my heart to withdraw my flesh from wine, that I might turn my mind to wisdom, and might avoid folly, till I might see what was profitable for the children of men: and what they ought to do under the sun, all the days of their life." *

This resolve marks the first period of the young king's reign, when his heart sincerely sought to know and follow the divine Will. Here now is the description of his downward career:

"I made me great works, I built me houses, and planted vineyards. I made gardens and orchards, and set them with trees of all kinds. And I made me ponds of water, to water therewith the wood of the young trees. I got me men-servants and maid-servants, and had a great family: and herds of oxen, and great flocks of sheep, above all that were before

---

* Ecclesiastes, ii, 1-3.

me in Jerusalem. I heaped together for myself silver and gold, and the wealth of kings and provinces. I made me singing men and singing women, and the delights of the sons of men, cups and vessels to serve to pour out wine. And I surpassed in riches all that were before me in Jerusalem: my wisdom [*i. e.*, learning,] also remained with me. And whatsoever my eyes desired, I refused them not: and I withheld not my heart from enjoying every pleasure, and delighting itself in the things which I had prepared: and esteemed this my portion, to make use of my own labor." *

The sequel indicates that the voluptuary's conscience troubled him in the midst of the paradise he had made himself. But the oscillations of Solomon's soul between unbounded enjoyment, "the vexation of mind" which follows guilty satiety, and the light of his faith pointing to the better road, only ended in his falling deeper and deeper in the slough in which he wallowed. He, long ages before Christ, came, as all our millionaire sensualists do, to ask himself the sceptic and materialist's question:

"The death of man and of beasts is one, and the condition of them both is equal; as man dieth so they also die. All things breathe alike; and man hath nothing more than the beast: all things are subject to vanity. And I have found that nothing is better than for a man to rejoice in his work, and that this is his portion. For who shall bring him to know the things that shall be after him?" †

Solomon went the way of the voluptuary, the cynic, and the materialist. Yet, the memory of his empire and its magnificence, as well as of his learn-

---

* Ecclesiastes, II, 4-10. * Ibidem, II and III, passim.

ing, has survived among the Semitic nations of Asia and Africa as those of a being who was superhuman in everything. Still, power, pleasure, pomp, and all the pride of kings he found to be but "vanity and vexation of spirit."

THE RAPID RISE AND FALL OF EMPIRES.

Vast as may be the empires founded by the sword of the conqueror, or the policy and wisdom of statesmen, they all fall away in due time and come to nothing. We travel over them, admire the cities with which they are studded, wonder at the mixed wealth and squalor of the various peoples, at the hideous misery underlying gigantic and thriving industries, at the armies which cannot secure peace, and the fleets which cannot secure plenty, even when their mints pour out unceasingly streams of gold and silver.

And the marvel is, that nations, who believe in Christ and the promises of eternity, will persist in not believing the present life to be only a brief period of trial instituted to merit life eternal, and that this earth is for us but the tent put up in the wilderness for the night, and to be taken down with the first light of morning; that here is not our home, nor our true country, our final resting place—the lasting and glorious city where we shall enjoy the true life.

The earthly Jerusalem, in her ruin and desolation, preserves many of the monuments of Solomon's provident rule and splendid munificence; her people cherish, as a pleasant and glorious dream of the past, the memory of all that he had done for the city and the nation. They were, mostly, the achievements of his better days, when the light of heavenly wisdom still shone upon his path. What would he not have achieved, if pride, and the love of praise, and the still more fatal love of pleasure, had not made the great king oppress and impoverish his people to maintain the shameful and criminal extravagance of his court and household?

DAVID'S UPRIGHTNESS OF HEART.

David—Solomon's father—had sinned, and sinned deeply; but he had sincerely repented, and accepted the bitter suffering sent as expiation. He could not long forget the God of his youth, who had taken him from the sheep-cot and made him shepherd of all Israel. Hence his cry: "What have I in heaven? and besides Thee what do I desire upon earth? *For Thee* my flesh and my heart hath fainted away: Thou art the God of my heart, and the God that is my portion forever! For behold they that go far from Thee shall perish. Thou hast destroyed all them that are disloyal to Thee. But it is good for me to adhere to my God: to put my hope in the Lord God." *

If such were the magnanimous sentiments of the shepherd king, "the Sweet Singer of Israel," who had not anticipated the life to come, and the beatitude of the clear light shed by Christ's teaching and that of the Christian ages, what should be our detachment from earth and all that it possesses of empire, wealth, power, and pleasures? What ideas should be those of a true Christian man on that other existence, in which God bestows upon us, as our eternal inheritance, the greatest, most immense, and most magnifi-

---

* Psalm LXXII, 25-28.

cent of all His works—the heaven of heavens, Himself as our portion, to be most truly the God of our hearts, our own God for evermore, in the land of the living?

CHAPTER XIII.

THE EMPIRE OF CHARITY.

THE BEAUTIFUL HARMONIES BETWEEN EARTH AND HEAVEN CREATED BY SUPERNATURAL LOVE.

After having satisfied our minds as to the existence of that divine society into which our dear departed enter after this life, and when they have purged off every remnant of sin's defilements, we may contemplate more leisurely and more profitably that heavenly city and its inmates.

Let us, then, draw near in spirit to that true "Mount Sion, and to the city of the living God, the heavenly Jerusalem, and to the company of many thousands of angels; and to the Church of the firstborn, who are written in the heavens; and to God, the Judge of all; and to the spirits of the just made perfect; and to *Jesus*, the Mediator of the New Testament; and to the sprinkling of blood which speaketh better than that of Abel. . . . Therefore receiving an immovable kingdom, we have grace: whereby let us serve pleasing God with fear and reverence."*

Ah! this glorious church of heaven, this city of God on high, seated upon the everlasting hills, far

---

* Hebrews, xii, 22-28.

and away above and beyond the remotest stars, have we not something of thy unity, thy universality, thy divine charities, thine eternity—aye, even of thy immovable security and peace, deeper and wider than the ocean—all foreshadowed in the Church Militant here below—in that city of God on earth, the mighty and fruitful parent of the Saints and citizens of the heavenly Jerusalem?

THE TWO CITIES.

As from some lofty mountain-peak between the two worlds, with the vision of the supernal Sion disclosed above, and the embattled multitudes owning Christ's spouse as their mother and mistress, encamped in the wilderness below, one can see that these are but the mortal and the immortal phases of God's kingdom.

In the blessed city on high, where God, seen clearly, loved perfectly, possessed eternally, is the light and life of every human and angelic spirit there, I behold, with St. Paul, not only "many thousands of angels," but also their myriads of myriads in ninefold array standing adoringly around the intolerable splendors, ready to do His will; I see with them "the Church of the First-Born," the millions of millions whom the Son has redeemed, and who have gone before us to take possession of their inheritance. I see that altar, described by St. John, on which is the Lamb—ever slain, but still immortal—the sprinkling of whose blood "speaketh better than that of Abel." It crieth for forgiveness and mercy, not for punishment and retribution. It is poured out, only that in its divine fecundity men may be born anew as children of the living God.

So, the mighty figure in heaven is that of *"Jesus, the Mediator of the New Testament,"* the "Heir of all things," the Brother of men, according to the flesh, the Adored of angels as God and Man, the Glory and the Joy of these exultant multitudes. Oh! what happiness, what peace, what unity, what love are there!

THE CHARITY OF HEAVEN.

What diversity of merits, what brotherly exultation in the lowest angel and the lowliest Saint at the deserved glory of the highest and nearest to God! What love and reverence in the bosom of the divinest seraph and the heart of her who is the Mother of the Lord, toward the babe dead in its baptismal innocence, or the sinner, like the thief crucified together with the Redeemer, and justified only at life's latest hour! For God is all in all to them. *He* it is who is loved by each in all, and by all in each; and who loves all and each with a charity which fills and overflows angels and men, and surrounds them on every side with an immensity of love and tenderness exceeding their need and capacity as far as the utmost limits of created space is distant from this spot of earth. So appears from afar the eternal city.

And I look down upon this city of God on earth, this Church which, in every successive generation until the end of time, is appropriately called "the Church of the Latter Born;" and how closely her divine order, beauty, worship, and holiness make her resemble the city of God on high!

THE CITY OF GOD ON EARTH.

There she is dispersed all over the globe—"a great multitude which no man can number, of all nations, and peoples, and tribes, and tongues;" all professing one faith, reciting one creed, obeying one united hierarchy, under Christ's Vicar; all "standing before the throne and in the sight of the Lamb." As in the heavenly, so in the earthly city, there is but one altar, upon which the "Lamb, slain from the beginning of the world" in the figurative victim of Abel's offering, slain on Calvary for the fulfillment of all prophecies and the completion of all atonement, is still slain unbloodily, but in very deed, a "perfect oblation," from the rising to the setting sun.

To this Eternal Shepherd of souls, who "laid down His life for the sheep," belong the elect, the faithful servants of God, from Abel the Just to the latest born into the bliss of the life above. His fold, His Church, claims the Saints of the Old and those of the New Testament—those who closed their pilgrimage before the day of Calvary, and those who belong to all succeeding ages. Jew and Gentile are equally His. Jewish hands laid the foundations of the Church after Christ's day. We who have been called from among the Gentiles owe our regeneration to the Apostles of Israel.

And, as in the Israel of old, so in the Church which succeeded to her inheritance, I see the armies of the living God, the angelic hosts, ever ascending and descending, encamped round about Christ's fold, wherever shepherds and flocks tarry on every land. The angelic citizens of the heavenly Jerusalem are ever mixed up with their human brethren in exile—ever busy in ministering to them, watching over them with unwearied love, warding from them a thousand unseen dangers, prompting them to lofty aims and holy deeds by continual inspirations.

We who have fallen upon evil days, like the servant of Eliseus of old, think God's Church beset with perils out of which no man may deliver her, surrounded on every side by the hosts of unbelief and hostile materialism. Each one of us sees "an army round about the city, and horses, and chariots." And in our despair we cry out: "Alas, alas, . . . what shall we do?" But if some prophet were near to open our eyes, what a sight would be that of the invisible and spiritual world we make so little account of?

We, too, should behold "the mountain full of horses and chariots of fire round about." * Who can number the legions of these mighty and helpful spirits who, on every point of the globe, where the children of the Church are fighting the battles of the Lord, camp about every Christian home, and altar, and cemetery, protecting the living from evil and guarding the sacred ashes of the dead?

THE BLESSED VISION OF PEACE.

Divine constitution of that kingdom of God here below, how immovable it stands while revolution succeeds revolution, shaking the earth to its centre, blotting out empires, principalities, and peoples! The Church resembles the temple, beheld by St. John in his vision, where all is peace, praise, and thanksgiving evermore around the altar of the Lamb, as He remains a perpetual Oblation, the

---
* 4 Kings, vi, 15-17.

Blood offered by our divine Abel pleading incessantly for all the needs of earth. So is it here below; as the sun unweariedly goes on his circuit round our globe, so does the Oblation of Christ's commemorative Sacrifice follow it in its rising over every land. There is no setting of our Sun of Justice and Mercy. It is ever morning in the Catholic Church. Her morning Sacrifice is never interrupted. The river of purifying grace and vivifying love, which issues from beneath the altar of the ever-present Lamb, pours unceasingly round the globe like the streams of ocean, cleansing all, giving life to all. Though "all nations, and tribes, and peoples, and tongues," stand in prayer and praise in that Veiled Presence, theirs is one language, because the One Victim is the object of their worship and love. In the most glorious cathedral, as well as in the log-church of the American forest, or in the missionary's open-air altar of the Brazilian desert or the South Sea Island, the worshipers know *who* it is whose Blood cries there from earth to heaven.

Oh! if we, who are still blundering along the road amid the mists of this cold world, could only see what is ever really passing beneath our eyes—this glorious and most blessed communion between the Saints on high and their pilgrim-brethren struggling onward in God's service!

THE ARMIES OF CHARITY.

And, to the enlightened eye of faith, to the sense of the spiritual man, accustomed to look beneath the surface of things—how worthy of the admiration of heaven itself are these millions of holy souls, who labor obscurely to sanctify themselves, to live up to

Christ's teachings and examples, amid the seductions of the present life, in spite of the fearful corruption of mind and heart which carries souls away as in the triumphant waters of a mighty deluge! How many bishops and priests; how many of the aristocracy of birth, and intellect, and wealth; how many of the sons and daughters of toil in every walk of human industry; how many of the very poor in the crowded slums of our cities, are living the lives of angels! To every one of these souls are applicable the words of the great early martyr, the disciple of the Apostles: "Let me desire nothing of all that is seen and unseen, in order that I may gain the possession of Christ Jesus. . . . Let me open my soul to that pure Light which, if I only reach, will make me a man of God. . . . My Love hath died on the cross; wherefore there remaineth in me no spark of desire for any other love. But the spirit which lifts me up as on a living wave, saith to me, 'Come to the Father!'"*

Heaven, by the best writers of scientific and ascetic theology, has been called the kingdom of perfect charity. How could it be otherwise, since the Beatific Vision makes of the existence of every spirit there a life only differing in degree from God's own life—one of supreme knowledge and supreme love of God Himself? We have, in a preceding chapter, endeavored to describe that divine charity, whose pulsations throb in the bosom of the Deity, as well as in that of every angel and Saint in these realms of eternal bliss.

See now in what a wonderful manner charity in the Church here below seems a participation of the love which made God give His Only-Begotten Son to

---

* St. Ignatius, Martyr, "Epistle to the Romans."

the cross for mankind, which makes the Son give us as our own possession both His Father and His own Spirit, together with all the infinite stores of glory and happiness of His own everlasting kingdom.

The lesson of love which the history of revealed truth has taught us means that the charity of the Triune God consisted in preparing man and angel to receive in eternity the gift of *Himself*—of all that He is and has.

The great events which mark the course of His providence in the Old Dispensation and the New are the syllables by which we are taught to spell and to understand that love ineffable—that giving of Himself to the world.

So have ever done all those whose souls have been touched by the divine fire of His love; so do they do now all over the world—they give themselves and all that they have in loving their brethren for the love of God.

APOSTLES OF EDUCATION AND MERCY.

Two great armies, whose legions cover both hemispheres, are devoted to the divine works of charity— that which devotes itself to education, and that which professes to remedy, as far as human devotion can, all the spiritual and bodily ills of suffering humanity. Both of these hosts of devoted men and women often undertake to accomplish both purposes—to form the young after the ideal of Christ, creating them in the living image of the Man-God, while ministering to the bodily needs of the poor and suffering.

But, oh! how beautiful are the hosts, and how blessed the labors, of these apostles of education! And, if possible, how dearer and nearer to the sympathies and gratitude of the Christian people is that other and more numerous army of charity, properly so-called! Under a hundred different names—but all claiming to work under the immediate patronage and direction of the Mother of Christ, the Mother of Fair Love—these embattled legions of holy women, the *élite* of the race, and the beautiful flower of their sex, are night and day employed, among all the nations and tribes of earth, in doing the work of the divine Samaritan.

HOW CHARITY MULTIPLIES ITSELF.

I write these pages in the capital of the land most famed for undeserved and interminable suffering in ancient or modern times. While the immense majority of the people are still heroically struggling for the most sacred of human rights, amid the ruins accumulated by centuries of strife between race and race, and creed and creed, the sons and daughters of the old and long-oppressed faith are wholly mindful of building up the moral ruin, of pouring oil and wine into the festering wounds of the people, of rearing the young to be true children of God, of teaching brother to love and to help brother, of making of earth an image of heaven.

Sisters of Charity, Sisters of Mercy, Sisters of Our Lady of Loretto, Sisters of the Sacred Heart, and so many others—who can describe their labors, or estimate all the good they do? Angels of God on earth—surely, were our eyes opened to see what is passing in our midst and all over the land, we should see these holy toilers in school-room, in orphan asylum, in hospital, in squalid hovel, at the bedside of the sick or the dying, attended by angels of light sent from on high to help and sustain them in their ministrations. Where is the form of human suffering which these angelic women do not alleviate all around me in the great city and its beautiful and wide-spreading suburbs? Where can human anguish and woe lurk, that their divine instinct will not detect it, and their divine tenderness find means of giving comfort and light to the soul in despair?

Here they have created for the dying of every class, and clime, and creed, a hospice—a sort of outward court of heaven—where the weary and agonizing wayfarer, at the end of life's journey, enters and reposes in the very shadow of the peace eternal, with the doors of heaven almost visibly ajar, and angel-voices reaching him from within, and the radiance of the eternal day falling on head and heart. One needs no effort of the imagination to lift the veil, and to see the place filled with God's angels, with the blessed ones who have gone before, and who come to whisper peace and forgiveness and immortal hope to these dying ones, ere they accompany them to the judgment seat—the throne of mercy, rather.

And here, again, another band of these angels of earth are solely devoted to sick and deformed infants—the poor waifs cast up on the shore by the ebb and flow of that tide of cruel selfishness, which all the charities of Christian civilization cannot dry up in great cities. No; Christian charity cannot extinguish sin upon earth, but it can labor and suffer, devote itself and die, to remedy the evils of sin.

In another place—alas, in more than one place— the Sisters of Charity give their pure lives to the service of those of their own sex, who have fallen victims to the seductions of evil. Oh! with what chaste and tender hands they touch and cure the wounds of these blighted and mortally stricken souls! With what a supernatural tenderness and infinite intelligence do they not labor to create a clean heart and a right spirit where evil had passed, destroying, one might think, the very roots of all goodness and holiness! And, surely, here, too, God's holy angels delight to dwell, helping invisibly the divine work of sincere and lasting repentance.

What shall we say of these homes of the blind, where children, girls, women—picked up from the bye-ways, rescued from poverty, and the helplessness of their own condition—are as tenderly reared, as carefully educated, as lovingly maintained to their dying day, as if they had been born to wealth and independence. Ah! they find here what is not unfrequently absent from the homes of the wealthiest and the greatest—treasures of love unfailing in their benefactresses and in the companions into whom the Sisters of Charity breathe their own spirit of divine unselfishness.

Or what, again, should we not say of these nightly refuges where the homeless are so hospitably received, so generously entertained, so securely guarded amid the manifold temptations and perils of a great city? Even the penniless waif and the friendless wanderer are looked upon and entertained by these angels of mercy as if in each Christ Himself knocked at the door, asking a place to lay down His head and be sheltered for the night.

There is not a land bathed by sea or ocean, known to geographers, which is not enlightened and warmed by this active charity, whose spirit and labors ever tend to make of earth an image of heaven.

But work what miracles we may by devotion and self-sacrifice, the transformation effected by this twofold apostleship only foreshadows dimly and most imperfectly the charity of the everlasting home.

APOSTLESHIP OF MEN AND WOMEN OF THE WORLD.

But you men and women of the world will say, that such charity as this, such devotion to good works, such a keen insight into the needs of the society around you, and the energy necessary to meet these needs, are things to be left to persons consecrated to God. They are all beyond your sphere of action, you think—certainly beyond your sphere of duty.

Do not speak so positively, or hug so closely a false conviction. The field in which, outside of their own home, men and women of the world, married and unmarried, can exercise a true apostleship, and one most fruitful in our day, is simply immense. We have known, on both sides of the Atlantic, a multitude of such apostles; but we point out only one—one already gone to her earthly reward.

AN ANGEL OF EARTH.

Yes; this young woman of the world is gone all too soon to heaven—so fruitful was her young life in the most beautiful domestic virtues, and in heroic labors undertaken for the spiritual good of those around her. Herself the daughter of parents who never neglected an opportunity to do God's work in souls, and reared amid a household where God was ever first, last, and middlemost in the minds and hearts of all, and where all the sweet charities of religion, and home, and society were performed as a daily offering to Him, the young maiden was the servant of the neighboring poor, the devoted teacher of the children of the African slaves, the soul of every good work in her own native city. A wife and a mother, torn away from the parents she worshiped, the brothers and sisters and friends who idolized her—her young heart riven by the loss of her first-born babe—she rose above all her sorrows, as she was on her way to her husband's far-off home, to devise plans for restoring the reign of religion and the splendor of suppressed religious worship in that God-forsaken land. Dearly as she loved her own country, then plunged in the horrors of the most gigantic civil war of modern times, and strong as was her affection for her own afflicted countrymen, the spiritual desolation and debasement of the people to whom she was going engrossed all the zeal of her lofty spirit and enlightened piety.

The mortal homesickness which oppressed her, the almost uninterrupted series of illness which impaired or paralyzed her bodily strength, could not prevent the generous young heart, to which the cause of God was as the breath of life, to undertake and to accomplish for the populations around her everything which could renew effectually their moral and intellectual condition.

How the name of the young stranger, "The Angel," as the grateful natives called her, flew far and wide, and bore a blessed influence with it!

But, lo! while just mourning for the death of her noble father, and a few weeks after the birth of her third child, the yellow fever invades the city, and attacks her own household. The servants who are spared by the plague fly in terror to the mountains; the others are lying at death's door. She begs to be taken to them. The physician resists. "You are very weak and unwell yourself, madam," he says, "and you are not acclimated. That you will take the sickness, predisposed as you are, is almost a certainty; and it is equally certain that you will die of it, if you take it. You owe your life to your husband and children. It would be very wrong to expose it."

So reasoned he. But the little apostle was only mindful of what she had been taught, of her duty to God and to immortal souls, when no other spiritual help was nigh. "I only ask myself," she replied, "what mamma would do, if she were in my place. I know she would not let her servants die without preparing and strengthening them, if she were here." And so the generous husband did not withstand her purpose, and the physician had to yield. They bore her to where the fever-stricken were lying. With a mother's tenderness she cheered them, and lifted their souls to God. She had been an angel of light and consolation before this at many a death-bed in that city, and had brought the thought of the dread judgment, with the fear and love of the just Judge, to souls that had utterly forgotten Him. And now her whole heart went out to the dying ones of her own household.

It was her supreme effort. The plague forthwith seized herself, and she died, blessing and blessed, leaving her babes motherless, her husband inconsolable, the city in mourning, and the whole country bereft of her bright examples and God-given zeal.

And the mother, of whose very heart she was a part, though thus doubly widowed and bereaved, never once regretted that she had given her oldest and dearest to do God's work in that distant land.

So much will true hearts undertake and do for God and for the souls who are dear to Him while still travelers only on the road to heaven. And if such be some, and some only, of the innumerable instances of supernatural charity which in every generation grace this earth of ours, what must be the charities of that most blessed society above? Who can conceive the ardor with which they evermore yearn and pray for our salvation here below? Who can describe all the loveliness of that charity which binds them to each other, and makes the social intercourse of the heavenly city a source of such exquisite happiness?

CHAPTER XIV.

THE BELIEF IN THE RESURRECTION OF THE BODY.

THE RESURRECTION OF CHRIST THE FOUNDATION OF OUR FAITH.

The Christian religion is supernatural. Its great Founder, Jesus Christ, unites in His Person both the divine and the human natures. This stupendous union is supernatural. His conception and His birth were supernatural. The three years of His public or missionary life were filled with extraordinary miracles—supernatural in their agency and tendency. His death, repeatedly foretold in its principal circumstances, was attended by the same supernatural occurrences. The sun was darkened, although there was no eclipse; the earth was shaken; the dead arose and appeared to many in Jerusalem.

He had also foretold that on the third day after His Crucifixion He should arise from the grave in the fullness of a new life. This prediction, known to His enemies, the Pharisees, to the Roman authorities who had consented to His Crucifixion, and also to His Disciples, caused the former to set a military guard over His sepulchre, in order to prevent the possibility of a fraud. And yet one does not see how, in the case of a Man publicly executed as a criminal, and well known to the people and the magistrates, a fraud was possible in the present instance.

The people had beheld his death; they had seen the centurion, sent to examine and certify the fact of His death, cause one of his soldiers to pierce the dead body of Christ with a lance. This assurance, made doubly sure, was reported to the authorities. Meanwhile, the governor authorized, late on the eve of the great Jewish Sabbath, the body to be taken down from the cross, embalmed, and entombed, with the precaution that the tomb should be sealed and jealously guarded.

Nevertheless, on the third day Christ arose; appeared to His Apostles and Disciples; remained among them for forty entire days, conversing with them, teaching them; and then, in their presence, ascended visibly into heaven.

To this double fact of His death and Resurrection, the men and women who had beheld it bore solemn and repeated witness at the risk of being scourged publicly, of being excommunicated by their co-religionists, banished from their own country— most of them sealing their testimony with their lives.

We are bound to believe such witnesses. We are bound to believe the mighty fact so attested, especially as their witness was also attended with miracles publicly, solemnly performed as the authentic sign of God's confirmation of the truth of their assertion.

In the light of these mighty facts, which happened in Jerusalem more than 1850 years ago, we are now to study the consequent fact of the general resurrection of all mankind at the end of time.

THOSE WHO ROSE FROM THE DEAD BEFORE CHRIST.

It was not altogether a new doctrine which Christ taught when He first spoke of a general resurrection of the dead. The care with which all peoples, in historic as well as prehistoric times, buried their dead, embalmed them (as in Egypt), treasured up their ashes, and jealously watched over these dear remains of their departed, would seem to be no unconvincing argument that they believed that life should one day re-visit this sacred deposit of the grave.

Among the chosen race—the descendants of Abraham—selected to guard the truths of the primitive revelation, together with the promise of the future Redeemer, and the faith in the restoration to be effected by Him, the belief in a resurrection was carefully inculcated. Still, whatever may have been, on this point, the faith inherited from antediluvian ages, or bequeathed by Noe to his family, it is certain that, in course of time, the belief in a resurrection was limited to the just alone. David Kimchi, one of the most authorized teachers of the Synagogue, affirms that "it is disputed among our sages" whether the resurrection shall be general; but adds that the "ways" or style of the Talmud favor the belief that it is the just only who will rise. Weber, in modern times, says that, although the resurrection of the dead is the thirteenth article of the Jewish creed, the doctrine of a resurrection of both good and bad cannot be proved from the Talmud or Midrashim. He confirms this assertion by quoting the words of Maimonides: *"The resurrection of the body is a fundamental article of Moses, our teacher, ... but it only belongs to the just."* *
We know that the Sadducees denied altogether the resurrection.

---

* Weber, "Altsynag. Theol.," p. 372, as quoted in the "Catholic Dictionary;" art. "Resurrection."

The rebuke administered by Christ to these heretics of His day is recorded by St. Luke: "Jesus said to them: 'The children of this world marry, and are given in marriage. But they that shall be accounted worthy of *that world*, and of the resurrection from the dead, shall neither be married nor take wives. Neither can they die any more: for they are equal to the angels, and are the children of God, being the children of the resurrection.' Now, that the dead rise again, Moses also showed, at the bush, when he called the Lord: *The God of Abraham, and the God of Isaac, and the God of Jacob.* For He is not the God of the dead, but of the living: for all live to Him." *

In the Old Testament two of the great Prophets who bore in their lives and their very name a close resemblance to our Lord—Elias and Eliseus—each raised the dead to life. And it is recorded of the lifeless remains of the latter, that the dead body of a man being cast by accident into his tomb, was forthwith restored to life. Thus the souls of three persons, at least, among the people of God in pre-Christian times, were miraculously recalled from the other world to inhabit the bodies they had before animated. In Christ's Transfiguration the two great Prophets of the Old Law—Moses and Elias—were summoned by the Lord of Glory to bear Him company and witness before the three most beloved and most privileged of His Apostles. Moreover, ere He consummated His own mortal life, He was pleased to raise two persons from the dead—the son of the widow of Nain, and His own devoted Disciple and friend, Lazarus.

---

* St. Luke, xx, 34-38.

CHRIST RECALLING MEN FROM BEYOND THE TOMB.

Most memorable and most touching was the scene enacted near the tomb of the latter. To the bereaved and weeping Mary, falling at the Master's feet and saying, "Lord, if Thou hadst been here, my brother had not died," He replied, first, by the manifestation of deep human sympathy. "Where have you laid him?" he says to the Jews, who wept with the sisters. "Lord, come and see," they simply answer. "And Jesus wept. The Jews therefore said: 'Behold how He loved him.' But some of them said: 'Could not He that opened the eyes of the man born blind have caused that this man should not die?'" They had now come to the rocky sepulchral chamber in the hill-side, and removed the stone which closed the door. The elder sister, Martha, in her despair, or half-faith, as the odor of advanced putrefaction filled the air, exclaimed: "Lord, by this time he stinketh, for he is now a corpse of four days." And yet, but a few moments before, and ere they had left the house, Jesus had said to her: "I am the Resurrection and the Life: he that believeth in Me, although he be dead, shall live. And every one that liveth and believeth in Me shall not die forever. Believest thou this?"

Surely, we believe Him to be the Lord and Life-giver, who is the Master of heaven and hell, the Judge who holds the keys both of the life eternal and of the everlasting death. From mere temporal death He can and will restore the departed at the prayer of living faith, and when it is for the glory of His Father. From the eternal death He will preserve all who believe in Him with that same living faith which binds the believer to the Author and Finisher of his faith in the chains of loving fidelity.

He "weeps" there, above the grave of Lazarus, and almost on the very eve of His own cruel death, at the thought of how little the miracle He was about to perform, and the shedding of His atoning Blood, would avail to open the eyes, to soften the hearts, or save the souls of the proud and self-justified generation around Him.

Still, he proclaims, amid the "trouble" of His Spirit, and the sweet human tears of His brotherly sympathy: "I am the Resurrection and the Life. . . . . Believest thou this?" And then comes the command of Him, whose word created the world: "Lazarus, come forth! And presently he that had been dead came forth."*

And in the face of all these facts, we who profess to believe in Christ, and cherish for the Bible an almost idolatrous reverence, do not hesitate to say, in speaking of the life to come, of heaven and of hell: "What do we know about a future state? Who has ever come back from the regions of death to tell us about it?"

CHRIST HIMSELF CAME BACK FROM THE OTHER WORLD.

But He—the Resurrection and the Life—did Himself taste of the bitterness of death, and dwell amid its dark shadow, visit and tarry with those who, after this life, had been exiled from heaven, till He had purchased for them in His own Blood the right to enter there. He returned to His sorrowing Mother and His grief-stricken Disciples, from the

---
* St. John, xi, 43-44.

very jaws of the grave, to converse during forty days with them both of the kingdom they were to found for Him on earth, and of the kingdom of heaven, of which He was soon to take possession in their name.

Do we believe in Him? Do we give faith to the witnesses of His Resurrection, the parents of the Christian world, the founders of the civilization of which we are so boastful? And shall we continue to say: *"Who has come back from beyond the grave to tell us of the other world?"*

The great supernatural fact of Christ's Resurrection is the corner-stone of our faith and hope as regards the life to come. It was felt to be so by the men to whom He had committed the charge of making the religion of the Gospel the religion of the world.

THE WITNESSES TO THE FACT OF HIS RESURRECTION.

Let us go back a few moments to Jerusalem, to the cradle of Christianity, just as the Apostles, filled with the Spirit of God, issue forth the first time from the upper chamber, and through their spokesman, Peter, dare to preach Christ Crucified and risen from the dead. Hear the first witness of the Fisherman of Galilee to the divinity of his Master and the reality of the Resurrection:

"Ye men of Israel," Peter exclaims, "hear these words: Jesus of Nazareth, a Man approved of God among you by miracles and wonders and signs, which God did by Him in the midst of you, as you also know: this same Being delivered up, by the determinate counsel and foreknowledge of God, you by the hands of wicked men have crucified and slain:

whom God hath raised up, having loosed the sorrows of hell, as it was impossible that He should be holden by it." * He quotes, as bearing on the Resurrection of Christ, the famous prophecy of David in Psalm XV.

"Foreseeing this, he spoke of the Resurrection of Christ; for neither was He left in hell, neither did His flesh see corruption. This Jesus hath God raised again, whereof all we are witnesses." †

MIRACLES CONFIRMING THEIR WITNESS.

The conversion and baptism of three thousand persons were the result of this first discourse on Christ Crucified and risen from the dead, delivered publicly in the city which had so recently been the theatre of His cruel death, and had afterwards been startled by the announcement of His return to life.

These were facts fresh in the memory of all.

Then came the great miracle—the cure of the cripple at the Beautiful Gate of the Temple, performed in sight of the multitude by St. Peter and St. John.

"A certain man who was lame from his mother's womb was carried, whom they laid every day at the gate of the Temple, which is called Beautiful, that he might ask of them who went into the Temple."

"Silver and gold have I none," St. Peter says to the expectant beggar. "But what I have I give thee: In the name of *Jesus Christ* of Nazareth, arise, and walk!"

The man forthwith leaps to his feet, and follows the Apostles into the Temple, "walking, and leaping, and praising God," in the ecstatic consciousness of the new powers bestowed on his limbs.

---

* Acts, II, 22-24.   † Ibidem, 31-32.

The vast portico of Solomon, with its colonnades and the adjoining court, is soon filled with the wondering crowd, who throng to gaze upon the restored cripple and his benefactors.

Again Peter addresses them:

"Ye men of Israel, why wonder you at this? or why look you upon us, as if by our strength or power we had made this man to walk? The God of Abraham, and the God of Isaac, and the God of Jacob, the God of our fathers, hath glorified His Son *Jesus*, whom you indeed delivered up and denied before the face of Pilate. . . . The Author of Life you killed, whom God hath raised from the dead, of which we are witnesses."

Ere Peter had done speaking "the priests, and the officer of the Temple, and the Sadducees, came upon them, being grieved that they taught the people, and preached in *Jesus* the Resurrection from the dead. And they laid hands upon them, and put them in hold till the next day, for it was now evening."

On the morrow there was a great assembly of the priests and magistrates under the High Priest. And again Peter, "filled with the Holy Ghost," raises his voice: "Ye princes of the people and ancients hear: If we this day are examined concerning the good deed done to the infirm man, by what means he hath been made whole, be it known to you all, and to all the people of Israel: that by the *name of our Lord Jesus Christ of Nazareth*, whom you crucified, whom God hath raised from the dead, even by *Him* this man standeth before you whole. This is the stone which was rejected by you the builders, which is become the head of the corner."*

---

* Acts, iv, 8-11.

Vainly did the Jewish Council forbid the Apostles "that they speak no more in this name to any man." The fear of imprisonment or of the infamy of public scourging could not seal the lips of men whose sole purpose was to fulfill the divine mission intrusted to them. Nor did the terror inspired by the persecutors prevent the increase of the multitude of believers. The miracle-working power granted to the Apostles as the divine seal of the truth of what they preached concerning *Jesus* of Nazareth, His divinity, and His Resurrection from the dead, was productive of the most marvelous results. "They brought forth their sick into the streets, and laid them on beds and couches, that when Peter came, his shadow at the least might overshadow any of them, and they might be delivered from their infirmities. And there came also together to Jerusalem a multitude out of the neighboring cities, bringing sick persons and such as were troubled with unclean spirits: who were healed."*

THE WORLD HAD TO BELIEVE SUCH WITNESS.

Here was a new Power, that of *Jesus* of Nazareth crucified and risen from the dead, which asserts Itself as divine. It claims the adhesion of the Jewish Church authorities, inasmuch as *Jesus* had constantly declared that He was the Messiah promised in the sacred books of the Jews and expected by the whole nation. The Jewish Church withstanding the evidence of a claim supported by this display of supernatural power, has no alternative but to persecute the new faith.

The Apostles are cast into prison. "But an angel of the Lord by night opening the doors of the

---
* Acts, v, 15-16.

prison, and leading them out, said: 'Go, and standing speak in the Temple all the words of this life.'" *

The Council held on the morrow was a most memorable one. "You have filled Jerusalem with your doctrine," says the High Priest to the courageous preachers of the Resurrection, "and you have a mind to bring the Blood of this Man upon us. But Peter and the Apostles, answering, said: 'We ought to obey God rather than man. The God of our fathers hath raised up *Jesus*, whom you put to death, hanging Him upon a tree. . . . We are witnesses of these things.'" †

The influence of Gamaliel could not prevent these purblind rulers of the Jews from inflicting on the Apostles the degrading punishment of the rod. But attempted degradation only glorifies the truth, and humiliation serves only to increase tenfold the energy of its apostles. "And they indeed went from the presence of the Council rejoicing that they were accounted worthy to suffer reproach for the name of *Jesus*. And every day they ceased not, in the Temple, and from house to house, to teach and preach *Christ Jesus*." ‡

ST. STEPHEN BEHOLDS CHRIST IN GLORY.

The drama went on increasing in tragic interest till its first act ended with the death of St. Stephen, the first to bear solemn witness by his death to the sincerity of his convictions and the divinity of Christ Crucified. "A great multitude of the priests also obeyed the faith." ‖ Most eloquent was the discourse addressed by the youthful martyr to the Great Council and in answer to his accusers. At its close,

---

* Acts, v, 19-20.
† Ibidem, v, 28-32.
‡ Acts, v, 41-42.
‖ Ibidem, vi, 7.

and while the members of the assembly writhed under his inspired denunciations, "he, being full of the Holy Ghost, looking up steadfastly to heaven, saw the glory of God, and *Jesus* standing at the right hand of God. And he said: 'Behold I see the heavens opened, and the Son of Man standing on the right hand of God!'"*

Shall we, of this nineteenth century after Christ, when we hear His divinity proclaimed, the existence of a supernatural heaven taught as the consequence and consummation of His redemption, and the resurrection of all flesh set forth as founded on His Resurrection—shall we, like the Jews in the Great Council, stop our ears, cry out against this sublime doctrine, and violently assail the teacher?

Let us pause, rather, while we read and meditate this sole early and authentic record of the first growth of Christian faith and life in the city of David, and reflect that the existence of a future world, the glory of a heaven in which Christ arisen from the dead thrones in His humanity and divinity, were the cardinal doctrines to which the truth of such heroic and persistent witness was borne.

The return to life from the realms of death, the restoration of the body to new life, *the Resurrection*—such are the doctrines, the dogmatic facts—real historical facts, before they were inculcated as doctrines—which stand face to face with us at the very cradle of Christianity.

With the eyes of the inspired Stephen, as he is about to seal his witness with his blood, we shall look into that *heaven* into which he is about to enter, and gaze fondly on that promised "glory" and on

---
* Acts, vii, 55.

"*Jesus* standing at the right hand of God." We shall say with him now, as we hope to say with our latest breath: "Lord *Jesus,* receive my soul!"* For He, too, is the God of the "departing;" and death is only the gateway to the life in which He awaits us.

ST. PAUL FORCED TO BELIEVE STEPHEN AFTER SLAYING HIM.

But there stood one by those who stoned Stephen to death—one who fanatically rejoiced in the stoning, and heard the martyr's last prayer. To him, at that moment, Stephen appeared to be only a blasphemer—an enemy of God and of God's chosen people. With all the ardor of a youthful spirit bent on crushing out this budding heresy— as he deemed it to be—Saul, a disciple of Gamaliel, sets forth for Damascus, empowered by the High Priest and the Jewish magistrates to do for the Apostles and Disciples of Christ what he had just done for Stephen in Jerusalem.

On the road, amid his armed escort, a divine power casts him to the earth, Christ appears to him, converts him, changes him from a persecutor into the most energetic and eloquent of Apostles.

So to Saul, at the very height of his incredulity and anti-Christian hatred, *One* comes back from the dead—from the land of the living, rather—to touch with His hand the eyes, the head, the heart, of the persecutor—to open to his soul a new world of truth, new aspirations, affections, and supernatural achievements.

ST. PAUL'S WITNESS.

Let us hear this mighty witness, also, as he testifies about the Resurrection of the dead and the

---

* Acts, vii, 58.

existence of that life eternal beyond the grave. He is writing to the new Christians of Corinth, the most beautiful and the most infamous city in the heathen world:

"I make known unto you, brethren, the Gospel which I preached to you, which also you have received, and wherein you stand; by which also you are saved, if you hold fast after what manner I preached unto you, unless you have believed in vain.

"For I delivered unto you first of all, that which I also received: how that Christ died for our sins, according to the Scriptures: and that He was buried, and that He rose again the third day, according to the Scriptures: and that He was seen by Cephas, and after that by the Eleven: Then was He seen by more than five hundred brethren at once, of whom many remain until this present, and some are fallen asleep. After that He was seen by James, then by all the Apostles. And last of all, *He was seen also by me*, as by one born out of due time. . . .

"Now, if Christ be preached that He arose again from the dead, how do some among you say that there is no resurrection of the dead? For, if there be no resurrection of the dead, then Christ is not risen again. And if Christ be not risen again, then is our preaching vain, and your faith is also vain. Yea, and we are found false witnesses of God: because we have given testimony against God, that He hath raised up Christ, whom He hath not raised up, if the dead rise not again. . . . . Then they also, that are fallen asleep in Christ, are perished.

"If in this life only we have hope in Christ, we are of all men most miserable." *

---
* 1 Cor., xv, 1-19.

The difficulty opposed by mere reason to the possibility of a resurrection is here met without flinching. Paul and his fellow-Apostles are witnesses to the fact of having seen Christ living again in the body after His death upon the cross. As to the fact of this death, the Apostles are not alone to testify to it. All Jerusalem beheld it. The High Priests, the magistrates, the Pharisees, as well as the Sadducees—the whole nation, in a manner, concur in affirming that *Jesus* of Nazareth died on the cross, was taken lifeless from it, and buried. This fact the Roman governor, in his turn, certified to the emperor at Rome.

IMPOSSIBILITIES.

It would seem as if the Redeemer permitted the death of Lazarus to happen a few days only before His own, and that the brother of Martha and Mary should be buried amid the lamentations of his numerous unbelieving friends from the neighboring capital, and that he should remain dead four entire days, before the other public occurrence of his being recalled to life—summoned to come publicly forth from the tomb—should have startled the entire community.

Those who had not seen Lazarus dead, but who believed in the truth of the common report of his demise and burial, refused to believe in his coming to life again. But all such as had witnessed his burial, and again beheld his wonderful restoration to life, could not resist the evidence of their own senses. They could no more deny either the fact of their friend's death and burial or that of his coming forth from the grave, its putrefaction, and bandages, than the man born blind and cured by Christ could deny the fact of his own identity, or that his parents, when questioned, could gainsay the fact that he had been born blind, and had continued so up to the day when the hand of the Master touched his sightless orbs and gave them light and life.

Vain is the objection of the materialist, the rationalist, the unbeliever—that the resurrection is against the laws of nature; a thing impossible. What is impossible, what is against all the laws of rational nature, is not to credit the evidence of one's senses when one sees the man, publicly buried amid the grief of his own family and the lamentations of neighbors and friends, coming forth, after an interval of three or four days, from the corruption of the grave and standing a living, speaking, healthful man before the eyes of the crowd. What revolts all the instincts of human nature is to say—when a cripple who, since infancy, since the hour of his birth, never was able or was known to make a single step unaided, whose limbs were manifestly unfit for all purposes of motion, stands up at the sound of a single word, walking, leaping, running—the thing is impossible!

He, in whose ever-blessed name such miracles were performed in the sight of an entire people, had said that He would voluntarily submit to die a shameful death, and, that by His own divine power, He would rise and return to life again. He arose, according to His promise; He clothed with preternatural courage the poor fishermen who were His Disciples; He gave them the power to perform such miracles as those described—all for the sole purpose of proving that He was truly God, and that he was truly risen from the dead.

The world—the *élite* of the Roman empire, of the human race—did believe both of these things on the faith of such miracles. It would have been the most stupendous of miracles to have so believed without any real miracle.

We, at this day, nineteen centuries after Christ, believe that He has so risen, and that He is very God. On the strength of His Resurrection and of His word, we believe that, at the end of time, all men shall rise as He did; and in the bodies in which they lived, labored, and died, appear in judgment.

And what a magnificent horizon this belief opens up to the mind, the hopes, and the affections of man! How this belief in the resurrection of the dead harmonizes the past and the present of our race with the future—the trials and sacrifices and heroic labors of a virtuous, a saintly life, with the greatness, the goodness, the justice of God, and the yearnings of man's own soul!

"Now Christ is risen from the dead, the first fruits of them that sleep." So death, in this prospect of the life to come, is but a momentary, or, at most, a brief "sleep," as compared to the countless cycles of the eternal life which follows. Hence, the sweet name of *cemeteries* (a Greek term) given from the birth of Christianity to the resting places of the dead. All who died in the peace of Christ were laid to sleep, to rest there, tenderly, reverently, with their faces looking up to that heaven from which, in His own time, the Judge would surely come. His sign, or His name, marked the tomb to which the sleeper was consigned. "For by a man [Adam] *came* death, and by a man [Christ, the second Adam,] the resurrection of the dead. And as in Adam all die, so also in Christ all shall be made alive. But every one in his own order, the first fruits, *Christ:* then they that are of Christ, who have believed in His coming. Afterwards the *end:* when He shall have delivered up the kingdom to God and the Father."*

CHAPTER XV.

THE NEW BIRTH OF MANKIND.

And darkness and doubt are now flying away,
  No longer I roam in conjecture forlorn;
So breaks on the traveler, faint and astray,
  The bright and the balmy effulgence of morn.
See truth, love, and mercy in triumph descending,
  And nature all glowing in Eden's first bloom;
On the cold cheek of Death smiles and roses are blending,
  And beauty immortal awakes from the tomb.
                                    —*Beattie.*

We have the faculty, when imagination prompts or feeling strongly moves us, of transporting ourselves in thought across seas and continents to the remotest parts of the globe, where is the home we left awhile, and where our dear ones dwell. So can we, when we please, pass over centuries upon centuries in time, and fancy ourselves present at some mighty event in which our interests and affections are deeply involved.

---

* 1 Cor., xv, 21-24.

We believe in the resurrection of the dead at the end of time, as Christ, our Lord, has taught us. Let us, for one hour at least, shut out the world around us, and force ourselves to be present in spirit at the last tremendous assizes, in which all angels and men shall stand before the judgment seat of the Creator and Lord of all things.

We may take the words of Paul and of his Master to guide us in this contemplation, and to make us feel sure that what we are about to see and hear is not a dream.

THE RESURRECTION OF LIFE.

"Behold, I tell you a mystery," the great Apostle says to his sorely-tried Corinthians. "We shall all indeed rise again, but we shall not all be changed. In a moment, in the twinkling of an eye, at the last trumpet: for the trumpet shall sound, and the dead shall rise again incorruptible: and so we shall be changed. For this corruptible must put on incorruption: and this mortal must put on immortality. And when this mortal hath put on immortality, then shall come to pass the saying that is written: 'Death is swallowed up in victory. O Death, where is thy victory? O Death, where is thy sting?'" *

Here are the words of the Master Himself:

"As the Father raiseth up the dead, and giveth life; so the Son also giveth life to whom He pleaseth. . . . . Amen, amen, I say unto you, that the hour cometh, and now is, when the dead shall hear the voice of the Son of God, and they that hear shall live. For as the Father hath life in Himself; so He hath given to the Son also to have life in Himself. And He hath given Him power to do judgment,

---

* 1 Cor., xv, 51-55.

because He is the Son of Man. Wonder not at this: for the hour cometh wherein all that are in the graves shall hear the voice of the Son of God. And they that have done good things shall come forth unto the resurrection of life; but they that have done evil, unto the resurrection of judgment."

Let us, first, consider "the Resurrection of Life." We shall treat afterward of "the Resurrection of of Judgment."

ANTECEDENT EVENTS.

As we have said repeatedly, we must, in dwelling on all that relates to God's final retribution to both the wicked and the just, enlarge our minds and consider everything in the light of the infinite and the eternal.

Of the series of events, more or less dimly foreshadowed in Scripture, and discussed by the most authorized interpreters, which are to take place before the general resurrection, we need say nothing here. It is sufficient for our purpose that the resurrection itself, the subsequent judgment, and the separation between the just and the lost, have been described by our Lord and His Apostle with a minuteness of detail that leaves the intellect and imagination no room for misconception or false fancies.

Time, as we now reckon it, by the measure of human life and the revolutions of our globe, will have given way to a very different period of duration, with far different elements of calculation. Ere the Judge makes His appearance, every human being on the surface of the globe will have closed his earthly career, and passed beyond the limits of time into that eternity where all is to be estimated in duration and greatness on the being and life of the Infinite God.

The Word Incarnate was not reading a lesson in astronomy when He thus summed up the mighty cosmic revolution which shall precede His coming as Judge and Remunerator:

"Immediately after the tribulation of those days, the sun shall be darkened, and the moon shall not give her light, and the stars shall fall from heaven, and the powers of heaven shall be moved. And then shall appear the sign of the Son of Man in heaven: and then shall all tribes of the earth mourn. . . . They shall see the Son of Man coming in the clouds of heaven with much power and majesty. And He shall send His angels with a trumpet, and a great voice: and they shall gather together His elect from the four winds, from the furthest part of the heavens to the utmost bounds of them." *

St. Paul, delivering to the Corinthians the revealed doctrine on this point, thus supplements what St. Matthew omits:

"We shall all indeed rise again, but we shall not all be changed. In a moment, in the twinkling of an eye, at the last trumpet: for the trumpet shall sound, and the dead shall rise again incorruptible;" † that is, with bodies thenceforth exempted from death and the corruption and dissolution which follow close upon death in the present stage of human existence.

It is the Almighty Creator who is consummating His own work in the physical and moral world. We are to take His account of His mysterious operation on matter and spirit, as well as the course of

---

* St. Matthew, xxiv, 29-31.   † 1 Cor., xv, 51.

events as they occur at the beginning of that final transformation of all things.

"As the lightning cometh out of the east and appeareth even unto the west, so shall also the coming of the Son of Man be." *   This accords with the "moment," the "twinkling of an eye," measuring the mighty "change," from the dust and immobility of the grave to the fullness and activity of bodily life, wrought in the countless myriads of the human race by the simple word of the Son of God—the glorious King of humanity.

THE NEW CREATION.

We who pride ourselves on our reason, make a most feeble use of its light in our "reasonings" about the divine Power, Its efficacy, and Its wisdom. Estimating in thought the past human generations, whose mortal remains slumber in the dust of earth from which the Almighty Hand originally drew them to associate them with the life and destinies of immortal spirits, we are appalled by the thought of how even Omnipotence could command all this lifeless clay, this scattered dust, to arise, and live, and stand forth under the canopy of heaven, more innumerable, far and wide-extending than the trees of the American forests when Vespucci first touched the continent—forests covering the land from Cape Horn to the ice of the northern polar regions, waving green along the shores of mighty river and sea-like lake between the tides of the eastern and the western oceans!

There was an epoch when these same continents bore not the germ of tree, or shrub, or grass, nor had ever been trodden by the foot of living thing—

---
* St. Matthew, xxiv, 27.

when not even an insect troubled the silent air with the hum of its wings, and not a germ of life stirred within the depths of these desolate waters. And then, at His bidding, who is the Fount and the Lord of Life, earth, and air, and sea are filled with life, and beauty, and the joy of animate existence.

And we hesitate to believe that the Power, the Wisdom, and the Love, from whose creative action man sprung into being and covered the earth, could recall past generations from the grave! We who, with all the experimental science of the past and the present at our command, can study the first forms of life in the primitive cell of vegetable or animal tissue find in the one and the other an insoluble problem; we who can admire the grass of our fields and the flowers of our gardens are, with all our treasures of knowledge, powerless to create either the tiniest blade of grass or the simplest flower! And yet we ask: "How can God bring the dead to life? How can He recall from the grave the untold generations of men?"

THE OBJECTIONS REFUTED BY ST. PAUL.

The Corinthians, to whom St. Paul addressed his two wonderful Epistles, had heard a like difficulty opposed to the revealed doctrine of Christ, for Paul answers it thus:

"But some man will say: 'How do the dead rise again? or with what manner of body shall they come?'

"Senseless man! that which thou sowest is not quickened except it die first. And [in] that which thou sowest, thou sowest not the body that shall be, but bare grain, as of wheat, or of some of the rest.

But God giveth it a body as He will, and to every seed its proper body. All flesh is not the same flesh: but one is of men, another of beasts, another of birds, another of fishes.

"And there are bodies celestial, and bodies terrestial; but one is the glory of the celestial, and another of the terrestial; one is the glory of the sun, another the glory of the moon, and another the glory of the stars. For star differeth from star in glory. So also is the resurrection of the dead. It is sown in corruption, it shall rise in incorruption. It is sown in dishonor, it shall rise in glory. It is sown in weakness, it shall rise in power. It is sown a natural body, it shall rise a spiritual body;"* that is, a supernatural body, endowed with new powers, which seem to assimilate it to the nature of spirits.

Such is the doctrine of St. Paul, which one might aptly call the *Gospel of the Resurrection.*

Let us look into each utterance it contains; for each is an abyss of truth so deep that no sounding line can fathom it.

"WHAT MANNER OF BODY WILL RISE AGAIN?"

In the first century of the Christian era, as in the nineteenth, a rationalistic philosophy, or the self-sufficient science of the day, asks: "With what manner of body shall they [the dead] come" to life again in the resurrection?

And here we must bear in mind what modern physicists affirm as a fact of observation which cannot be gainsaid—that every particle in the human frame changes periodically, and more than once, during the fifty or seventy years allotted to our

---
* 1 Cor., xv, 35-44.

existence here below. It is affirmed positively, arrogantly: "Who can say that the fact has been proved, demonstrated beyond the possibility of a doubt? No reputed man of science, whose testimony on this matter could be accepted by the calm judgment of those who are most competent to pronounce on this question."

THE MOST PROBABLE OPINION.

Shall we say—as appears to be what reason and Christian instinct point out as most probable, if not morally certain—that it is the body from which the soul parts in death, and which is consigned to the grave, that the Creator will re-unite to the soul in the resurrection? If we follow the customs of all peoples, civilized and uncivilized, so far as they can be traced in sacred and in profane history, even from prehistoric ages down to our own, we are met by the fact that the great majority of nations preserved the dead body with reverent care, taking the most scrupulous precautions to save it from corruption by embalming, or its repose from being violated. Even when the body was consumed by fire, the ashes and bones were gathered up, sprinkled with fragrant essences, bestowed in urns or vessels, and the tombs which guarded these deposits so constructed as to secure them against violence or profanation.

We know, however, that the instinctive veneration of mankind watched everywhere, and in all ages, over the repose of the dead. Not till the unnatural lust for plunder, and the impious hatred of their religious past, begotten by the revolt of the Eighth Henry, had changed the hearts and souls of the men who served him, had the civilized world been horrified by the wholesale profanation of the tomb. Avarice, we may believe, had more to do with these abominable sacrileges than even religious fanaticism. The Roundheads of the following century only imitated the example set by the commissioners of Henry. And the French revolutionists, at the end of the eighteenth century, had, in the violation of the shrine of Edward the Confessor, of St. Thomas of Canterbury, and so many others in Great Britain and Ireland, a precedent, excusing the horrors committed at St. Denis and throughout France. It was this same generation which invaded the cemeteries of Egypt—cemeteries till then respected by the Moslem. The custom obtained the sanction of science; and then were ransacked in succession the sepulchres of extinct peoples in the East and the West, and in both hemispheres.

This violation of the grave, become a custom within the memory of living man, stands forth as a thing condemned by the unanimous voice of all past peoples and ages, and condemned as well by the Catholic Church, the mother of regenerated humanity, the divinely-appointed guardian of the dead, as well as the guide of the living. In baptism she anoints with chrism the bodies of those who are born anew in those waters which typify the Blood of Christ, because the body of the Christian is the living temple of the Holy Ghost. At the approach of death she anoints them again, both to cleanse them from every stain contracted on the road of life, and to sanctify and consecrate them still more in anticipation of the hoped-for immortality. Where she is free to do so, she loves to have the bodies of her children reposing around her temples. Her cemeteries are solemnly consecrated, in order that those who sleep there may rest in the peace of Christ, amid the prayers, the love, and reverence of the faithful, until the sound of the last trump summon them to that final birth, which is only the dawn of the true, perfect, and everlasting life.

The Christian belief and practice, therefore, in all that relates to the burial of the dead, and the touching reverence for their remains, only resumes in their completeness and true significance the hallowed customs of the human race both before and after Christ.

THE BURIAL OF THE DEAD AN ACT OF FAITH IN THE RESURRECTION.

The Church of Christ inherited the belief of the Synagogue—that the dead were destined to be one day recalled to life. Christ cleared up by His revelation what was obscure and doubtful in the Jewish tradition. St. Paul, as we have seen, gave additional fullness to the scanty details left us by the Evangelists of the Master's teaching on this head.

So, then, both before Christ and after, those who believed in revealed truth considered that in consigning to the grave the inanimate bodies of their dear ones, they were doing as does the husbandman, depositing in the furrow grain which, in germinating, would lose its own proper form to assume, as it grew up, the perfection of a new life. Hence the wonderful appositeness of St. Paul's words in replying to the objectors of the first century: "That which thou sowest is not quickened, except it die first. And [in] that which thou sowest, thou sowest not the body which shall be."

We had no part in the forming of the grain and its vital germ; no part in framing the laws by virtue of which it germinates, puts forth its green leaves, grows up into stalk and ear, and ripens into the golden sheaves of harvest. We can only help toward the unfolding of the mystery of life in the grain of corn; but the mystery shall remain for man's utmost science an abyss, to the bottom of which no sounding line of his can reach on this side of the grave.

He from whom come the beginnings of human life—He whose hand framed that wonderful being, man, from the first unconscious, helpless stages of his existence to perfect manhood—will keep watch and ward of every atom consigned to the tomb. As He develops the lordly oak from the little acorn which we bury in the ground; so from our body of clay laid to rest in the grave will He unfold an immortal and glorious body in His own appointed time, on the resurrection day, at the new and divinest birth of mankind—the dawn of the everlasting spring-tide.

It is the duty of each living generation of mankind to entomb with loving reverence and awe the bodies of those to whom, under God, they owe their own existence. If no sacrilegious hand disturbs the repose of the grave, the deposit will be sacredly kept till the resurrection morn. But even when the sacred dust has been dispersed, can a single atom of it perish for Him in whom all things have their being, or escape the eye of His providence or the hands of those angels who are the ministers of His love toward mankind?

St. Paul next hints at the wonderful variety offered by the animal world—every species and variety from man down to the lowest zoophyte deriving its characteristics and wonderful beauty from the Infinitely

Wise and the Infinitely Powerful. Even in the boundless universe of inorganic matter there reigns the same prodigious variety. "And there are bodies celestial and bodies terrestial; but one is the glory of the celestial, and another of the terrestial. . . . . Star differeth from star in glory. So also the resurrection of the dead."

Do not pass over these sentences lightly. To the eye of mortal man during this present stage of brief life, limited observation, and imperfect knowledge, the spectacle of the earth around him and the worlds which float in space, is a mighty book, every page and character of which tells of that Infinite Power and Wisdom. Even this little globe of ours is a volume, no one page of whose wonders has yet been perfectly conned by any one man, or by all the children of men, since the world began. So magnificent are the works of God in the visible world, of which we obtain only imperfect glimpses.

But of that new creation which is to be ushered in by the resurrection, what magnificence, what variety, what glorious forms of life can we not predicate?

HEAVEN COMES DOWN TO OUR EARTH.

The angelic and the human worlds are brought face to face in their entirety. Not one of the mighty spirits created at the very birth of time but will be present at that assembly convened by the Creator. The hosts of the faithful angels, marshaled under Michael's leadership, will extend their shining ranks around the seat of the divine Majesty. What a glorious sight, even for the eye of seraph or Saint to contemplate, will be this noblest portion of His creation—these armies of His ever-loving servants and ministers!

From heaven have also come down with the King and His angels the countless multitudes of blessed human spirits, admitted to the Beatific Vision through Christ's merits, and now eager to be reunited to their bodies, and thus bear the last resemblance to their divine Head, the Son of God and of the Virgin Mary. He is, in heaven, true Man, the integrity of His human nature enjoying, in its union with the Godhead, the highest degree of glory and bliss; and this elder Brother of ours reigning there in body and soul, is also very God. No human spirit in the vast family collected in heaven with Adam and Eve, with Jesus and Mary, but yearns, as the day of the new birth is about to dawn, to be like the second Adam and the second Eve, united with the body—with a body in every way resembling theirs.

There is another portion of the angelic and the human world which has been bidden to the scene as a preliminary to the general resurrection—those eternally excluded from heaven. Among these, such as have departed this life unstained by any deadly guilt of their own, but not engrafted on Christ by baptism, or a living faith in Him as the promised Redeemer and Restorer, will, indeed, never enjoy the society of the blessed or the Beatific Vision. But they will not be condemned to the torments of the wicked. Nay; it is not improbable that their final abode shall be, not the region of the eternal death, but the *Limbus*, or "fringe," of the Fathers—a world skirting this latter, or midway between heaven and hell; whose inhabitants, enjoying a real immortality, are blessed with a knowledge and love of God, such as the soul is fitted for by nature, and blessed too with the social charities begotten by intercourse with the good; for such we suppose this portion of the human family to be.

But it is to the unhappy tribes of the eternally lost that the summons to meet the Judge, and the thought of reunion with the body, shall be alike dreadful.

To both fallen angels and fallen men, this meeting with the blessed company of heaven, and the Man-God King over all, apply the words of Scripture, in which the guilty call upon the mountains to fall upon them and hide them from the face of the Lamb.

QUANTUS TREMOR EST FUTURUS!

Brief as the interval between their being thus brought together and the resurrection may be, ages of thought and feeling will be crowded into it: the thought of their God, infinite in His greatness, His love, mercy, and justice—a thought most blissful to his faithful servants—a thought overwhelmingly bitter to His enemies: the feeling in the blessed that this hour is only the solemn triumph of their Master's wisdom, justice, and power, so long blasphemed by the wicked—the last splendor added to their own glory—the filling up and overflowing of their cup of delight—and the feeling of humiliation and despair in the lost at the manifest evidence of their own unnatural wickedness, at that persevering perversity of will which turned them away from God in life and in death, and which is to remain for all eternity.

Then as the dread trumpet sounds—the signal which God's angels have been waiting for during ages—the Almighty Virtue, which is infinite at every point of creation, from the centre all round to the circumference of the universe, by the ministry of these faithful angels brings together each particle of the body from which every human soul has parted in death, and makes of it in an instant an organic whole. Into their bodies the souls of the just lovingly, rapturously enter, at once communicating by this reunion, in accordance with the divine Will, the supernatural qualities which shone forth in Christ's own body on that Easter morning when He burst the barriers of His sepulchre.

And the fairest sight that even God's own eyes beheld, the myriad myriads of Adam and Eve's descendants stand forth on this earth of ours, immortal, glorious, triumphant, in the consciousness of their possessing the perfection, the fullness, of that bliss and that life for which humanity was created and destined from the beginning.

When the traveler, after passing through the snows and ice of winter and the frightful Alpine solitudes of the Splugen, comes suddenly with the dawn of morning upon some lofty eminence, overlooking Upper Italy, arrayed in all the loveliness and glory of her spring-tide, he may well pause, enraptured, and fancy that he stands at the gates of the earthly Paradise.

But no spectacle of splendor, magnificence, and sublimity afforded by the fairest region of earth, at its sunniest season, can afford any point of comparison to the glories of the resurrection morn, when, around the Parents of the new life—the Redeemer and His Mother, together with the assembled angelic hosts—shall stand Adam and Eve, with the countless millions of their blessed children, just clothed with the additional splendors of their immortal and spiritualized bodies. The revival of nature yearly, after the long winter of our northern latitudes, and within the tropics the reflorescence of vegetation in forest and plain, when the rainy season has passed away, always, from the beginning, pointed to this new birth of humanity, this final triumph of life over death, this perfect restoration of all things in Christ and through Christ.

Oh! the song of exultation and thanksgiving which bursts from the lips of these million millions of human beings just restored to the completeness of life, immortality, glory, and happiness! What a flower is that which blossoms forth from the grave!

> Let us sing to the Lord, for He is gloriously magnified;
>
> The Lord is my strength and my praise,
> And He is become salvation to me;
> He is my God, and I will glorify Him;
> The God of my father, and I will exalt Him!

O hope, which has lived in the dust of untold generations, all through the slowly passing centuries—hope in the living God, the firm trust in Him who should raise us up in the last day—how magnificently thou art fulfilled! Let your eyes run along these myriads regenerated in the Blood of the Lamb, signed with His name, sealed with His blessing in death, and now raised up into a participation of His immortality, His eternity, His felicity. O Father of the world to come, what a family is Thine, what a kingdom, what a triumph!

CHAPTER XVI.

THE GENERAL JUDGMENT.

THE ENTIRE ANGELIC AND HUMAN WORLDS FACE TO FACE WITH THEIR CREATOR AND JUDGE.

> Thou hast given me, O Lord, a delight in Thy doings:
> And in the works of Thy hands I shall rejoice
> O Lord, how great are Thy works!
> Thy thoughts are exceeding deep.
> The senseless man shall not know,
> Nor will the fool understand these things.
> When the wicked shall spring up as grass,
> And all the workers of iniquity shall appear:
> That they may perish forever.
> But Thou, O Lord, art most high for evermore.
> —*Psalm XCI,* 5-9.

The resurrection—the new birth of mankind—is only the prelude to the general judgment. This mighty drama has both its joyous and its terrible part. The birth of the elect to the new life of eternity is the triumph of the divine Love and Mercy. The resurrection of the wicked to judgment is only the beginning of the eternal death. The judgment, which we are now going to assist at, is the vindication and triumph of the Infinite Goodness, Wisdom, and Justice.

HOW OUR FATHERS LOVED TO THINK OF THE JUDGMENT.

No subject within the scope of human thought has been more frequently treated by sacred orator, poet, painter, and sculptor, than this last day, with its assizes, in which the entire human race have to appear and give an account of their lives—of the use or misuse of God's magnificent gifts. This was a subject with which our forefathers were more familiar than we are, with all our boasted civilization, our professed worship of the Scriptures, and the millions yearly spent to scatter copies of the mutilated versions of them over heathen and Christian lands.

In those magnificent temples, for the erection of which a whole people loved to labor in those ages when faith and its mighty truths were better known by the peasant than by prince and noble, when religion regulated the lives of the guilds of workmen, who had created every city in Christendom almost, the very walls inside and outside were graphic, speaking histories of man, and his destinies, and his deeds. The last judgment was most frequently the subject vividly represented by the sculptor over the principal door of the church, so that no one could enter there and lift up his eyes to the magnificent portal, with its world of statuary, without beholding, as on the title page of an illustrated book, the Judge seated on His throne, the dead arising, the good separated from the wicked, heaven open to receive the just, and hell beneath swallowing up its doomed inhabitants. Inside the sacred edifice the same subject was repeated by the painter, within the very sanctuary sometimes, and near the altar, that the worshipers might be reminded that the God of the Temple, so near them, so lavish of His gifts, so desirous of their salvation, should one day judge them with inexorable justice. And to this day, on many of the glorious stained-glass windows which shed on the interior so soft a radiance, judgment, heaven, and hell look down upon the people beneath, reminding them of the goal toward which they are traveling.

It was merciful thus to keep before the eyes of every generation of Christians the terrible responsibility that was hanging over them for the use of time and its opportunities, for their own fidelity to conscience and the light that was in them, for the discharge of their duties to God and themselves, and to their brethren for the love of God. These churches were a book ever open to the people in times when a manuscript Bible cost a fortune.

THE PART CONSCIENCE WILL PLAY.

But for the past generations, as for the present and the future, we know that there shall be but one Judge on that last day, and that for each man, woman or child there shall be one principal accuser and witness—*conscience*.

It is a sad, a terrible, a mysterious, and yet a glorious story—that of free will granted from the beginning to angel and to man. If the greatest minds that have ever shed the light of their genius and their virtues along the path over which mankind has been traveling, have only seen in our innate freedom to choose between good and evil the root of all man's moral grandeur; if they have endeavored to show, both by their own reasoning and by the shining examples of their lives, that God's law is easy of execution, and that He has provided a thousand helps to encourage the willing, a thousand motives to dissuade the weak and the wicked from wrong-doing; others, on the contrary, have either denied that essential freedom altogether, or have made the divine law a thing impossible of observance, or of salvation a work in which God does everything—man's co-operation nothing.

To those who read these pages, and who believe as the writer does, there can be no question of God's having done everything for man that God could do.

GOD'S EFFORTS TO SAVE US.

He set before Him from the beginning the sublime destiny and the unspeakable felicity which we have endeavored to describe and explain in the preceding chapters. Towards the attainment of heaven and its happiness, we have the royal road of God's Commandments, of Christ's precepts and examples, the ever-present sources of grace in the Sacraments by Himself instituted, the unfailing light which His Spirit pours on our mind to make us see what is good, or better, or best, and the unfailing impulse and strength given at the very same time to our heart to be true to the light within us. And to those who are earnest in following that royal road to heaven, how many other helps are afforded in the words and conduct of God's true servants around them!

And if the knowledge of this glorious destiny, if the attraction of this eternal existence, with all its glory and felicity, should be insufficient to stimulate the generosity of men's souls and to awaken all that is noble in them, God has set before men's eyes the certainty of eternal punishment for those who refuse to serve Him, and to secure thereby their own everlasting happiness.

We who believe in Christ Crucified, in the love of the Father who gave His Son to such a death for our sakes, can never forget that such a death must have been endured to save fallen man from infinite misery, as well as to gain for him happiness without end.

CHRIST CRUCIFIED PLACED ACROSS THE GATE OF HELL.

You who read this believe with me that Christ wished by His cross to close forever to mankind the gates of an everlasting hell, and to open the gates of an everlasting heaven. When you take up your crucifix, and look upon Him who is nailed to it, the thought must come to you that He paid a dear price for your eternal salvation. Can we think, believing what we do, and knowing all that we do about Christ's infinite generosity, that the man who, with his eyes open to the consequences of his conduct, lives so as to outrage Christ, to turn his back upon heaven, and to make hell the certain reward of his deeds, has any right to count on God's mercy? Has he any lawful claim to the pity of all who love generosity and detest ingratitude?

Take up the book of the crucifix, and read the lesson of love, infinite and incomprehensible, which these nailed hands and feet and that thorn-crowned head must teach the dullest and the most hardened; and say if hell, with its eternal separation from God, its irreparable loss of heaven and its beatitude, and all the consuming fire of remorse at the remembrance of His Blood shed in vain, and His unavailing agony of shame and bodily torture, are too deep a punishment for the impenitent and unloving sinner?

This infinite love, mercy, and generosity—the light on the soul coming from the lesson of the cross and the Crucified Saviour—shall be that in which the myriads of lost Christians will read their own guilt on the last day, and acquiesce in the sentence which banishes them forever from the society of God and His faithful servants.

THE CROSS ILLUMINES THE SCENE OF JUDGMENT.

Recalling, therefore, what is in itself indescribable, because everything in the scene of the resurrection and the general judgment partakes of the infinite, the immense, we must endeavor to force our imagination to picture the two worlds— literally the two worlds which face each other in presence of the Judge—the angelic and the human. Their numbers He alone at present knows who is their Creator. Every intelligent being called into existence throughout the uncounted cycles of time shall stand in that presence.

Let the God-Man Himself now tell us in His own words how this judgment is to proceed:

The Preliminaries.—"And then shall appear the sign of the Son of Man in heaven: and then shall all tribes of the earth mourn: and they shall see the Son of Man coming in the clouds of heaven with much power and majesty. And He shall send His angels with a trumpet and a great voice: and they shall gather His elect from the four winds, from the farthest part of the heavens to the utmost bounds of them."*

The Judgment Itself.—"And when the Son of Man shall come in His majesty, and all the angels with Him, then shall He sit upon the seat of His majesty.

---

* St. Matthew, xxiv. 30-31.

And all nations shall be gathered together before Him; and He shall separate them one from another, as the shepherd separateth the sheep from the goats. And He shall set the sheep on His right hand, but the goats on His left.

"Then shall the King say to them that shall be on His right hand: 'Come ye blessed of My Father, possess you the kingdom prepared for you from the foundation of the world; for I was hungry and you gave Me to eat: I was thirsty, and you gave Me to drink: I was a stranger, and you took me in: naked, and you covered Me: sick, and you visited Me: I was in prison, and you came to Me.'

"Then shall the just answer Him, saying: 'Lord, when did we see Thee hungry, and fed Thee: thirsty, and gave Thee drink? And when did we see Thee a stranger, and took Thee in: or naked, and covered Thee? Or when did we see Thee sick or in prison, and came to Thee?'

"And the King, answering, shall say to them: 'Amen, I say to you, as long as you did it to one of these My least brethren, you did it to Me.'

"Then He shall say to them also that shall be on His left hand: 'Depart from Me, you cursed, into everlasting fire which was prepared for the devil and his angels.

"'For I was hungry, and you gave Me not to eat: I was thirsty, and you gave Me not to drink: I was a stranger, and you took Me not in: naked, and you covered Me not: sick and in prison, and you did not visit Me.'

"Then they also shall answer Him, saying: 'Lord, when did we see Thee hungry or thirsty, or a stranger, or naked, or sick, or in prison, and did not minister to Thee?'

"Then He shall answer them, saying: 'Amen, I say to you, as long as you did it not to one of these least, neither did you do it to Me.'

"And these shall go into everlasting punishment: but the just into life everlasting." *

Such, on this great drama of divine justice, is the simple but all-pregnant description of the Eternal Word made Man.

CHARITY IS THE FULFILLMENT OF THE LAW.

One law was imposed on mankind from the beginning—that commanding man to love God with all his soul and all his strength, and all mankind, his brethren, as himself. This is what the divine Lawgiver expressly affirms elsewhere in the Gospel. "Which is the great commandment in the law?" asks one of the Jewish doctors. Christ answers forthwith: "Thou shalt love the Lord thy God with thy whole heart, and with thy whole soul, and with thy whole mind. This is the greatest and the first commandment. And the second is like to this: Thou shalt love thy neighbor as thyself. On these two commandments dependeth the whole law and the prophets." †

We know how Christ, the very last day of His life, added to this twofold law His own complement: "This is my commandment, that you love one another as I have loved you. Greater love than this no man hath, that a man lay down his life for his friends." ‡

We are glancing back along the road over which the human race has traveled since its cradle in Eden—glancing back at it, as we listen to the award

---

* St. Matthew, xxv, 31-46. ‡ St. John, xv, 12-13.
† Ibidem, xxii, 36-40.

meted out by the just Judge to both the good and the wicked of the entire race. It is striking to find, in the history of God's people, how often this law of charity, which, if observed, would make a heaven of earth, and effectually close the gates of hell, was reiterated, and its practice enjoined, now in one respect, and now in another.

God had in a particular manner insisted on paying back to Himself in the person of the stranger, the poor, the suffering, the debt of love and gratitude due to Him. Christ expressly identifies Himself with all who stand in need of the kindly offices of this brotherly love.

"He," [the Lord,] says Moses, "doth execute the judgment of the fatherless and widow, and loveth the stranger, in giving him food and raiment. Love ye, therefore, the stranger; for ye were strangers in the land of Egypt." * And elsewhere: "The stranger that dwelleth with you shall be unto you as one born among you, and thou shalt love him as thyself." † A few centuries before the coming of Christ another inspired writer says: "Offer to the Lord . . . . the sacrifice of sanctification and the first fruits of the holy things. And stretch out thy hand to the poor, that thy expiation and thy blessing may be perfect. A gift hath grace in the sight of all the living, and restrain not grace from the dead. Be not wanting in comforting them that weep, and walk with them that mourn. Be not slow to visit the sick: for by these things thou shalt be confirmed in love. In all thy works remember thy last end, and thou shalt never sin." ‡

---

* Deut., x, 18-19.
† Leviticus, xix, 34.
‡ Ecclesiasticus, vii, 35-40.

Is this not foreshadowing the grounds on which we shall all be judged on the last day? It is not that men in every age shall not have other duties to fulfill, and that there are not other sins for which our souls shall have to answer besides those against charity and the obligations of bodily and spiritual mercy; but our Lord evidently supposes that a man who loves God with his whole heart will also love his brother-man, and fulfill both to the one and the other every sacred duty. He also points out that one who loves neither God nor his brethren will not only neglect all the duties he owes to both, but open his soul to every evil influence and defile it with every crime.

TO LOVE CHRIST IN OUR BRETHREN.

This is the age to proclaim it on the housetops. The fruits of true civilization and the divinest virtues of religion are tested by ministering to the sad needs of body and spirit in the suffering millions around us. Never, since the world existed, was it more imperative to dispense to sick souls, to Godless lives, and to bodily needs ever growing wider and deeper, the ministrations of the divinest Christian charity, of mercy, infinite and indefatigable.

If we study Christ, and take Him into our hearts, our minds, our strength in every word and deed of ours, we shall be to all around us the embodiment of His gentleness, His kindness, His untiring and far-reaching love. We must school and accustom ourselves to see *Him* in all who need the edification of a Godly life to lift them out of sin and worldliness; *Him* in all whose souls are darkened by doubt and unbelief; *Him* in the hearts embittered and angered by the inequality, the iniquity, the pitiless greed they have met in those above and around them; *Him* in every form of poverty, infirmity, and suffering. We shall find every day, and every hour, and at every step, the needy in spirit, in heart, in soul, and in body, the cry of whose sore distress will be the cry of *Christ Himself* appealing to us.

Do not turn away. You are offered a golden opportunity.

HOW FRANCIS OF ASSISI EMBRACED CHRIST IN THE LEPER.

St. Francis of Assisi was a wealthy, gay, and youthful cavalier, when riding forth one morning, he was suddenly startled, amid the green fields and the flowering shrubs of the wayside hedges, by a stench so horrible that he looked around for the cause of it. Lo! crouching in a hole, at a short distance, was a leper, so hideous, so deformed, that the very beast Francis bestrode refused to advance, rearing and plunging furiously. The young soldier —such he then was—had perceived the appealing look cast at him by the forlorn wretch. He had wheeled his horse round from the spot, where the leper contaminated earth and air. But these beseeching eyes followed him; and he remembered Christ who was made a leper for our sakes. So, dismounting, he went back, cast himself on his knees, and tenderly embraced the sufferer. But that instant the frightful odor disappeared, and his own soul was flooded by a sense of overpowering sweetness. Having bestowed a large alms on the leper, and said comforting words to cheer him, he remounted his horse. Turning round to wave adieu to the object of his compassionate kindness, he was surprised to see that the leper had disappeared. He sought for him, but it was a vain search. It was our Lord Himself who had thus tried the generosity of a soul destined to do great things for God and man, and which, from that moment, became aflame with the love of Christ Crucified.

Let us learn to find *Him* on our daily road. How sweet it will be to find Him on the last day, and to hear: "As long as you did it to one of these My least brethren, you did it to *Me*."

While the King, with His imperial escort of the twofold heavenly world, ascends on high, and the other world of the doomed are sinking into everlasting punishment, we can throw further light on the great facts we have been contemplating, and help to strengthen our own faith in Revealed Truth, by comparing the description of the general judgment, as we have taken it from St. Matthew, with a fragment from one of the most ancient literatures of the East.

LIGHT FROM THE PAGAN EAST.

It dates from a period when Persia was peopled by a race entirely devoted to agricultural and pastoral pursuits. The existing world is described as "the world of herds and happy homes." As the writer has been lately studying the condition of his own native land in pre-Christian times, the conditions and manners of the race which had come from Central Asia to colonize it, as they are painted by the most authentic records, would make of the Ireland of 1000 before Christ "a land of herds and happy homes." The extract brings us back to an epoch resembling that when Abraham and Lot pastured their flocks amid the fertile valleys of Palestine.

Singularly consonant with what the Gospel then teaches concerning the equity of the divine judgments, and the eternal nature of both the final punishments and the final rewards, are the religious traditions of the ancient Asiastic nations, among whom the dogmas of the primitive revelation have survived the revolutions and ruin of centuries, and the overlapping of so many successive creeds.

THE JUST MAN'S CONSCIENCE.

In the fragment of the Avesta, alluded to and recently published, the expectancy of the just soul after death, the judgment which follows, and the description of heaven and its bliss, are given with a surprising simplicity and beauty. The fragment purports to be a dialogue between Zarathustra (the Zoroaster of Rollin), the great religious teacher of the ancient Persians, and Ahura-Mazda (Ormusd), the Creator of the world. Zarathustra questions:

> "Say, when a just man dies, where dwells his soul
> In that first night that follows after death?"

> "It takes its place beside the dead man's head,
> Singing the gladsome Ustavaiti hymn,—
> *Blessing and happiness to each and all
> Of those Ahura-Mazda wills to bless.* . . .
> And through the night that soul is filled with joy—
> Joy great as all the joy of all that live."

Thus, waiting, singing, and filled with ecstatic joy, the second and the third nights pass.

> "But as the third night whitens to the dawn,
> It seems unto the just man's soul as though
> He stood mid plants and flowers; and from the flowers
> There comes a perfume borne upon a wind,
> A sweet wind, from the region of the south,
> Fragrant, more fragrant than the winds of earth."

Here comes upon the soul the wonderful impersonation of the just man's conscience, or better self, which is, even in the Christian interpretation of the general judgment, the light and the voice of the Supreme Truth and Justice.

"Then there comes
Advancing towards him with the fragrant wind
A maiden, youthful, radiant, beautiful,
Shapely her arms, her port and tread majestic,
Tall and erect, of perfect form, as one
Sprung from some glorious race, in early youth
Fairer than all that is most fair on earth.

THE JUDGMENT.

"Then does the just one ask her: 'Who art thou,
Fairer than all the maidens I have seen?'

"And she replies: 'I am thy own good thoughts,
And words, and deeds—thy conscience and thy self.'

"And who has made thee thus, so beautiful,
Fragrant, and tall, with this triumphant air,
Like one that conquers, as I see thee now?"

"GOOD THOUGHTS, GOOD WORDS, AND GOODLY DEEDS."

"'Tis *thou* hast made me thus, 'tis thou thyself
With thy good thoughts, good words, and goodly deeds,
Drawing thy nature forth in excellence,
Beauty, and fragrance, and triumphant might,
That gave thee victory o'er thy enemies.
When thou didst see, on earth, an evil man
Dealing in magic, following after lust,
Or shutting up his heart against the poor,
Or felling fruitful trees, then thou wouldst kneel
And sing the holy hymns aloud, and praise
The pure bright waters and the sacred fire,
Ahura-Mazda's son, and grant an alms
To faithful men who came from far and near.
So thou hast made me, lovely as I was,
Still lovelier; beauteous as I ever was,
More beautiful. A lofty place was mine,
Thou hast advanced me to a loftier one
By thy good thoughts, good words, and holy deeds."

This, in truth, is remarkably in accord with what Catholic theologians teach of the general judgment, where the book, open to the eyes of men and angels, in which each individual can read the record of his own good or evil deeds, is conscience—is man placed face to face with his own good or evil *self*. From conscience, from this terrible and truth-telling self, comes the sentence which forestalls that of the divine Judge, and confirms the estimate formed of each virtuous or each wicked life by the assembled hosts of angels and men.

And most beautiful is that Persian delineation of the good man's *self*, ever growing from good to better, from better to better still, advanced by the holy use of God's grace from one lofty place in merit and sanctity to a still loftier.

Such is the award of a good conscience. Now listen to this brief and pregnant description of the just spirit's entrance into eternal felicity:

AFTER THE JUDGMENT HEAVEN.

"And then the soul uprises. With one step
It gains the region by the gate of heaven
Sacred to holy thoughts; with one step more
It gains the region of all holy words;
One more, the region of all holy deeds.
Then with another step it enters in
To the fair realm of uncreated light.

"Then one who died before him speaks to him—
One of the just: 'Art dead? How didst thou come
Out of the world of herds and happy homes,
Out of the world of sense to that of soul,
Out of the world that passes, into this
That passes not away? How came to thee
This lasting happiness?'"

It is simply put. Holy aims and thoughts, holy deeds, as well as words, must lead us to the everlasting gates and beyond to "that fair realm of uncreated light," the world that passes not away.

With no less simplicity, truth, and graphic power the story of the wicked soul is told, in its downward progress far away from light and bliss:

THE WICKED MAN'S SOUL MEETS HIS CONSCIENCE.

"Say, when the wicked dies, where dwells his soul
In that first night that follows after death?"

"It hovers restless round the dead man's head,
Wailing and crying, '*Whither shall I go,
Or what shall be my refuge?*' All the night
That soul is filled with woe and bitterness—
Woe great as all the woe of all that live.

"But as the third night whitens to the dawn,
It seems unto that evil soul as though
He stood in some strange region, drear and dark,
And evil odors come upon the wind—
A cold wind blowing from the bitter north,
Foul-scented, foulest of the winds that blow;
He breathes its foulness, and he asks himself,
'Whence comes this hateful wind, the foulest wind
That I have ever breathed?'"

Of course, the reader feels that the "hateful wind" heralds the approach of the man's conscience, of that abominable *self*, with whom he is presently to be confronted in judgment. It is a tremendous passage:

THE WICKED SOUL JUDGED BY HER CONSCIENCE.

"Then there comes
Advancing towards him with this evil wind
A woman, old, decayed, with gaping mouth,
Lean, wasted limbs, plague-spotted skin, bent down
And bowed with age, foul-scented, horrible.
Then asks the evil soul: 'Say, who art thou?
Than whom I ne'er saw aught more horrible,
'Mongst all that God or demon made on earth?'

"And she replies: 'I am thy own bad thoughts,
And words, and deeds—thy conscience and thy self.
'Tis thou thyself hast made me what I am.
When thou didst see good men, with prayer and praise,
Offer the sacrifice, and keep with care
From all that soils the water and the fire,
And guard the cattle and the fruitful trees,
And all good things that wise Ahura made,
Then thou wouldst do the wicked demon's will,
Still serving Angro-Mainyus.* When the good
Gave alms to faithful men from far and near,
Then thou wouldst close thy heart against the poor.
So hast thou made me, evil as I was,
More evil; hateful as I was, more hateful;
Driving me northward to the demon's land
By those bad thoughts, and words, and deeds of thine.'

AFTER THIS JUDGMENT EVERLASTING HELL.

"And then the soul uprises. With one step
It sinks into the hell of evil thoughts;
One more, into the hell of evil words;
A third, into the hell of evil deeds;
A fourth, and lo! the everlasting night.

"Then one who died before him speaks to him—
One of the damned: 'Art dead? How didst thou come
Out of the world of herds and happy homes,
Out of the world of sense to that of soul,
Out of the world that passes, into this
That passes not away? How came to thee
This day of lasting evil?'

"Then the fiend,
Dark Angro-Mainyus, cries: 'Nay, question not
This soul, new come from out the weary way,
The last dread journey when the soul and flesh
Are parted. Let them bring him fitting food,
Poison and mixed with poison, as beseems
The man of evil thoughts, and words, and deeds,
Whose life on earth was ever bent to ill.'"

—*From The Month, October,* 1885.

---

* Angro-Mainyus is the author of all evil—the enemy of God and all good.

CHAPTER XVII.

CHRIST'S HUMAN EMPIRE AFTER THE RESURRECTION.

WHAT MAN CAN BE.

"That was not first which is spiritual, but that which is natural: afterwards that which is spiritual.
"The first man was of the earth, *earthly:* the second man, from heaven, *heavenly.*
"Such as is the *earthly*, such also are the earthly: and such as is the *heavenly*, such also are they that are heavenly.
"Therefore, as we have borne the image of the *earthly*, let us also bear the image of the *heavenly.*"
—1 *Corinthians*, xv, 46-49.

There are among those who claim to profess a superior or exclusive reverence for the words of Scripture not a few unwilling to admit any interpretation of its sense at variance with their own private judgment, or with the rationalistic notions by which they are guided even when they think they are following the light of revelation.

They refuse to accept the doctrine here plainly taught, that the bodies of Christ's elect, after the resurrection, will be endowed with the supernatural qualities possessed by His own after He had issued from the tomb.

The pretty general tendency of all who, down to the present century, followed the light of private judgment, in opposition to the authoritative teaching of the Church and her careful interpretation of Holy Writ, to reject from revealed religion and Christianity itself everything that can be rightly defined as supernatural, has become almost universal among them since German rationalism, French scepticism, and the scientific materialism of the English schools have come to tyrannize over the intellectual world.

Catholics, with their unchanging and unerring guide, the spouse of Christ, cherish the ancient belief of the Patriarchs, inherited by the Hebrew Church, completed and reaffirmed by Christ, and here so eloquently, so clearly expounded by St. Paul.

SUMMARY OF CATHOLIC DOCTRINE ABOUT THE RISEN BODY.

As man in his first or earthly stage has a body subject to the laws and necessities of his present condition; a body gross, growing from the first germs of organized life to its full maturity, and then decaying till the separation from the soul gives it up to corruption, the worm, and its original dust; a body needing meat and drink, repose and sleep, and a thousand precautions against disease and hurtful accidents; so in the second or heavenly stage of his existence, where both soul and body attain to their supernatural destiny and the divine life of the Beatific Vision, the change effected in man's soul and in all its faculties requires a corresponding change in the body united with it in this heavenly existence and the truly divine life it bestows.

"*The first man Adam was made into a living soul; the last Adam* [Christ] *into a quickening Spirit.*"

Like the inferior animals, who derive their very name from the soul or immaterial principle which gives them life, his body was subject to the laws of organic growth and decay, of sensual appetite, and the struggle for existence. This is what St. Paul calls the "natural body"—a body doomed to death and subject to the cravings of sensual appetite and necessity; and the "living soul" is thus the slave of animal needs.

In the second creation—or heavenly and eternal phase of human existence—we are born, in soul and in body, after the image of the last or divine Adam, Christ Jesus. Our body, in that divine life to which we are raised in Him and through His merits, is to be a *supernatural* or "spiritual" body, fitted and adapted in every way to the uses of that exalted existence, in which the carnal love of the present life has no place, and the present necessities are superseded by the fruition of a blissful immortality, and a divinely spiritual life. It may truly be said of Christ, the meritorious Cause of that life, that both in body and soul He is "*a quickening Spirit.*"

The natural body which each earthly generation deposits in the grave, as the husbandman casts his seed into the furrow, will, at God's own appointed time, rise from the earth "a spiritual body," created anew on the model of His, who, on the resurrection day, comes down as the "quickening Spirit" from heaven, and so rises from the dust "heavenly." "Such as is *the heavenly,* such also are they that are heavenly."

And then we have, for the instruction and consolation of all who believe in Christ, and hope firmly in the fulfillment of His promises on the last day, the solemn affirmation of the great Apostle, so near his end:

"Therefore, as we have borne the image of the earthly [Adam], let us bear also the image of *the heavenly*" [Christ.] But, as we shall see, each blessed soul on that day will be come to its body "a quickening spirit."

CHRIST'S TRANSFIGURATION AND OURS.

Now, what is the image of that "last Adam," and His "heavenly" body, which is to be the model on which the Creator, at the beginning of the new and everlasting era of human existence, is to mould and perfect the bodies of Christ's elect? Only St. Matthew and St. Mark describe His transfiguration. Yet the body which shone on the Mount with such surpassing brightness was only His mortal body. It had not then passed through the fiery furnace of His Passion, and thereby merited for itself and for the bodies of His faithful followers the glories of the resurrection.

St. Matthew says: "His face did shine as the sun, and His garments became white as snow." St. Mark adds: "His garments became shining and exceeding white as snow, so as no fuller upon earth can make white."

Of His body only the face was seen, as dazzling as the noonday sun. This was the glory due to the hyposlatic union, the union, namely, of our humanity with the Person of the Son, and to the Beatific Vision consequent upon that union. It was only by a miracle—a miracle necessary to the fulfillment of His missionary career—that this natural effulgence was concealed. But, besides the splendor thus due to the body of the Incarnate Son, the sufferings of His Passion merited additional glory. This He does not appear to have shown to His Disciples after His Resurrection.

We can only repeat here the words of St. John, that when He, the Redeemer and the Judge, will "appear," or come solemnly at the end of time to complete His work upon earth, "we shall be like to Him," the body of each one of us "made like the body of His glory," as St. Paul declares to the Philippians.

HAPPINESS COMPLETED BY THIS TRANSFIGURATION.

The happiness of the soul will then be complete; for the human soul has the varied powers of sensibility, which imply its union with the body and the exercise of the organs of sense. These—these in particular that minister to the intellect and the imagination—will have additional perfection and enjoy their own share of blessedness in the new life.

It is a righteous compensation. For during the battle of life, and the long career of self-denial and self-crucifixion undergone by the Saints on earth, the bodily senses bore their part, and were the willing instruments of the generous spirit. In that life of ecstatic knowledge, bliss, and joy, of imcomprehensible social beatitude, what will not be the special satisfaction of sight and hearing, and even of taste and smell! For, as the body in general is so spiritualized as to be associated with the soul in the Beatific Vision, and in the enjoyment of all the secondary causes of bliss we have above enumerated; so will each exterior sense have become more and more identified with the interior. The eyes will be the supernaturalized instruments of the intellect in the clear sight of the divine Essence, and the contemplation of the divine perfections. And what rapturous sights will await them in the divine humanity of our Lord, in the sweet majesty of His Mother, in the glorious bands of saintly personages of every age, and country, and sex; of the entire family of the elect, in their various degrees of merit and glory, in their varied differences of nationality and character. Our fancy will not mislead us if we permit it to revel in representations of all that is most wonderful and most magnificent in the numbers, the appearance, the beauty, and the loveliness of these blessed multitudes, and the realms which they inhabit.

While our minds are yet full of the glorious spectacle of the new birth of mankind, and while Christ is ascending, to take anew a more solemn and final possession of His empire, escorted by the triumphant hosts of angels and men, let us examine more carefully the "change" which has taken place in the bodies of the just.

SUPERNATURAL QUALITIES OF GLORIFIED BODIES.

The first supernatural quality, or divine gift, bestowed on the glorified bodies both of Christ and of all His human subjects in heaven is "immortality," and with it the "impassibility," or exemption from disease, or pain, or any elemental force, or created living agency, that can hurt, or bruise, or wound. This is what St. Paul means when he says: "The dead shall rise again incorruptible: and we shall be changed. For this corruptible must put on incorruption: and this mortal must put on immortality." *

---

* 1 Cor., xv, 52-54.

The change, therefore, is from the condition of this present life, in which we bear in our bodies from the cradle to the grave the germs of corruption, decay, and death, to that heavenly condition, where nothing can weaken, hurt, corrupt, or age any part of our bodily organism; it is from mortality to immortality—from the perpetual fear and peril of death to that everlasting life, secure from all danger, disease, or destroying agency.

Such is not the "incorruption" or "immortality" with which are endowed the bodies of those who are doomed to share with the fallen angels the punishment due to mortal sin deliberately committed against the voice of conscience and the light of reason and revelation—sin separating the sinner from God, the Supreme Good and the Supreme Justice—sin unrepented of in life and death.

The bodies reunited at the resurrection to these guilty and lost souls are, indeed, immortal in this sense: that death never will separate them. But their condition is not one of impassibility, or exemption from pain. Far from it. Just as their will never has returned with all its force, and with the sorrow due to the magnitude of their offences, to the Author of their being, the Source of life, and light, and all good; so the material world and its elemental forces are not withheld by a special interposition of Providence from avenging His cause on these rebellious transgressors.

The second gift, likening the bodies of the elect to that of Christ their King, is *lightsomeness*—that is, an inherent brightness, of which nothing here below can give us an adequate notion. This is what is meant by St. Paul when he says of the human body: "It is sown in dishonor, it shall rise in glory."* That men now die at all, is due to the fall of Adam, who dragged us all down with him in his dishonor. And there is a dishonor in the ruin which death and sin thus bring on the fair organic structure which the Creator from the beginning destined to be the living and beautiful temple of His Holy Spirit.

The glorious effulgence with which the Creator invests the human body at the resurrection, is alluded to by our Lord Himself where He says: "Then shall the just shine like the sun in the kingdom of their Father."† St. Paul, writing from his prison in Rome to the Philippians, exhorts them, as an encouragement to endure all the ills of this life, to think of what is promised them in heaven. "Our conversation," [that is, our manner of living,] he says, "is in heaven, from whence we look for the Saviour, who will reform the body of our lowness, made like the body of His glory."‡

The promise is too clearly, too explicitly expressed to leave any room for question or doubt.

The next or third gift of glorified bodies is termed "agility," and implies both the power to traverse, like purely spiritual beings, vast spaces with the speed of the lightning, and the power to move great material masses. To this quality applies the text: "It is sown in weakness, it shall rise in power." ‖ In this sense, as speaking of the supernatural agility and might bestowed on the bodies of the just, is understood the passage of Isaias: "Youths shall faint and labor, and young men shall fall by infirmity. But they that hope in the Lord shall renew

---
* 1 Cor., xv, 43.
† St. Matthew, xiii, 43.
‡ Philip., iii, 20-21.
‖ 1 Cor., xv, 43.

their strength; they shall run and not be weary; they shall walk and not faint." * These words of the Prophet may, however, be understood of the strength, vigor, and unwearied energy which God often bestows on earth on His living servants, who spend themselves in holy ministrations. Nevertheless, this great degree of energy vouchsafed by the Creator to mortal bodies may, with exceeding propriety, be conferred on the immortal, and in a state of existence where they are indispensable to the soul. The text of Isaias from verse twenty-five down to the passage we have quoted exalts the attribute of God's infinite power, and may be very appropriately quoted in referring to the resurrection and its effects: "It is He that giveth strength to the weary: and increaseth force and might to them that are not." † Here, again, we see the action of the "quickening Spirit."

St. Jerome does not hesitate to quote the text of Isaias as describing accurately the transformation, from our present heaviness and infirmity to the agility and energy of angels, of the bodily forces of the just.

St. Augustine thus expresses his sentiment: "If the angels can, without effort, carry off the bodies of living beings and put them where they please, why should we not believe that the souls of the just can move their own bodies and place them where they wish?" ‡ In another passage the great doctor says more positively: "It is certain that wheresoever the spirit wills the body to be, there it will be forthwith." ‖

---

* Isaias, xl, 30-31. ‡ August., "De Civitate Dei," L. XIII, 18.
† Ibidem, xl, 29. ‖ Ibidem, L. XXII, cap. ult.

The energies of the glorified bodies of the just will, undoubtedly, in this resemble those possessed by the body of our Lord.

THE SPIRITUAL AND HEAVENLY BODY.

The fourth and last attribute or gift of the risen bodies of the just is termed "subtility" by theologians. It is designated in the text of St. Paul, contrasting the gross, opaque, impenetrable, and heavy body laid in the grave, with the "spiritual" body, called forth from it by the command of the Creator.

This quality is that which raises the human organism to the closest resemblance with spiritual beings. For to a purely spiritual being no material substance is impenetrable.

HELPS TOWARDS UNDERSTANDING THIS POINT.

This is not the place to discuss the discordant theories of physicists regarding "impenetrability." Experience teaches us that one hard substance may be divided rather than penetrated by a still harder. This apparent penetrability comes of want of perfect cohesion in the particles of the less hard body. Where there is this perfect cohesion, or intimate union, of atom with atom forming a molecule, and of molecule with molecule composing a mass of sensible dimensions, there ought to be perfect physical impenetrability.

We know, on the other hand, that heat and electricity will not only penetrate the hardest known substances, such as the diamond, but disintegrate and decompose them. Not merely that; but electricity will separate the molecules of the diamond itself, and those indeed of all known substances.

The experiments of the chemist, as well as those of the physicist, go to establish the fact that no body with which we are acquainted is able to resist the disintegrating and decomposing energy of these subtile fluids called electricity, magnetism, etc. Now, the theory is that a universally diffused substance called *ether*, filling all space and interposed in the hardest and simplest substances (such as the pure diamond), between the molecules themselves, if not between the atoms proper, is the medium by which light, heat, electricity, magnetism, and motion itself, are communicated. The waves or vibrations of this ether, according to their various degrees of rapidity, cause the phenomena of light, electro-magnetism, etc. Pervading, as they do, the substance of metallic or other bodies, they make them more or less apt to communicate the magneto-electric currents over great spaces. Thus, these "ethereal" waves, in a copper wire across a continent or an ocean, can cause the molecules of the wire, by vibrations of such astonishing rapidity, to convey messages by sign or by sound—that is, by a mode of motion—in an instant of time.

We do not explain; we suggest. We point out what degrees of unimaginable velocity, as well as of real "subtility," the almighty and all-wise Creator gives to certain material substances or agencies, of whose existence modern science discourses so learnedly. This, then, is our position: If the Creator of matter and spirit has made a substance as spirit-like as the universal ether just described, bestowing on it such a constitution that it fills all space and interposes itself between the component elements of the hardest metallic or mineral bodies, and that it flows through every portion of every living organism, while it can convey the waves of light, of electricity, of sound, of heat, in an instant of time from one end of the earth to the other; why could not that same Creator endow the human body with similar or superior spirit-like properties, enabling it, as well as the glorified soul animating it, to pass, at the will of the latter, from one end of creation to the other, without finding in material space or material masses any obstacle to its progress?

We suggest the analogy, and the inevitable conclusion, and pass on.

FROM REASON TO REVELATION.

To this quality of "subtility" in the glorified human body apply the words of St. Paul: "It is sown a natural body, it shall rise a spiritual body. . . . . The first man was of the earth, earthly: the second man, from heaven, heavenly." *

The Apostle clearly vindicates for Christ's body as it exists in heaven, and for those of His elect, which are there formed anew after "the image" or model of His heavenly body, conditions of existence, assimilating their organism as nearly as may be to the nature of a spiritual substance. Who will question the power of the Creator to effect such a change? Or who will speak of impossibilities in the face of the wonderful phenomena and agencies daily discovered on this earth—the narrow abode of "the first Adam" and his progeny?

---

* 1 Cor., xv, 44-47.

WHAT THE EARLY FATHERS TAUGHT.

This "subtility," which makes St. Paul call the body recalled to life by the resurrection "a spiritual body," was discussed by the early Christian writers with that freedom and fullness which characterize the works of these great men. Naturally, their scientific and physical views were those of their contemporaries. But they were not narrow or illiberal views.

St. Epiphanius, in his exposition and refutation of the various heresies about the resurrection, sets forth the accepted teaching of the Christian schools on the very point we have just now touched. "When our Lord Jesus Christ," he says, "arose from the dead, He brought up with Him no other body than that which He had before, bestowing on it in the change a spirit-like subtility, and composing therewith one spiritual whole, by which He could enter a room through closed doors. This we cannot now do with these gross bodies of ours, which have not yet been made the subject of such a spiritual union." In another place the Saint says: "So the body, which was a true body composed of subtile elements, was the same that had formerly consisted of gross material parts." *

We translate this passage from the Latin quotation of Lessius: "He [St. Epiphanius] expresses the same opinion in Heresy XX," says the great Jesuit theologian. "Where the words *spirit-like fineness of parts* and the absence of *grossness* are used we must not understand him to mean an attenuation of the material particles, or a rarefaction of the body—

---

* St. Epiphanius. "De Hæresibus." Hæresi LXIV.

such a change being repugnant to the constitution of the flesh and bones. We can only give one meaning to his words: that the glorified body is freed from that imperfection which prevented it from penetrating another—an imperfection that we might call material grossness, since we lack appropriate terms in which to express this condition of things. Wherefore, a body freed from this imperfection may be called spirit-like and subtile, because it can penetrate other bodies as a spirit does."*

HEAVENWARD! HEAVENWARD!

Let your imagination soar, allow your fancy to borrow all the colors that the material universe in its utmost magnificence ever wore, either when God laid the foundations of the earth, "when the morning stars praised God together, and all the sons of God made a joyful melody," † or when heaven, and earth, and all creation put on their fairest vesture for the new birth of mankind—for the vindication and triumph of God's justice, mercy, and unfathomable goodness toward men and angels. Can any created intelligence understand the grandeur, the glory, the immensity, of either of these two worlds which Christ leads upwards beyond the orbit of the remotest perishable star, to that imperishable and immutable empire where He, with the Father and the Holy Spirit, is to reign eternally over subjects outnumbering the stars in multitude, outshining them in glory, and partaking of God's own felicity and eternity? Can the sublimest imagination conceive or describe the splendors of that triumphal train?

---

* Lessius, "De Summo Bono," L. III, c. vii.
† Job, xxxviii, 7.

Let us follow them with eye, and mind, and heart, as they sing:

> "The earth is the Lord's and the fullness thereof:
> The world, and all that dwell therein!
> Who shall ascend into the mountain of the Lord?
> Or who shall stand in His holy place?
> The innocent in hands, or clean of heart,
> Who hath not taken his soul in vain,
> Nor sworn deceitfully to his neighbor,
> He shall receive a blessing from the Lord:
> And mercy from God His Saviour.
> This is the generation of them that seek Him.
> Of them that seek the face of the God of Jacob.
> Lift up your gates, O ye princes:
> And be ye lifted up, O eternal gates!
> And the King of Glory shall enter in.
> Who is this King of Glory?
> The Lord who is strong and mighty:
> The Lord mighty in battle.
> Lift up your gates, O ye princes,
> And be ye lifted up, O eternal gates:
> And the King of Glory shall enter in.
> Who is this King of Glory?
> The Lord of Hosts, He is the King of Glory."*

You who believe in the glorious realities of this unseen world, which I have been disclosing to you with awe and reverence, oh! be Godlike in your life and your charities!

---
* Psalm XXIII.

CHAPTER XVIII.

THE TRIUMPH OF CHRIST.

"Misericordias Domini in æternum cantabo."
—*Psalm LXXXVIII.*

The mercy of the Lord,
'Twas the subject of the singer—
'Twas the the theme he loved the best;
He had known that mercy long.
Could he measure or define it?
Oh, no mortal could describe it.
But he sought to tell the wonder
And the work of it in song.

THE CONQUEROR AND HIS TRAIN.

Can the mind of man conceive, can the tongue or hand of man express, the glory of Christ's entrance into the heavenly Jerusalem, after this final triumph over the enemies of God, and this victorious vindication of the divine Justice, Mercy, and Patience? He had given His soul to shame, humiliation, and agony unutterable upon the cross and in the streets of the earthly Jerusalem, that He might thus merit for His brethren the everlasting glory, joy, and exultation of the new life now beginning; He had delivered up His body to the buffeting and the blindfolding, to be spit upon by the vilest, to be scourged at the pillar and crowned with thorns; He had bowed his bleeding shoulders to the wood of the cross, and carried it a while up the steep ascent, which Isaac had trodden before Him, bearing the wood of the Sacrifice; He had lain down meekly on the self-same spot where Isaac had reared the altar and suffered Himself to be bound and laid on the pile by the hands of His sorrowing parent. How lovingly were the hands and feet of the second Isaac stretched out to the cruel nails which there pierced them! How lovingly, from the highest heaven, did the eternal Father look down on His Only-Begotten Son made Man for us, and for us given up there to death the most shameful and the most terrible!

THE BATTLE AND THE VICTORY.

The sublime drama of filial obedience and fatherly generosity enacted on that mountain-top by Abraham and Isaac was only a foreshadowing of that infinite love for mankind manifested in that other Sacrifice on the same spot, where the Father of angels and men offered up His beloved One, and no angel interfered to stay the sacrifice.

O charity, charity! O love unspeakable, what a sacrifice was that! And for what a purpose!

Try to ascend in spirit to the verge of that most glorious realm, where the cross is borne before the *Crucified*, as He takes possession, for Himself and His followers, of the empire awarded to Him and them by the Father. Forget the spectacular triumphs of Roman consuls, generals, and emperors; forget the Napoleonic pageants of the first years of the present century, and the half-million citizen-soldiers who—the great civil war over—marched through Washington in 1865. Nothing that earth or heaven ever beheld can compare with Christ's triumphal entry into heaven after the general resurrection and the last judgment.

Who can number the angelic hosts who attend Him? Who can count the millions of His Saints and elect?

THE NUMBERS LIBERATED BY THE VICTOR.

How long, from the present year of grace, will human life be prolonged till the last babe is born, and the last human being gathered into judgment by death? Will it be ten thousand years? or a hundred thousand years? or two hundred thousand? Who will dare to limit the experiment of human free-will upon this earth to his own narrow conceptions of time? Christ did not die on the cross to extend the saving benefit of His truth and charity to a fragment only of the race. And when, in His own appointed time, all nations will have heard and embraced the Gospel; who will presume to limit to one generation, or even to a hundred, the reign of Christian morality, the growth of a true Christian civilization?

CHIEF OBSTACLE TO THE CHURCH'S INCREASE IN THE PAST.

Down to the close of this nineteenth century, the natural, lawful, logical action of the Gospel and the Church on mankind and civil society has been marred chiefly by that feudalism which sprang up after the fall of the Roman empire, and was implanted by the Barbarians in every part of Christendom. The Church and the supernatural life which she imparts to the children of God have struggled on for more than a thousand years against the hostile spirit and oppressive might of feudalism—just as a magnificent tree of the Southern forests lives on in spite of some mighty creeper which wound itself long ago around its young trunk, grew with its growth, fed upon its substance, and would have strangled it in its embrace had the life of the noble tree been a mere natural life.

Feudalism is old, decrepit, dying. But the Church is ever young. The parasites which had wound themselves round her, and seemed to be to her a support and an ornament, are being cut away and detached, not without rending away a part of the bark of the lordly tree. Patience! The separation only means freedom, new life, vigor, and beauty.

PROSPECTIVE INCREASE IN THE FUTURE.

Give us the blessed and glorious era when the Church, at liberty to speak to all the tribes of earth, to set before them the story of Christ's infinite love for mankind, will make them embrace and practice the law of life, and look up to the eternal promises as the sole reward worthy of true piety, devotion to duty, and self-sacrifice—as the only goal fit to tempt the ambition of men and women regenerated in the Blood of Jesus Christ. Who will limit to a few centuries this era of liberty for the Church, this true millennium—extending, it may be, over ten or twenty times a thousand years—during which Christ will indeed reign on earth over the hearts, and minds, and lives of men? This, in one dim shape or another, has been the dream, the hope, the prophetic instinct of all Christian ages from the beginning. Let us not belittle God and His plans by measuring with our own tape-line the road over which He intends the human race to travel. He is the Everlasting, the Infinite, the Eternal. Why should we say: "Within this narrow circle shalt Thou display the wonders of Thy goodness and Thy wisdom. Here is the limit beyond which human existence may not go."

Let us leave to that Love Eternal to work out Its own designs. What are a million of years to Him who knew no beginning and who can know no end?

THE MIGHTY FLOCK AROUND THE GOOD SHEPHERD.

So, then, around our King, Christ, in His supreme triumph, our imagination may behold glorified human beings in body and soul numerous enough to people all the orbs and clusters of worlds in the firmament above and around us; myriads of the Saints and elect, vieing in number with the angelic hosts, and, in the splendor of their re-born bodies, outshining the sun itself.

Oh, the prey won by the cross from hell and the grave! the spoil obtained by these pierced hands from the prince of this lower world and his allies, sin and death! Oh, the immense flock, appalling the mind in its immensity, which the bleeding feet of that Good Shepherd sought far and wide!

And now He brings them, gathers them, at length —at length into His fold, and around the feet of His Father!

THE GODLIKE PURPOSE OF CHRIST'S SUFFERINGS.

To impart to the myriads of myriads of human bodies, which shine and gravitate around His own, the splendor and the spirit-like qualities described in the last chapter; was it unworthy of the all-foreseeing Son of God to give up His body to the cold of the manger, to the long fast of forty days and nights, to the night-long vigils on hill-top or desert, after the consuming labors of a missionary day, to the night of torture and humiliation in the house of Annas, and to all the sufferings of that dreadful morrow, ending with the three hours upon the cross?

To bestow on every human soul gathered into His kingdom the bliss and glory of the Beatific Vision, and a share in the very life and eternity of the Triune Godhead; was it too dear a price to endure all the shame of His Passion, all the ignominy heaped upon His head by the nation assembled in Jerusalem for their most solemn feast, and the unutterable agony of these awful three hours of lingering death on the cross, while the multitude scoffed, derided, blasphemed around?

So, advance the victorious banner of our King. Let the cross flame high before the advancing ranks of the two great armies, which follow His triumphal car borne by seraphim and cherubim, where the "strong woman," * who stood by His cross in that agony, now shares His triumph, the mother of the new life, the second Eve and parent of all Christ's redeemed. Patriarchs, Apostles, martyrs, confessors and virgins—all ye sublime souls, who, before Christ and after Him, have kept living before the world the ideal of the Godlike life which man can lead here below—surround the throne of your Chief.

THE BANDS OF HIS CLOSEST IMITATORS.

Pause awhile, and contemplate, as the Conqueror of death and hell advances, and the feet, the bodily feet of His followers, tread for the first time the soil of His heavenly empire—the sacred cohorts of those whose pre-eminence in sanctity gives them the right to be nearest to His Person—holy men and holy women gathered from every generation since the world began, and from every clime beneath the sun; Adam and Eve, whose tears of sorrow and anguish fell, during so many centuries, on the furrows in

* Proverbs, xxxi, 10.

which they sowed their grain, while the earth, on which their great sin had brought a curse, produced a great crop of iniquity and inhumanity; and then Seth, and Henoch, and Noe, with their families, who kept their souls above the rising and resistless tide of surrounding corruption; then Abraham and his descendants, with their checkered fortunes, their alternations of fidelity to God and desertion of His law. But what a glorious harvest from the Hebrew race He has gathered into His everlasting home! And then count, since the midnight glory and the songs of angels thrilled the shepherds around Bethlehem, how many, from age to age, have trodden in the footsteps of Jesus of Nazareth, in voluntary poverty, suffering, and self-sacrifice, to santify their own souls and help on His work of salvation! Count, if you can, the holy men and women who are the spiritual progeny of Anthony and Benedict, of Bruno and Romuald and Bernard, of Francis and Dominick, of Angela de Merici and Ignatius Loyola and Vincent of Paul. How many other glorious religious families glitter, like the clusters of the Milky Way, among these great orders, the foster parents of every Christian generation, the blessed auxiliaries of the Church in saving and sanctifying the world!

THE TE DEUM SUNG IN THAT PROCESSION.

We have often heard in seasons of great joy the Christian hearts of the people pouring out their gratitude in the holy place, and around the altar of the Lamb, for some mighty benefit received from on high. Even then the sublime chant of the *Te Deum Laudamus* was an earthly echo of the perpetual hymn sung in heaven. But, on the return of Christ triumphant into heaven at the head of the Church, complete in the number of her children, and crowned with the perfection of life immortal, what strain more appropriate than that sung so often in exile?

> "Thee, O God, we praise;
> Thee we proclaim the only Lord.
> Thee, O Father eternal, the whole earth adores.
> To thee do all the angels; to Thee do the heavens
> With all the powers of the universe;
> To Thee do the cherubim and seraphim,
> With unceasing voice sing forth:
> Holy, holy, holy,
> Lord God of Hosts!"

Oh, yes; He is the God of holiness, and heaven is the eternal abode of the holy. And see what hosts of the holy surround Him there!

> "Filled are the heavens and the earth
> With the greatness of Thy glory.
> Thee the glorious apostolic choir;
> Thee the blessed band of Prophets;
> Thee the white-robed army of martyrs
> Praise.
> Thee through all earth's bounds
> The holy Church proclaims
> The Father of Majesty Infinite;
> Worthy of adoration Thy true and only Son,
> Together with the Holy Spirit, the Comforter."

So may we behold them in spirit—these two mighty worlds in eternity—hymning the sovereign greatness and glory of the Triune Deity. And then hear them as they address the Son:

> "Thou, O Christ, art the King of Glory.
> Thou from eternity art the Son of the Father!
> Thou, in order to liberate man, didst take man's
> Nature on Thee, not recoiling from the Virgin's womb!
> Thou, when death's sharp dart was broken,
> To Thy believers openedst wide the realms of heaven.
> Thou it is who thronest in glory
> At the right hand of Thy Father."

THE WORK OF MERCY CONSUMMATED.

The remainder of St. Ambrose's glorious hymn is but the prayer of sinners expecting judgment, of exiles asking to be safely guided homeward, of children anxious to be gathered beneath the wings of Almighty Love and Mercy.

The work of mercy is now complete. She has not only removed from Christ's elect all the ills of earth and time, but conferred on them all the good things in God's own power—Himself and His most blissful life. Hence the blessed multitudes can well sing David's glorious psalm:

"The mercies of the Lord I will sing forever;

For thou hast said: 'Mercy shall be built up forever in the heavens;
Thy truth shall be prepared in them.'

The heavens shall confess Thy wonders, O Lord,
And Thy truth in the Church of the Saints.
For who in the clouds can be compared to the Lord?
Or who among the sons of God shall be like to God?
God, who is glorified in the assembly of the Saints:
Great and terrible above all them that are about Him.
O Lord God of Hosts, who is like to Thee?
Thou art mighty, O Lord, and Thy truth is round about Thee.

Thine are the heavens, and thine is the earth:
The world and the fullness thereof Thou hast founded:
The north and the sea Thou hast created.

Justice and judgment are the preparation of Thy throne.
Mercy and truth shall go before Thy face:
Blessed be the people that knoweth jubilation!
They shall walk, O Lord, in the light of Thy countenance:
And in Thy name they shall rejoice all the day,
And in Thy justice they shall be exalted." *

---

* Psalm LXXXVIII, 1-17.

JOY EXHAUSTS OUR MORTAL FRAME.

O joys of eternity, whose duration is measured by no revolution of earth or sun, what occurrence of time, what mighty outburst of popular or national sentiment can give us even a faint and shadowy notion of your fullness, your immensity, your height, and your depth? Our senses are dulled, our bodily strength is exhausted by a single day's celebration here below, in which the great waves of popular enthusiasm sweep by like the roaring, rushing waves of a great river hastening toward a precipice. The spectacle of a hundred thousand men in military or in holiday attire dazzles and dazes the eye as they pass before it. The most delightful or elevating music ever composed by the genius of man, or ever executed by the most perfect human skill, expressing itself in divinest song or exquisite instrumentation, can only be endured for half a day uninterruptedly, and may not be repeated day after day, like a succession of intoxicating banquets. In this life our capacity to receive pleasure, like our capacity to give it, is sadly limited. The human spirit, while on earth, is a small narrow-necked vase, into which the delicious liquor of joy and bliss must be poured carefully, drop by drop. Even when plunged in a deep and wide river, it can only be filled drop by drop; and when its capacity is exhausted, the waves above, beneath, and around it sweep by, profitless and unheeded. The heart of man here below, the heart of the best and the most gifted, is a beautiful and delicate flower, whose envelope alone receives the invisible droplets of the night-dew, and which a down-pour of rain overwhelms, destroys, or casts crushed and lifeless on the ground. Even the sunlight and warmth must be tempered to its frail and exquisite texture.

HEART AND SOUL ENLARGED FOR HEAVENLY JOYS.

But in the life to come, and when the resurrection sends men back to heaven in the fullness and perfection of bodily and spiritual power, not even the infinite greatness, light, and loveliness of the Deity, seen face to face, will overwhelm or crush the soul. As we have said repeatedly, the elevation and enlargement of the soul's capacity and power are a something so divine as to bring the creature near the Creator—to make of the human spirit a being so far above our present conceptions as to entitle it to be called divine. This sharing of the divine nature and the divine life is a fact expressly revealed in Scripture, and which we are bound unhesitatingly to believe, while discussing it reverently.

But the elevation and enlargement of the bodily powers and senses of man's entire organism, after the resurrection, are to be co-ordinate with those of the soul. The Innocents martyred by Herod's cruelty, and which his hatred of Christ caused him to baptize in their own blood, will preserve their identity in heaven. Their bodies will be ever the bodies of babes, without the helplessness and infirmities of infancy; their souls will have the maturity and wisdom, the supernatural fullness of knowledge necessarily bestowed by the Beatific Vision. Revered evermore by the entire body of the elect, their minds will be the minds of the angels, their bodies endowed with the qualities bestowed on those of the highest Saints, their hearts enlarged to the capacity of loving and holding the Infinite God, and their tongues loosened to sound and sing eternally the praises of Christ and the Father.*

ALL OUR SENSES ELEVATED AND PERFECTED.

The sense of beauty and harmony, in forms, and colors, and sounds, is one of those peculiar to human nature. It is at the very foundation of art. In heaven this sense shall be perfected and purified in all the blessed. Not merely shall we have there the faculty of enjoying what is most exquisite in physical form, most beautiful in color, and most ravishing in harmony, but we shall be able to pour out our whole soul in song.

THE MUSIC OF THE SPHERES.

What shall be in heaven, at the dawn of that eternal day of the new life, which shall never know evening or night, the rapturous harmony of that song resounding through all the spheres of the celestial kingdom, and celebrating the Father's mercy, the Son's love and power, and the fostering providence of the Spirit of Truth and Charity!

We try to find in the inspired canticles of Holy Writ, as sung in the solemn services of the Church, and applied to the triumphs of the Church in heaven, some of these divine strains, some echoes of the harmonies of the city of God on high, which may lift us upward to a conception or contemplation of the Reality.

Hear the Royal Prophet:

> Sing unto the Lord a new song!
> Sing unto the Lord all the earth!

---

* In the verse, Apocalypse, vi, 9, "I saw under the altar the souls of them that were slain for the word of God" is applied to the Holy Innocents by the Church. In the beautiful hymn of their feast, December 29, they are spoken of as "little ones playing beneath the altar with their palms and crowns."

Aye; let all these crowned and white-robed myriads, whom earth has sent to heaven as her fairest flowers and richest fruit, lift their voices together in that glorious canticle:

> Sing ye to the Lord, and bless His name!
> Show forth His salvation from day to day!

As if all the cycles of eternity could not suffice to exalt that name of *Jesus*, and to set forth the wonderful means by which He accomplished our salvation. Jews and Gentiles are confounded in those adoring throngs, and sing with one acclaim:

> "Declare His glory among the Gentiles,
> His wonders among all people;
> For the Lord is great, and exceedingly to be praised.
> . . . .
> Praise and beauty are before Him:
> Holiness and majesty in His sanctuary.
> Bring ye to the Lord, O ye kindreds of the Gentiles,
> Bring ye to the Lord glory and honor:
> Bring to the Lord glory unto His name!" *

THE FULLNESS OF HEAVEN'S BEAUTY APPRECIATED.

Not until this day of days dawned upon God's fairest creation—that other universe situated beyond the most distant stars—and ushered in the eternity of the new life, has the soil of the heavens of heavens been trodden by human foot, save only His who trod alone the wine-press for us, and the Mother's, who stood by Him, dying her raiment also in the purple blood of the grape. But now these Two have with Them all the immense family of the children of God. How every eye and mind among these countless millions can now take in the beauty, the magnificence, the splendor, of the new world which is to be their home. Even the blessed souls who, before the

---

* Psalm XCV 3-8.

resurrection, enjoyed the clear sight of the divine Essence and the joys of paradise, have now superadded enjoyment unspeakable in being able to see with their bodily eyes that glorious masterpiece of the Almighty's power and love; to gaze upon its unutterable loveliness; upon the ever-changing beauties of the supernal Eden, with its flowers, its fragrance, its colors; in being able to hear the music of all these voices attuned to one perfect accord of harmony, one divine and exhaustless unity and variety of theme; in finding body and spirit steeped in that celestial atmosphere of light that dazzles not, of warmth which cannot overheat or weary.

King David had sung of old:

> One thing I have asked of the Lord,
> This will I seek after—
> That I may dwell in the house of the Lord
> All the days of my life:
> That I may see the delight of the Lord,
> And may visit His temple.
>
> . . . .
>
> My heart hath said to Thee, My face hath sought Thee:
> Thy face, O Lord, will I seek. *

And elsewhere:

> The Lord ruleth me, and I shall want nothing;
> He hath set me in a place of pasture,
> He hath brought me up to the refreshing waters,
> He hath turned my soul [toward their delight.]

THE BEAUTY OF THAT REGION.

The spring-tide glory of Lebanon is given to that land of the living, as well as the beauty of Carmel and Sharon. Whatever men have ever beheld on this earth, beneath the tropics or in the temperate zones, of all that is most enchanting or sublime in the prospects of land or sea, of lake or river, of

---

* Psalm XXVI, 4-8.

forest or wood, of sunny verdant slopes or peaceful valleys; whatever of beauty the Creator has there displayed in tree or shrub, in all that flowers in field or garden—that, and much more than that, in a variety and a profusion of which He alone has the secret, has His hand scattered throughout that heavenly world.

HOW FLOWERS SPRANG UP WHERE ST. FRANCIS WALKED.

There exists in Italy and in Spain, wherever St. Francis of Assisi traveled, borne along, like a seraph, lent to earth for a while to breathe a message of divine love to the nations, most touching and most beautiful traditions relating to his influence over all animated nature. In the Diocese of Barcelona, it is said, and still believed, that in a desert glen into which the Saint sometimes withdrew to pray and meditate, the very earth became clothed with fertility, beauty, and flowers of most exquisite hue and fragrance. And the very springs in which he quenched his thirst and blessed were endowed with a healing virtue. All who have read his wonderful life know how the very birds and beasts were drawn to that Christ-like man, whose gentleness seemed to charm and hold them spell-bound. What wonder if beneath those feet, which bore the stigmata, or bleeding wounds, of our Crucified Lord, the earth put forth its sweetest flowers as he passed along, bearing on his person the image of the Saviour? What wonder if these nail-pierced hands could charm the fierceness of the wolf, or tame the eagle to his will, or beckon the birds to tree and hedge on his path to join with that seraphic soul in singing the praises of God the Most High?

In Milan, a touching reminder of this heavenly man, and his supernatural loveliness and goodness, was the feast which was celebrated formerly in that portion of the city which surrounded the Church of San Francesco, then the most splendid of all the Milanese temples. During the three first days of October all the streets, squares, and thoroughfares of that quarter were transformed into a paradise of flowers. Ah! memories of the Christian ages, reverence for heroic of soul, and the pure and heavenly in life, how they strive to blot you out from the hearts and minds of the people, from the ruined shrines and desecrated soil of Italy!

What must it be in the true Eden on high as Christ advances with His triumphal train? Will not the very soil beneath the feet of the Crucified put forth flowers of the heavenliest hues and fragrance?

Not without a purpose shall nature in these spheres bear unceasingly the alternate bloom and fruit of all these most beautiful creatures of the vegetable world, which are, here below, the delight of the fairest of our bodily senses. Does not He, as Man, take pleasure in all the lovely creations with which He, as the Son, covers, and clothes, and adorns the face of inanimate nature? And will not His children, in that most magnificent of worlds, not share the enjoyment of their Master and Model, and adore the footprints of the Creator in all this wealth of beauty with which He decks out the heavens of heavens?

GODLIKE SPIRITS AND GODLIKE MEN.

As we contemplate, therefore, the triumphal progress of the inhabitants of these united empires of heaven—the angelic and the human—let us open wide to the overwhelming truth, to the splendor of this most real of all realities, every avenue of our souls. In the angelic hosts, as they pass by, marshaled in their hierarchies, there is not a glorious spirit whom men here below would not deem worthy almost of adoration if they could only behold him in his own native beauty, or witness the display of his might, his wisdom, his goodness. But these sublime beings, from the highest to the lowest, only reflect and set forth to our intelligence, in ascending and descending degrees, the perfections, attributes, and glory of the Creator. Compared to them, in their nature and moral excellence, the popular deities of the heathen world were like the rude delineations of the human form made by our Northwestern savages, as compared with the sculptures of the Parthenon and the designs and paintings of Lionardo da Vinci.

More than that. As we may behold in spirit, following close in the footsteps of the God-Man, *Jesus*, all those successive hosts of His human kindred, each member of them perfect in body and in soul, and adorned with all natural and supernatural excellence, how far the lowliest and least in the kingdom of heaven surpasses in goodness, greatness, and power the fabled deities worshiped by Greece and Italy, by Egyptian and Babylonian, by the dreamy millions of Buddha's followers in India, China, and Japan!

Impeccable, infallible, immortal, impassible—with bodies made like the most spiritual substances, with souls transformed by knowledge and love to the very likeness of God Himself, and made partakers of His life and happiness—how far above the conceptions of pagan poets or philosophers, when they describe the Godhead, is the height of grandeur and glory to which Christ has raised His own!

And this triumphal entry into heaven of Christ and His angelic and human followers, is only the prelude to what He describes Himself as the wedding feast which the King of kings has prepared for His Son. These are the bridals of the Lamb which were shown afar off, in the Apocalypse, to the beloved Disciple, who had reclined on the breast of Jesus in the Last Supper. This glorious assemblage of the two heavenly worlds is the Church Triumphant, the bride of the Lamb; and not till now, not till the resurrection has united every human spirit with the flesh it had cast off in death, was Christ's bride ready for the everlasting espousals, or could this perfect union of the Infinite God with our deified humanity take place.

THE DIVINE REALITY.

To poor sinners yet in the flesh, and endeavoring to lift themselves up by thought and meditation to some shadowy notion of the Eternal Reality, even the shadows which conceal while outlining that Reality Itself overwhelm the mind by the forms they reveal and the splendors which struggle through the mist of our intelligence. Even to the beloved Disciple, St. John, when lifted up in spirit to the everlasting gates, the veiled vision of the place, of its inhabitants, and the life therein led, was too much for mortal intelligence to bear, for human language to express. His efforts to describe what he has beheld are like those of one intoxicated or half-delirious to convey to others the impressions of what he beholds and feels:

"After these things, I heard, as it were, the voice of much people in heaven, saying: Alleluia! Salvation, and glory, and power is to our God. . . . . And I heard, as it were, the voice of a great multitude, and as the voice of many waters, and as the voice of great thunders, saying Alleluia [praise ye the Lord.] For the Lord our God the Almighty hath reigned. Let us be glad, and rejoice, and give glory to Him; for the marriage of the Lamb is come, and His spouse hath prepared herself. And it is granted to her that she should clothe herself with fine linen glittering and white. For the fine linen are the justifications of Saints.

"And he [the angel] said to me: 'Write: Blessed are they that are called to the Supper of the Lamb.' And he saith to me: '*These words of God are true.*'

"And I fell down before his feet to adore him. And he said to me: 'See thou do it not! I am thy fellow-servant, and of thy brethren who have the testimony of Jesus. Adore *God!*'" *

So much for the mighty multitudes and their *Alleluias*, sounding like the voice of many waters falling from cataract to cataract, or of thunders re-echoed from all the clouds of heaven and the mountains of earth.

Now read what St. John says of the mighty Victor over death and hell as He advances before the hosts he leads in happy captivity:

"And I saw heaven opened, and behold a white horse: and He that sat upon him was called *Faithful and True,* and with justice doth He judge and fight.

---

* Apoc., xix, 1-10.

And His eyes were as a flame of fire; and on His head were many diadems, and He had a name written which no one knoweth but Himself. And He was clothed with a garment sprinkled with blood: and His name is called *The Word of God*. . . . . And He treadeth the wine-press of the fierceness of the wrath of God the Almighty. And He hath on His garment and on His thigh written, *King of Kings and Lord of Lords*." *

Take away from this descriptive passage the gorgeous imagery in which the Eastern peoples clothe their thoughts, especially in poetry, and in that highest form of poetical inspiration, prophecy, and enough will remain to satisfy even our cold and calm northern intellects as to the grandeur of the pageant, when Christ, *King of Kings and Lord of Lords*, enters heaven, leading with Him the innumerable multitudes which He redeemed from eternal death, when, alone, with His Mother to encourage Him to conquer, He did "tread the wine-press of the fierceness of the wrath of God the Almighty." Let Him now, in that realm in which all our present notions and relations of space and time are totally changed, do for our liberated and redeemed humanity what the noblest, the most magnificent of lovers would do for his bride—set forth for her, in the most superb of palaces, the most sumptuous and regal of banquets.

That is a feast which is to last forever. It is called a "supper" because it closes the festivities and pageants of the day. It comes at the end of time, and fills with its magnificences and delights all the cycles of eternity.

---

* Apoc., xix, 11-16.

So, as in beginning this book we spoke of the house of God upon earth, and of the Sacramental Bread which the Church, the mother of His children, daily breaks to them at her table, let us now see how the Reality in every point fulfills and exceeds the figure and the pledge.

CHAPTER XIX.

THE UTMOST GOAL OF HUMAN ASPIRATION AND PROGRESS.

DRINKING IMMORTALITY AND DIVINITY.

They shall be inebriated with the plenty of Thy house:
And Thou shalt make them drink of the torrent of thy pleasure;
For with Thee is the *fountain of life:*
And in Thy light we shall see *the light.*
—*Psalm XXXV*, 9-10.

"We must not fancy," says Cardinal Bellarmine, in speaking of the Nuptial Supper of the Lamb, "that there shall be in heaven anything like the banquet set forth here on earth by sovereigns when they celebrate their bridals. In the kingdom of heaven we shall be like God's angels, who can neither marry nor be married, and who need not to feed on aliments necessary to our bodily sustenance. That Supper of the Lamb will, therefore, be filled with a display of wealth, of delights, of ornaments, and of splendor such as shall befit the condition of the blessed. The matter is set before us at present in that form, because our eyes can see on earth nothing better or greater. But from what is said about it we should learn that the heavenly Banquet shall transcend in excellence all our earthly feasts as much as heaven itself is above the earth, and as much as God, whose care it will be to prepare the Feast, surpasses in power and riches all mortal potentates." *

A WEDDING FEAST THE IDEAL OF JOY AND PLEASURE.

Truly, by meditating on what we are familiar with in this life, on what we know as conveying to the minds of all the idea of what is most magnificent, most joyous, most delightful, we can ascend to the contemplation of heavenly things. A wedding feast among the lowliest as among the highest, among the poor as among the wealthy, is an occasion for the display of hospitality, of the utmost outlay, and of generosity to the needy poor. If our Lord, in preparing our minds to conceive the loftiest idea of that life eternal, after the resurrection, in which all found faithful to God shall enjoy with Him and in Him such supreme felicity as Almighty Love can bestow, compares that life eternal to a royal wedding supper, it is because such a supper is on earth what men consider to be all that is most splendid and pleasing to the sense. Bellarmine, who was wont,

---

* Bellarmine, "On the Eternal Felicity of the Saints," Book V, c. v.: Neque tamen suspicari debemus, in caelo futuram esse coenam, qualem hic habent magni principes cum nuptias celebrant: siquidem in coelo erimus sicut Angeli Dei, qui neque nubent, neque ducunt uxores, neque vescuntur cibis ad vitam mortalem sustentandam necessariis. Erit ergo coena plena divitus, et deliciis, et ornamentis, et gloria Statui Beatorum conveniens. Haec enim dicuntur nobis hoc tempore, quia meliora et majora non vidimus. Sed ab his discere debemus, tanto fore coenam illam nostris coenis quamvis lautissimis meliorem quanto coelum distat a terra; et quanto Deus qui illam parabit, potentia et divitus mortalibus Regibus praestat.

toward the end of his life, to meditate yearly in solitude on this great subject of eternal felicity, says, in the same chapter, that kings in their nuptial banquets are at pains to unite, for their guests' enjoyment, all that can delight the senses, all that can show forth this world's wealth, power, and glory. He quotes, as an instance of this, the great banquet which Assuerus prepared for the princes who governed under him the one hundred and twenty-seven provinces of his vast empire. The sumptuosity and magnificence displayed on this occasion were deemed by the King of Persia to be the most convincing proof he could give these satraps of his greatness and power.

THE WEDDINGS OF THE POOR.

We need not, however, go to the palaces of sovereigns to obtain a clear knowledge of what a wedding supper or banquet may be, when the bridegroom or the bride, or their parents, possess such wealth as to permit a lavish expenditure for the entertainment. As we are anxious, from what strikes and gratifies the sense on earth, to form a true estimate of what the divine pleasures of the heavenly life will be, let us glance at our ideal wedding feast here below.

Who has not seen the homes of the wealthy decorated and prepared for a wedding? Everything in architecture and decoration which can charm the eye and satisfy the cultivated taste—painting, statuary, hangings, lights, the rarest flowers, the richest plate,—all is there. And to the pleasure of the eye is added that of that other sense which the most fragrant odors gratify. The most delicate perfumes and subtile essences of the East impregnate the air without loading it. And there is heavenly music, the blending of orchestral harmony with the divine melody of human voices, lifting the soul to the spheres. Of the lower and more animal senses I need say nothing, and yet it is to them that the crowd attends most. What profusion of viands, of liquors, of fruits, and all manner of delicacies invented to tempt and stimulate the appetite!

And in the banqueting-room the splendor and varied richness of apparel of the guests as well as of the bride and bridegroom and their friends—the finest cloths, the rarest and richest silks and stuffs, the blending of lovely colors, with the flashing of gems, and the glitter of burnished gold and silver—who can describe all this that has not seen it? And to those who have seen it often what need of describing it?

THE WEDDINGS OF THE GREAT.

Among the mighty and the wealthy, too, these nuptial festivities and costly entertainments are often prolonged day after day. So did Assuerus feast his subject princes and nobles for one hundred and four score days in succession. And this first series of entertainments ended, the king "invited all the people that were found in Susan [the capital], from the greatest to the least, and commanded a feast to be made seven days in the court of the garden, and of the wood, which was planted by the care and the hand of the king. And there were hung up on every side sky-colored, and green, and violet hangings, fastened with cords of silk and purple, which were put into rings of ivory, and were upheld by marble columns. The beds [on which the guests reclined at table] also were of gold and silver, placed in order upon a floor paved with porphyry and white marble, which was embellished with painting of wonderful variety. And they that were invited drank in golden cups, and the meats were brought in divers vessels one after another. Wine also in abundance and of the best was presented, as was worthy of the king's magnificence."*

THE WEDDING SUPPER OF THE LAMB.

Coming now to the heavenly Banquet—the Supper of the Lamb—what are we to understand by it?

This: The work of Christ being completed, having gathered into His heavenly kingdom the last born among His brethren on earth, and the Church of earth being merged in that of heaven, a new era, as it were, begins for that blessed society above, composed of angels, and of men now, like Christ and His Virgin Mother, enjoying in eternity the twofold bliss of body and of soul. Until the resurrection day, earth held the sacred dust of the human body from Adam to his latest descendant. Now, at the Creator's word, that dust has been reanimated, and the elect of the race have entered heaven, each happy soul bearing with it, as a spoil recovered from death and the grave, the body in which it had lived, labored, suffered for Christ. That restored body is made in all things like His, differing only from His in degree of glory, and all the Saints, both in body and in soul, differing from each other according to their degree of merit as "star differeth from star in glory." †

---

* Esther, 1, 5-7. † 1 Cor., xv, 41.

THE NUMBER OF THE GUESTS.

What numbers death, in the last age of the world, added to the ranks of the blessed, we know not. We may believe that our dear Lord will not, in those last days, withdraw His mercy, His Spirit, and His saving grace from the children of men. Among Christ's triumphal train, as He re-enters heaven, His glorious labors ended, we can behold millions who never till then tasted the joys of paradise.

Confining our contemplation, for the moment, to that Church of which Christ is the Head, to that glorified human society whose members claim Him as Brother and King, it now comes into His heavenly empire not only complete in its numbers, but complete in its nature. For all men in these blessed ranks are complete in body and in soul. Until now angels and blessed souls in heaven have only looked upon the glorified human countenances of the second Adam and the second Eve. Now our first parents follow Christ and His Mother in that triumphal procession, bearing with them to the throne of God the bodies which His own hand had fashioned in the beginning; and how fairer, brighter, more glorious they shine there than they did in Eden before sin had poisoned their blood and dimmed the lustre of both body and spirit! So shine the white-robed ranks of the generations who follow our great parents as they march on, glittering wave after wave, a mighty ocean stream beheld at dawn from a mountain top near the shore, when the sun has just come out of his tabernacle, and the East is resplendent with all its many-colored glories, and the living waves bound after each other, reflecting the magnificence of heaven, and all the shining ocean lifts up its voice in praise of the Lord of the earth and the sea. Oh! look at that stream of glorified and exultant human life as it flows through the land of the living!

The Lord hath reigned; He is clothed with beauty:
The Lord is clothed with strength, and hath girded Himself.
For He hath established the world which shall not be moved.
Thy throne is prepared from of old: Thou art from everlasting.
The floods have lifted up, O Lord, the floods have lifted up their voice.
>> The floods have lifted up their waves
>> With the voice of many waters;
>> Wonderful are the surges of the sea,
>> Wonderful is the Lord on high.*

THE PROCESSION TO THE BANQUET HALL.

These are the human generations marching in after Christ to share the Banquet set forth for Him and them by the Father. Try to use in advance these spiritual powers which enable the just in heaven to behold God's immense empire and its inhabitants as one now can take in the interior of the largest edifice or of the vastest banqueting-room with its guests. Fear not to assign to Christ some central position, toward which every eye can be directed, and from which His divine countenance can shed the radiance of its love over every face in those far-stretching ranks beneath, all round, above, tier upon tier of enthroned men and women, millions multiplied by millions, drinking in the ecstatic bliss of that Vision divine, that clear sight of the Deity, whose presence is like the tempered light and vital warmth of the sun, pervading, penetrating all.

---

* Psalm XCII, 1-4.

WHERE THE SUPPER IS SET OUT

Put away from you the thought of an earthly city, no matter how great or how splendid. Our earth itself, were its entire surface to be spread out by Omnipotence into the floor of one vast edifice, and were the relations of space to be observed with regard to the glorified bodies of the elect, would be insufficient for the numbers who sit down with the Lamb at His Wedding Feast. And the angelic society, incomparably more numerous than the human, is to share that Banquet. Where shall the imagination find place for them?

Ah! our imagination has in it something of the infinite! It can wing its flight high, and, from that height, enable the soul to see, and to see clearly, beyond the circumference of this visible universe. Let us force it now to contemplate that real abode of the angels and Saints, where their two worlds are united and blended into one exultant company, feasting with Christ on the supreme delights which God can, in His goodness and power, minister to the deified spirits of angels and men, and, through the enraptured spirit, minister to the glorified senses of the body.

We know that God is not a material light, no matter how dazzling or how subtile. We know that He is a personal being—nay, that within His infinitely rich nature Three divine Persons live and, reign in one undivided Essence. We know that they form a most blissful society; and that the life and bliss of both angels and men in heaven consist in seeing clearly and knowing perfectly these Three Co-equal and Infinite Persons in Their essence and nature; in loving them, and being loved by them; in being admitted—really admitted—to share in that life, in Their society, fully, securely, everlastingly.

COMING TO THE TABLE OF THE LAMB.

Human thought can conceive nothing higher than this; the human heart can aspire to nothing higher. Nor can the imagination picture to itself here below anything more sublime or more ravishing than this union of man and angel in one glorious, immortal society with this divine Trinity.

Indeed, intellect and imagination, while we are yet in the flesh, can only perceive these truths dimly, unsatisfactorily. They are revealed truths, however.

So, imagine now the inhabitants of the angelic and the human worlds united in one society—let us say it in the noblest, the divinest sense—in one social gathering, around that Triune God, these Three Infinite Persons filling up from the abysmal bosom of their own life the cup out of which every soul there drinks, only to be intoxicated with a delight so divine that the draught never satiates.

When He who from all eternity is the very centre of that Triune society—the Son, the infinite Object of the Father's and the Spirit's love—took our flesh, walked among men, and tried to lift up their minds to some dim apprehension of the life eternal, it was as if one endeavored to hold discourse with persons just awaking from a lethargy which held body and soul.

"Amen, amen, I say unto you: He that believeth in Me hath everlasting life.

"*I am the Bread of Life.*

"Your fathers did eat manna in the desert, and are dead.

"This [*i. e.*, Himself, the Bread of Life,] is the Bread which cometh down from heaven; that if any man eat of it, he may not die.

"I am the Living Bread which came down from heaven." *

We have already spoken, in a preceding chapter, of the Sacrament and Sacrifice instituted by Him, on the eve of His Passion, in memory of His death. It was his farewell Supper; and the Bread broken there, and the dread Reality partaken of in that Supper, and left to be partaken of as a divine perpetual ordinance till the end of time, surely is a reminder as well of this Supper of the Lamb, described by St. John.

Read and ponder this passage:

"And whilst they were at supper, Jesus took bread, and blessed, and broke, and gave it to His Disciples, and said: 'Take ye, and eat: This is My body.'

"And taking the chalice He gave thanks: and gave it to them, saying: 'Drink ye all of this. For this is My Blood of the New Testament, which shall be shed for many unto remission of sins.

"'And I say to you, I will not drink from henceforth of this fruit of the vine, until *that day* when I shall drink it with you new in the kingdom of My Father.'" †

DRINKING THE NEW WINE.

The *day* here announced has now come; and we see Him and them at table in the kingdom of the Father.

---

* St. John, vi, 47-51. † St. Matthew, xxvi, 26-29.

What is "this fruit of the vine" which He promises to drink with them "*new*" in the everlasting kingdom? The fruit of the vine in the chalice out of which He has bid them all to drink in the Last Supper is, He says, "My own Blood of the New Testament." Both the Bread and the Wine, in that Banquet, contained a divine Reality, and this was the pledge of the eternal and perfect possession. Possession of what? Of that which alone can satisfy the aspirations of man or angel—the Supreme Good, the Infinite God Himself.

Christ revealed to the world the existence in the Deity of the Three distinct and Co-equal Persons. He spoke of His Father continually; of Himself as one with the Father; and of the Holy Spirit. In the kingdom to which, after death, He was returning, "the house of His Father, there are many mansions." There is room for all God's faithful servants.

As Man, with a perfect soul and a perfect body, what was the divine life of Jesus Christ's humanity? The Beatific Vision, first, due to Him from the union of that humanity with the Person of the Son, and the additional felicity and glory due to Him as Man-God.

The intoxicating draughts from that Beatific Vision, and the divine love it begets, was the Wine which both He as Man, the Head of regenerated humanity, and they, His members and brethren, were to drink in the kingdom of the Father. In Him and through Him we possess the Supreme Good, see God face to face, and drink from His very bosom the life eternal. And, precisely because this clear sight of the divine Essence, this possession of God, this union with the Three divine Persons, makes us sharers of God's own nature and life, Christ, in the farewell discourse at the Last Supper, likens Himself to the vine, the Disciples and all His elect to the branches. It is the same vital currents which flow through the stem of the vine and every branch and spray. In heaven, the bliss, the glory, the ecstatic life, produced by seeing and possessing God, flows from the Man-Christ, the Head of the Church Triumphant, of all humankind congregated there, through the entire body. This divine life, this partaking of the divine nature, is the drinking the fruit of the vine in the kingdom of the Father.

Ah, what banquet can be compared with that? What can equal in delight the breaking and eating of *that Bread of Life?* What wine ever tasted by man here below can equal the savor and intoxicating sweetness of "the fruit of *that Vine*" partaken of in that kingdom where man is lifted up to an equality with the angels, and where angels and men live, in a manner, on the very substance of the Deity?

CALIX MEUS INEBRIANS QUAM PRÆCLARUS EST!

Can we understand what a cup that is out of which all drink there? Even God Himself does not, cannot, exhaust the infinite sources of His own felicity: how could man or angel drain to the bottom the cup of bliss there held to their lips? As well might an infant try to pour the ocean with its hand into the hollow that tiny hand has dug in the sands.

And in that Banquet the deep joy and bliss of each are, if possible, increased by seeing the happiness and glory of all. In those sweet circles composed, amid that blessed company, by those whom we loved best and benefited most on earth—in those living crowns of sainted human beings who surround those who were their true parents and guides—is realized in the highest degree the joy which we behold on earth in family celebrations, where the parents are true servants of God, and the children are the image of their parents. It is hard to say who is happiest, the father and mother while dispensing love with abundance, or the children whose souls and faces reflect back on mother and father the divine radiance of gratitude, reverence, and deepest love, together with the light of their own joy.

So in the kingdom of heaven. But this is only one little item—feebly, feebly expressed—in the immense whole of the felicity which floods there, around the very Well-Spring of Life and Felicity Eternal—the myriads of the two worlds seated at the Supper of the Lamb.

THE NEWNESS OF THAT CUP.

We cannot dwell longer on this spectacle.

We now ask, Why did Christ say that He would drink with them the fruit of the Vine *new* in the kingdom of His Father? In what consists this newness?

It is *new*, because not till the resurrection day did the bodily organism of God's elect have any share in the divine life enjoyed in heaven by the holy souls admitted to its felicity between the Ascension and the Last Day. Once risen from their graves, and reunited to their glorified souls, the currents of divine life—the intoxicating wine of the Beatific Vision and the Godlike energies imparted by our consequent participation in the divine nature—flowed through the veins of these transformed bodies. What a thought of new life, new strength, new joy, was that of these myriads of God's own children, when they arose, thus transfigured, and looked upon the very face of Christ and His Blessed Mother—the Parents of that new life—and then could look upon the radiant countenances of all that immense society of the blessed, now marshaled to the right hand of the judgment seat! What bliss ineffable, what gratitude to the Giver of all good, overflowed their whole being as they behold around and near them those who on earth were dearest, who had helped them most to serve God, and whom they had helped to the knowledge and practice of all godliness.

Can we not conceive somewhat of the new transports of that hour?

And then with bodily eyes—these same weak eyes which are now dazzled by the splendor of the sun or the brilliancy of artificial light—to see God clearly face to face, to see and know every individual in the angelic world, to look upon the sacred humanity of our Lord, to perceive without veil or hindrance the depths of that great soul that only lived for us, that bore the agony in the Garden, and the agony in Jerusalem, and the desolation upon the cross; to see clearly how the Person of the Son is physically united to the humanity; and all this, at a glance, in which is concentrated the knowledge and delight of an eternity! Do you now understand holy Job's sustaining hope, while the most loathsome leprosy made his body as horrible to the sense as a corpse in putrefaction: "I know that my Redeemer liveth, and in the last day I shall rise out of the earth.

And I shall be clothed again with my skin, and my eyes shall behold, and not another. This, my hope, is laid up in my bosom." *

It is now the hope of every one of us, who believe, that "our Redeemer liveth," and that "in the last day we shall rise out of the earth," and that our bodily eyes shall behold Him. Oh! the beginning of that new life, when the same divine virtue which brought forth Christ's own body immortal from the sepulchre, shall course through our veins and arteries, and every fibre of our being, like the sap of the *Vine*, diffusing vital vigor through all Its branches!

INTOXICATED BY THE JOY OF THEIR NEW POSSESSION.

Another draught of this new Wine will add to the divine intoxication of the blessed multitudes, when they behold, opening out its immensities to receive them in that heavenly universe, the masterpiece of the love and power of the Father, and when their feet tread its soil, taking possession of it as their own—aye, their very own, in its height and depth,

---

* Job, xix, 25-27. [The Latin Vulgate version of the Book of Job is due to St. Jerome, who had to guide him not only the very best Hebrew and Syriac texts then extant, but also the best Greek texts of the Septuagint. It is certain that the Hebrew manuscripts from which St. Jerome translated have all utterly perished. The present Hebrew Masoretic Bible dates from the ninth century; and, according to some scholars, one great purpose of its authors (the Masoretes, "holders of traditions,") was to doctor the text in such a way as to take from the Christians all Scriptural grounds for proving Christ to be the Messiah. From the very first century, seeing that the Christians quoted—as, indeed, Christ and His Apostles had quoted—the Septuagint Old Testament, the Jews, who until then had held this version to be authentic, and even inspired, now disavowed it, and impugned its authenticity. But, as it had been most solemnly accepted by the Synagogue and the nation as authentic, scholars cannot give it up to please Jewish prejudice or spite. The sense of the text, as quoted above, was that of the Septuagint and of the "ancient" Hebrew texts in Jerome's possession. Modern Jews and recent Protestant translators into English cannot shake our faith in the Latin Vulgate.]

its length and breadth, throughout all its glorious spheres—all their own, with its magnificence and its treasures, together with *Him* who made it!

Oh, that land of the living, that Sion above the skies, that imperishable Jerusalem, that City of our God, so dear to us under so many sweet names, sung of under so many lovely images of home and country, during the exile of our race here below—what joy there will be when the everlasting Reality lies before us in all its grandeur and glory!

It shall bud forth and blossom, and shall rejoice with joy and praise. The glory of Libanus is given to it—the beauty of Carmel and Sharon: they shall see the glory of the Lord, and the beauty of our God.

"Say to the faint-hearted: 'Take courage and fear not! Behold your God will bring the revenge of recompense. God Himself will come and will save you. Then shall the eyes of the blind be opened, and the ears of the deaf shall be unstopped. Then shall the lame man leap as a hart, and the tongue of the dumb shall be free. . . . . And a path and a way shall be there: and it shall be called the *holy way*. The unclean shall not pass over it. . . . . No lion shall be there, nor shall any mischievous beast go up by it, nor be found there: but they shall walk there that shall be delivered. And the redeemed of the Lord shall return, and shall come into Sion with praise: and everlasting joy shall be upon their heads. They shall obtain joy and gladness; and sorrow and mourning shall flee away." *

It will be new for Them—the Father of our souls, Christ Jesus, and for the Mother who gave Him to

---

* Isaias, xxxv, 4-10.

us on the cross, the Fruit of Life for the healing of the nations—to see the children redeemed by Their sufferings, Their labors, Their tears, and Their blood, thus reunited in the land of the living, in body as well as in soul—God's blessed family for evermore!

It will be new for Him, the Father of our Lord and Saviour, Christ, to welcome to His kingdom, to seat around His table, the elect of the race, now made perfect in nature and grace, made His friends, and His children, admitted to the most secret intimacy of His interior life, associated with Him in His councils, made one with Him and with each other in that incomprehensible charity which is the soul of God's own life.

THAT DAY! THAT DAY!

Oh, on that day, when our humanity, arrived at this crowning stage in its upward progress, is thus for the first time seated—really seated—at that heavenly Banquet, what a new tide of divinest bliss and divinest joy will that Father of mercies and God of all consolation pour forth on the united worlds of men and angels!

"The rush of the river maketh the city of God joyful: the Most High hath sanctified His tabernacle. God is in the midst thereof, it shall not be moved: God will help us in the morning early."*

Aye, He "will help us in the morning early," at the dawn of the new day of eternity for the heavenly worlds, to bear the rush of this infinite tide of newborn felicity, to understand what a destiny and what glory is ours. For none save God Himself can

---

*Psalm XLV, 5: Fluminus impetus lætificat Civitatem Dei; sanctificavit tabernaculum suum Altissimus. Deus in medio ejus, no commovebitur; adjuvabit eam Deus mane diluculo.

measure the height and depth, the length and breadth, of that glory.

He must also help us to bear the intensity of the joy which, like the mighty electric currents of the lightning, or even of artificial creation, destroy life wherever their flow is impeded. Sudden joy, as we know by experience, kills as surely as the rush of a great and sudden sorrow. Our human hearts can only endure the measured pulsations of a moderate emotion. Too rapid a vital action breaks them.

CHAPTER XX.

HOW TO FIND HEAVEN ON EARTH.

Thou hast led me by Thy right hand:
By Thy will Thou hast conducted me,
And with Thy glory Thou hast received me.
For what have I in heaven?
And besides Thee what do I desire upon earth?
[For Thee] my flesh and my heart hath fainted away:
Thou art the God of my heart,
And the God that is my portion forever.
—*Psalm LXXII*, 24-26.

HEAVEN THE END OF ALL THINGS.

We scarcely paused to behold Christ, our King, enthroned on high at His royal Feast, while in and around Him shine forth all the splendors of the Deity. Our poor mortal eyes were dazzled, and our imagination wearied and terrified by the efforts to behold the heavenly universe, from the centre, at Christ's throne, to every point of its circumference, filled with His guests. For throughout that most glorious creation there are no vacant orbs, no desert places. At either pole of this immeasurable sphere, with the starry clusters revolving within its periphery, there is no frozen ocean, no ice, no cold; nor, in its central regions, is there tropical heat, or desert spaces, or rank vegetation. All is attempered to the loving will of the Creator, and fitted for the felicity and enjoyment of His beloved servants and children.

Such, physically and morally, is the heavenly Jerusalem, the Church of Christ in her eternal repose and perfection, the society of the city of God.

The altar of the Lamb, on which St. John beheld Him, as ever slain in sacrifice, is now replaced by His throne at the Feast. There are no longer, in exile and mortal struggle upon earth, any of the children of Adam and Eve, for whom Christ's Blood need flow in intercession or in expiation. The ladder which the Patriarch beheld, reaching from heaven to earth—that luminous pathway along which angels ascended and descended in their ministrations to mankind—is now withdrawn.

All is repose, enjoyment, perpetual praise, adoration, and exultation throughout every province of that celestial empire. The eternal bridals, the indissoluble union of the Lamb with His spouse, is now consummated; and "God is all in all."

Yes, *God is "all in all."* *

Shall I, His anointed priest, after guiding you to the gates of His heavenly city, and endeavoring to set before you, though never so dimly, so confusedly, the mighty *Reality*, not tarry with you awhile along the earthly road, and teach you, and myself with you,

---
* 1 Cor., xv, 28.

how to keep that God of our hearts—our Portion in the everlasting years—constantly and sweetly present to the eyes of our soul while our pilgrimage lasts?

THE PRESENCE OF GOD.

Let me endeavor to teach you what divine Love does, even in this life, for the children of men, in order to prepare mind, and heart, and life for the eternal reward.

In a thousand ways, and at every moment of our lives, and in every place, attentive reflection will convince us that *God is all in all.* Oh! let the light of this truth penetrate gently, sweetly, through every avenue of our spirit, and what a powerful aid we shall find in it towards noble thoughts, high aims, heroic deeds, a Godlike, Christ-like life!

I.—It is a truth of reason—one which, stated to an intelligent child or an unlettered peasant, will be accepted by either—that God, being a Spirit, and One to whose substance no place, no other substance can oppose limits or obstacles, must be present in all places and all things. It is one of the first truths inculcated in the catechism.

Theologians and philosophers explain this presence of God in all places and things, by considering how many ways a person may be present; we have only to consider the most obvious truths. God is present everywhere by His essence and substantial being. Hear what He says of Himself in the Prophecy of Jeremias:

"'Am I, think ye, a God at hand,' saith the Lord, 'and not a God afar off? Shall a man be hid in secret places, and I not see him,' saith the Lord? 'Do not I fill heaven and earth,' saith the Lord?" *

---

* Jeremias, xxiii, 23-24.

In another inspired book it is said:

"Think of the Lord in goodness, and seek Him in simplicity of heart. For He is found by them that tempt Him not: and He showeth Himself to them that have faith in Him. . . . . The Holy Spirit of Discipline will flee from the deceitful; . . . . He shall not abide when iniquity comes in. . . . . For the Spirit of the Lord hath filled the whole earth; and that which containeth all things hath knowledge of the voice." *

Both of these passages help us toward understanding the distinctions made in Scripture and explained by theologians. It is evident that God, being in every way infinite, is everywhere present, by His very essence, and present with all His graces and gifts. He is present also by His power, because He created all things, keeps them in being, and governs them all to His own purposes. He is also present by His watchfulness; for His eye, which never sleeps, sees everything, pierces through and through everything, reading the thoughts, aims, sentiments, affections, of all spirits and all hearts.

Such is the teaching of Ecclesiasticus, speaking of the lustful sinner:

"Darkness compasseth me about, and the walls cover me, and no man seeth me: whom do I fear? The Most High will not remember my sins.

"And he understandeth not that His eye seeth all things, for such a man's heart driveth from Him the fear of God. . . . . And he knoweth not that the eyes of the Lord are far brighter than the sun, beholding round about all the ways of men, and the bottom of the deep, and looking into the hearts

---
* Wisdom, i, 1-7.

of men, into the most hidden parts. For all things were known to the Lord God before they were created: so also after they were perfected He beholdeth all things."*

SUBSTANTIALLY PRESENT IN ALL THINGS AND PLACES.

Therefore, if we believe in God, in His infinitude, immensity, and omnipresence, we must simply believe that He is substantially present in all things—their Creator, Preserver, Governor. In the heavens above me, on the earth around me, in the abysses of ocean, as well as in the interior of our globe, there is not a thing, nor a place, in which that infinitely rich, beautiful, wise, all-knowing, and all-powerful Spirit I call *God* looks not out upon me, looks not into my very being. If I love Him, I can meet Him everywhere, see Him in everything; for in all, His wisdom, love, power, watchfulness, and care of me can be manifest to the eye of my soul.

If I love Him, and love to seek Him, it is easy for the eyes of my soul to pierce the veil which, in all created things, hides His presence from me, easy for the hand of my faith to touch and hold Him.

Oh! the veil which covers Him is much thinner than we fancy, if we only knew it!

More than that. We need not go abroad, outside of the house of our own soul, to find Him, hear Him, converse with Him.

GOD PRESENT IN THE HUMAN SOUL.

For it is a truth of revelation, as well as one of reason, that God dwells in man as in His dearest, noblest temple. No abode, among all created things,

---

* Ecclesiasticus, xxiii, 26-29

can be more sacred to that divine Majesty, to that uncreated Spirit, "who loveth souls," than the inmost sanctuary of our spirit, where we can make a throne for Him, and keep the lamp of the holiest love ever burning in His presence.

When, therefore, we walk abroad we can find in everything that we see the work of His hands; His footprints are on the mountain, in the plain, on the seashore, and the mighty deep. Everywhere He is very near to us, if we will only believe it; everywhere we can walk in His presence, and everywhere feel that the eye of the Father, Benefactor, and Judge follows us sleeplessly, unweariedly. The light of that veiled countenance, the watchfulness of that awful Eye, should be a strength and a comfort unspeakable to us in trouble and temptation. It should be a terror to the evil-doer.

There is another Presence very sweet and very dear to the Catholic heart, in which the Incarnate Wisdom and Love found means to be in a special manner our Emmanuel.

THE EUCHARISTIC PRESENCE.

The belief in that Presence covered ancient Christendom with shrines more beautiful in all the creations of art than ever was the Temple of Solomon. It is now, like a plant transferred to the soil of the New World, multiplying its offshoots everywhere, and blossoming forth into flowers of beauty. But the Presence is as dear to our hearts in the log-chapel of the Canadian woods, as it is in the marble cathedral of New York city. Blessed are those who love His tabernacles; the spell which draws them and holds them there is a mark of predestination.

II.—So Infinite Love speaks to willing ears from every part of earth and sky. But it is not satisfied with the mere passive presence. It also works for us in every one of those countless forces, energies, activities, that fill the physical, the intellectual, the social, and religious world.

HOW GOD WORKS IN ALL THINGS FOR US.

This truth opens out a marvelous field of study for every serious-minded person who has once perceived its significance—an exhaustless source of sweetest enjoyment to a heart set upon divine things.

St. Paul, writing to the Church of Corinth, utters these golden words: "All things are yours, whether it be Paul, or Apollo, or Cephas, or the world, or life, or death, or things present, or things to come: for all are yours. And you are Christ's: and Christ is God's." * And, writing to the faithful in Rome, he says: "We know that to them that love God, all things work together unto good, to such as according to His purpose are called to be Saints." † Do not, as these words meet your eye, allow the fearful phantom of the doctrine of predestination to rise up from this page, and cause you to close the book. Pedestination, as explained by her who is the tender mother of the children of God, and the unerring expounder of His revealed truth, is not the frightful thing which self-sufficient and self-guiding pride hath made it. St. Paul is teaching the Romans the beautiful scheme of God's supernatural and natural providence over all those who are baptized, and are heartily working to save themselves in accordance with their professed faith in Christ and the light of the Holy Spirit within them.

---

* 1 Cor., iii, 22-23. † Romans, viii, 28.

Surely, it is not for those who are turning their backs on the light, and walking persistently in the ways of evil, that we are to claim the manifold blessedness promised by Christ here and hereafter to His faithful followers.

Listen, then, to what St. Paul says of God's wonderful way of making all things on earth and in heaven work to secure the eternal felicity of those "who love Him" and who seek to do His will sincerely. We, who have been amid the splendors of heaven, who have been reading in the light of Calvary and the judgment seat the mystery of the divine Justice and Mercy, must have no difficulty in understanding every line of the following passage:

"I reckon that the sufferings of this time are not worthy to be compared with the glory to come. . . . For the expectation of the creature [*i. e.,* all creation,] waiteth for the revelation of the sons of God. . . . Even we ourselves groan within ourselves, waiting for the adoption of the sons of God, the redemption of our body. . . . Likewise the Spirit also helpeth our infirmity: for we know not what we should pray for as we ought: but *the Spirit Himself* asketh for us with unspeakable groanings. . . . What then shall we say to these things? If God be for us, who is against us? He that spared not even His own *Son,* but delivered Him up for us all, how hath He not also, with Him, given us all things?" *

A WONDERFUL DISPLAY OF GOD'S LOVING CARE.

Now consider the following points:

1. That, whereas all things are destined to be ours in the life to come—God, and all that He is

---
* Romans, viii. 18-32.

and all that He has; so now all creation, with all its elemental and vital forces, are so controlled and directed by the Creator that they shall co-operate with us in saving our souls, and that nothing, absolutely nothing, can or shall prevent our fulfilling God's design over us but our own willful neglect or abuse of His graces.

In the case of every one of us who reads this page, the truth, in so far as our soul is concerned, is this:

We know we are called to the service of God here, and to His eternal possession hereafter. In that service our poor weak will, to prevent it from making an ill-use of its innate and inalienable freedom, has ever before its eyes the terrors of an eternity of punishment as the award due to the willful abandonment of God's service—the contemning, in practice, the eternal inheritance of glory awaiting the faithful Christian, the contemning, as well, of Christ's death and redemption, the contemning of the unspeakable love of Father and Son as manifested in that work of redemption, and the spurning of the mighty helps toward fidelity, generosity, and self-sanctification supplied by Christ's ordinances, by God's ever-present and fatherly providence.

MAN INEXCUSABLE FOR NOT SERVING GOD.

Where human infirmity in a Christian man or woman is so divinely upheld, aided, set forward, and changed into Godlike strength by the use of graces which are given with a liberality proportioned to the good use made of them, and given with a liberality increasing ever as we lean more firmly on the Hand that gives, and walk more rapidly in the royal road of Christ's examples—what excuse can there be for losing one's soul?

Looking at what is highest, divinest, first, in this grand providential scheme for changing man's infirmity into Christ-like virtue and strength, we see that God places Himself, in a manner, at man's disposal in this struggle to attain to life eternal.

Not only are we assured that nothing, absolutely nothing—no power, no combination of circumstances we can think of—can prevent us from maintaining our union of mind and heart with God in this life, or from reaching in the other the sublime reward promised to fidelity; but all the Three divine Persons, all the influence of angels and Saints in heaven, all the action and ministrations of the Church on earth, are so ordained, so directed, as to help us positively, powerfully, continually, in serving God, sanctifying ourselves, and securing our salvation.

This statement is of indisputable certainty in every particular.

Still, when we consider this stupendous truth, and look into our own lives and consciences, we are appalled by our own lukewarmness, by our backwardness, by our utter lack of generosity, in corresponding with that infinite and ever-present Love, whose entire providence is planned to help us to rise and to lift up others with us to the divine height of goodness required by our quality of adopted children and servants of the Most High God, and of co-heirs with Christ to that everlasting kingdom we have been describing.

THE MYSTERY OF FREE-WILL.

Here is the deep, deep mystery of free-will; the mystery that God should leave us free to serve Him or not to serve Him; to make ourselves worthy of heaven, or to deserve hell by our refusal to comply with His will. Here *we* can meditate the mystery of man's weakness and perversity, in rejecting such a destiny, in neglecting such mighty helps toward its attainment. And here, too, shines forth the Godlike strength of the men and women who, enlightened by the knowledge of God's unspeakable goodness and greatness, filled with an insatiable ardor to win the glorious prize awaiting them in eternity, and inflamed with a holy zeal for the salvation of their brethren's souls, as well as their own, set forth on the road of God's service like giants running a race, and appear among men as if the Spirit of Christ lifted them up and carried them forward.

HOW ST. FRANCIS XAVIER CO-OPERATED WITH GOD'S DESIGNS.

Once Francis Xavier had firmly grasped the fact of the divine reality of the life to come, and clearly perceived all the means provided to enable him to attain its possession, his whole soul was fired with the love of the Saviour who had won for us so glorious a kingdom, with the desire to make His name known to the ends of the earth, with a consuming zeal to save from eternal separation from Christ the untold millions of the new worlds recently rediscovered by Vasco de Gama and Christopher Columbus.

See him leaving Rome, at the bidding of the Pope, traveling on foot all the way to Lisbon, passing, as if borne, like Isaias of old, in a chariot of living flame, along the western and southern coasts of India, along those of Java, Sumatra, the West

Indian Archipelago to Japan, and from Japan back again to Hindostan. Of course, wherever that holy man passed, like a celestial vision of goodness, gentleness, and saving power, the pagan multitudes were drawn to him, and through him to Christ. Compelled to return to Europe, he contemplated doing so by the way of China and the entire Asiatic Continent, converting on his way the peoples of these vast countries.

He only saw the good to be done, and put himself in God's hand as an instrument for doing it. And what cannot, will not, God do with man as His instrument, if man will only be in that Hand a willing, docile instrument, perfectly united to the almighty Energy which wields it?

The prodigies effected by Xavier's apostolic zeal during the few years he labored in the East would have been eclipsed by those which he purposed accomplishing in China, were it not that he succumbed within sight of its shores—the bodily frame exhausted by its gigantic labors, and consumed by the seraphic fire which burned within.

IN THE HAND OF GOD.

In one of his journeys by sea, the vessel which bore him was submerged by a cyclone, and evidently saved by a miracle. Xavier, in a letter, describes his own sensations as the waves closed over the ship. He was calm and in sweet communion with God. "He was but an instrument and in His hand, and whether on sea or land he only wished to be in that almighty Hand."

Those who have read his letters and his life know how uninterrupted was his communion with God, in spite of the devouring activity, which filled almost every hour of the night as well as the day. He seemed to be not a mortal man, but one of those angelic messengers invisibly busied on earth with merciful ministrations towards mankind, and who, in all places and in every occupation, never cease gazing on the face of God.

Thus, without wishing it, have we been led to state the practical purpose of these remarks—to work with God with our whole heart and soul in sanctifying our own life, and then to devote our whole energy to His service. Yes, we should so purify mind and heart—our aims, sentiments, actions, and entire life—if we would serve Him well. Let love of Him, and zeal for His glory, and the salvation of our brethren, detach us from *self*, if we would serve Him aright and do the work He has for us to do. We cannot be selfish and be God's efficient and helpful workmen.

A DEEPER CONSIDERATION OF THESE TRUTHS.

But to incite us to become thus worthy of serving the God of our souls, we have to think over and weigh well the fact, that in every living thing around us, in our homes and outside of them, there is not one which, in some way or other, does not work for our good.

HEAVEN HELPING EARTH TO SERVE GOD.

When, at the beginning of this chapter, we spoke of heaven as it will be after the last day, and the closing of the present era of trial, and said that the ladder beheld by the Patriarch in his vision, reaching from earth to heaven, would be withdrawn, we did not need to remind the reader that the ladder is still in existence. There is a road of light and love between God's family here below and the everlasting gates of our heavenly home, along which His angels are ever ascending with the petitions and thanksgivings of His children, and descending with His gifts and graces—along which, too, the spirits of the just mount to receive their reward, and come down, when He so permits it, to fulfill some errand of love and mercy toward their dear ones here below.

If the veil of mortality were withdrawn from our eyes for a single hour, what a sublime and consoling spectacle would be disclosed of the perpetual intercourse between the Church on earth and the Church of heaven!

At any rate, let every one of our readers believe that for every soul working earnestly, with God's grace, to secure its own sanctification and salvation, the entire city of God on high is perpetually making intercession. The entire course of His natural and supernatural providence conspires to help us in this work. Do we live and act as if we believed this?

WORK LIKE A TRUE CHILD OF GOD.

Then think of the folly and wickedness of becoming dismayed or discouraged by the obstacles created by our own weakness or inconstancy of purpose, or by temptations from without and the terrible influence of evil or worldly example. We should recall the memorable words of one * who, unbaptized and carried away by the tide of the surrounding pagan corruption, had long weakly believed virtue to be a

---

* St. Augustine.

thing impossible: "Behold, if I only will it, I even now become a child of God!"

Then read over attentively these words of another great convert: "What shall we then say to these things? If God be for us, who is against us? *He that spared not even His own Son, but delivered Him up for us all, how hath He not also, with Him, given us all things?*" *

To enforce his appeal to our generosity in co-operating with God and His Son in the work of our sanctification, St. Paul reminds us that, at our last dread account, no one but God, the Author of our being and the Giver of all gifts, natural and supernatural, has the right to stand as our accuser. "Who shall accuse against the elect of God? God that justifieth." †

Aye, He alone, our Father, who, at this very moment, places Himself and all creation at our disposal, if we will only consent to do our part and work with Him.

And who is to be our Judge when the day of accounting has arrived? "Who is He that shall condemn? Christ Jesus that died, yea that is risen also again, who is at the right hand of God, who also maketh intercession for us." ‡

While the Father directs the whole order of heaven and earth so as to help us to attain to our glorious destiny and gain our inheritance, He, the Son, who died to give us a right to it, is here represented as sitting at the Father's right hand, perpetually pleading for us, making His Blood and His wounds speak in our favor.

---

* Romans, viii, 31-32.   ‡ Ibidem, xiii, 34.
† Ibidem, viii, 33.

"Who, then," Paul asks the Romans under Nero, "shall separate us from the love of Christ? Shall tribulation? or distress? or famine? or nakedness? or danger? or persecution? or the sword?"

The persecutor even then was busy at work; and the day was not far distant when Nero's sword would strike the Apostle himself, and the fires which lighted the streets and squares of Rome by night would each consume a Christian martyr.

Still the prospect will not deter Paul from hastening to Rome, or from thus infusing his own heroic spirit into the faithful of that city:

"But in all these things we overcome [*i. e.*, gain the victory,] because of Him that hath loved us. For I am sure that neither death, nor life, nor angels, nor principalities, nor powers, nor things present, nor things to come, nor might, nor height, nor depth, nor any other creature shall be able to separate us from the love of God, which is in Christ Jesus, our Lord." *

This glorious spirit of generosity—giving back to God deeds for deeds, life for life, love for love—has never died out of the world. The words of the Psalmist, which St. Paul here applies to the Christians of his day—the first offerings to God of Christendom at its birth—are literally true as applied to our own times: "For Thy sake we are put to death all the day long. We are accounted as sheep for the slaughter."

The privilege of dying for Christ, however, is only that of the very, very few; that of living and laboring for Him and His cause is the scarcely less enviable lot of very many, as it ought, indeed, to be

---
* Romans, viii, 37-39.

the ambition of all Christians. If we would only remember the prize!

THE DIVINEST AMBITION.

And, truly, apart from the mere motive of gratitude and love to our divine Benefactor, apart even from the generosity which should prompt to noble aims and nobler deeds the adopted sons of the living God—the co-heirs with Christ to His kingdom—the very ambition of winning and securing that kingdom itself should be a motive force more than sufficient to lift us above the seeking of worldly pleasures, of temporal fame and honors, of a perishable wealth—only useful as a means to serve God and help our brethren—and to fire our souls with sentiments and passions becoming such as aspire to eternal glory and bliss.

St. Paul, when he wrote from Corinth his Epistle to the Romans, had in view, among other things, to sustain the Jewish Christians who were there subjected to bitter persecution. They were truly like men who went continually about with their lives in their hands. Every day beheld, throughout the Roman empire, numbers added by persecution to the army of martyrs. Christians were like sheep on their way to the slaughter-house. But they braved danger, distress, torments, and death for the sake of Christ.

When, later, he fell himself into the hands of Nero, and was in hourly expectation of his death sentence, how aptly and irresistibly he could, from his prison, appeal to the Corinthians in these eloquent words:

"All things are for your sakes. . . . . For which cause we faint not: but though the outward man decays [giving way to old age, exhaustion, torture, and imprisonment,] yet the inward man is renewed day by day. For that which is at present momentary and light of our tribulation, worketh for us above measure exceedingly an eternal weight of glory."

WHAT MEN DARE, AND DO, AND SUFFER TO GAIN THIS WORLD'S GOODS.

In our country men are more than eager to make a great fortune in a short time. For this purpose they dare everything, undergo everything. The mining regions of the Rocky Mountains, of California, and now the frozen wilds of distant Alaska, could tell incredible tales of hardship heroically borne, and often borne in vain, to secure the golden prize apparently within the grasp of the toilers. Of the many on whom fortune shed its golden showers, how few, comparatively, have retained possession of permanent wealth! What numbers have remained poor in spite of the down-pour! How many others have dropped the treasure they held, in their greed to possess themselves of a greater, which glittered in the treacherous stream of speculation beneath them! And to how many did not their speedily-gotten wealth prove the deadliest of all life's curses!

To be sure, the acquisition of a noble fortune is an object of laudable ambition to the man who wants to found a family, and secure its independence when he is no more. But both in the pursuit of wealth and in its possession and enjoyment all is uncertainty and insecurity. How many fathers are blessed with sons who will make a right use of the riches and lands acquired by the toil and sacrifices of a life-time? And, even when one has reached the summit of one's hopes, when boundless wealth, a princely home, a broad domain, and the esteem of the community are a present certainty, one looks forward, and says, "How long?"

Aye, there is the canker-worm in the very core of the golden fruit gathered from the tree of prosperity—the prospect of only enjoying all these things for a few years at most. Not one ounce of our gold shall follow us to the judgment seat, or avail to turn the scales in our favor. Not one foot of the soil of all our broad lands can profit the possessor beyond the space occupied by his coffin.

There is no perpetuity in the titles by which we hold, no permanent security in either possession or enjoyment, no infallible certainty in the prospects of happiness which open up beyond the grave.

Consider, therefore, as the fitting conclusion of this book, the *Eternity* of the Kingdom of Heaven, which Christ died to purchase for His own, and which we should so earnestly labor to secure.

CHAPTER XXI.

THE ETERNITY OF HEAVEN.

"An *inheritance* incorruptible, and undefiled, and that cannot fade, reserved in heaven for you."
—1 *St. Peter*, i, 4.

HOW THE WORLDLY WISE CALCULATE.

Let us look around us and see what precautions the wisest and most experienced in worldly economy daily take to provide against the loss of a fortune acquired by life-long toil, and to secure just profits from the investment of their money.

How carefully men of sound business habits examine the safest ways of turning their hoarded gold either into real estate or into shares in some commercial enterprise! Real estate—property in land and houses—has, at the present moment, to undergo a revolution. There was a time when men looked upon their broad acres as upon a source of wealth more reliable than the gold mines of the Oural or the Rocky Mountains—upon their possession as a basis of independence as imperishable as the foundation of the earth itself. In the wealthiest country on the face of the globe all this assurance, all this security so firmly held to in the past, are now giving way to insecurity and inevitable change.

SECURITY AND STABILITY FOR INVESTMENTS.

Men who do not so much value the prospect of a large and speedy return for their investments, but who seek for security and permanence in the returns yielded, will prefer to have the established governments as their debtors, and the public funds as their source of revenue. Provided the gold they give will bear fruit longer and for an indefinite period, they are content to receive less. They find ample compensation in their feeling of security, and in that assured stability which has nothing to fear from speculation or private dishonesty.

So—to borrow an illustration from what are called the best business principles in temporal affairs—we can help ourselves to reason on things which are eternal.

We cannot but approve of the wisdom which, in managing worldly interests, provides against loss, change, revolution, instability of every kind, and seeks what is safe, certain, lasting. The farmer, who needs a constant supply of wholesome water for his household and his cattle, will seek a spring whose flow never stops in the summer heat or is interfered with by the severest winter frosts. The miller and manufacturer who rely on water-power, for a steady supply of driving force, will build rather near the constant stream which is not over-swollen by the spring rains or dried up by the drought of the dog-days, than by the mountain torrent, or the rushing river, whose periodical inundations sweep away factory and mill.

We like what is unfailing, constant, and enduring for ever. We should like our homes, our fortunes, and our institutions to be imperishable, everlasting. In many ways God has planted in our souls, our instincts, our lives, a vain wish to impart eternity to the work of our hands, since we cannot, by any effort of our will or exercise of our power, obtain for ourselves the boon of immortality.

MAN SEEKING GREATNESS AND PERPETUITY INDEPENDENTLY OF GOD.

Twice in the history of our race do we find it recorded how men endeavored to make their existence on earth independent of their Creator, and their lives secure against the utmost exercise of His power. The first is recorded in the third chapter of Genesis: "Behold, Adam is become as one of us," so speaks the Almighty, "knowing good and evil. Now, therefore, lest perhaps he put forth his hand and take also of the tree of life, and eat and live forever." . . . The fragmentary narrative then says: "The Lord God sent him out of the paradise of pleasure to till the earth from which he was taken."

Alas! we know it well by this time, the tree of experimental knowledge of good and evil does not yield fruits of life, still less of immortality—unless it be the immortality of despair. What the tree of life here mentioned is, we know not, unless it be the clear knowledge of God's will and our own duty, and the loving accomplishment of the same. That tree of duty bears immortal fruit; for it makes man eternal like God Himself.

The other attempt is recorded in the eleventh chapter of the same sacred book: "Come, let us make a city and a tower, the top whereof may reach to heaven. . . . And the Lord came down to see the city and the tower, which the children of Adam were building. And He said: 'Behold, it is one people, and all have one tongue: and they have begun to do this; neither will they leave off from their designs 'till they accomplish them in deed. Come ye, therefore, let us go down, and there confound their tongue, that they may not understand one another's speech."

Christ made us anew into unity. Born, by baptism, in His Blood, we have a right to feed on that tree of life and immortality, of which Adam tasted not in Paradise. We are made the inhabitants of a city whose foundations are laid on earth, but from whose towers stretch up to heaven that ladder seen by the pilgrim Jacob, and along which the children of God are evermore ascending to the everlasting city, whose foundatians are above the stars, and whose life and duration are those of the eternal God.

"WE KNOW IN WHOM WE BELIEVE."

Christians who have set their hearts wholly on the possession of that "inheritance incorruptible, undefiled, and that cannot fade, reserved in heaven" for all who serve the Lord with their whole soul and strength, have even in this life that deep, abiding sense of security in the fulfillment of the divine promises. They "know in *whom* they believe." They have placed their trust for this life and the next in Him who is Truth Itself and cannot deceive; they have built their hopes on the Rock of Ages. St. Peter's words convey, therefore, unspeakable comfort to the souls sorely afflicted by this world's losses and disappointments, or tempted in their faith by the triumphs of error, impiety, wickedness, and oppression.

"By the power of God," he says, "you are kept by faith unto salvation, ready to be revealed in the last time. Wherein you shall greatly rejoice, if now you must be for a little time made sorrowful in divers temptations: that the trial of your faith (much more precious than gold tried by the fire) may be found unto praise, and glory, and honor at the appearing of Jesus Christ." *

To the immense majority of those who battle against this world's manifold evil, in the hope of a happy eternity, how much less formidable are the labors and sufferings of their every-day life, than the self-imposed sacrifices, hardships, and the bitter disappointments faced by the fortune-seekers already mentioned! And yet it depends on us to make that eternity secure. Let us weigh well the meaning of this single word. If we can only turn it round and round to grasp its mighty significance; if, like a heaven-sent gem, it only sheds on our minds the magic light it contains, and enables us, with the aid of that light, to view and estimate the things of earth, and to consider aright those of heaven, no talisman ever mentioned in Eastern story can open up to us such hidden treasures, or arm our soul with such power over our spiritual enemies.

CHRIST AND HIS APOSTLES SPEAK.

What, then, is the *eternity* of heaven?

If what has already been said on the nature of heavenly bliss, and of the supernatural, the divine life enjoyed in the land of the living, has been understood by the reader, this much must be now evident: that the life in heaven for the blessed is a partaking of the very life of the Deity.

That life is, therefore, *eternal*.

---
* 1 St. Peter, 1, 5-7.

Such, indeed, it was called by Christ Himself; for our English version of the New Testament makes "everlasting" the equivalent of "eternal." *

"*Eternal life*" was also placed at the end of that short and pregnant symbol or formula of faith called the "Apostles' Creed," and adopted by all the Churches of Christendom, from the fifth century, at least.† But the revealed truth it expressed had been so clearly formulated by our Lord that it was always an object of universal belief. The quibbling of the restless Eastern disputants gave occasion to place it at the end of the "Apostles' Creed" as the crowning truth of all faith and hope.

Let us unite here, as in a focus of light, the clear utterances of our Lord and His Apostles on the heavenly life and its eternity:

"They that shall be accounted worthy of *that world*, and of the resurrection from the dead, shall neither be married nor take wives. Neither can they die any more: for they are equal to the angels, and are the children of God, being the children of the Resurrection." ‡

---

* St. Matthew, xxii, 40: "Supplicium æternum, . . . vitam æternam." . . .

† St. Irenæus ("Adversus Hæreses I," ix, 4,) informs us that through the doctrine handed down from the Apostles, Christians have one belief, since "all teach one and the same *God the Father*, and believe the same economy of the *Incarnation of the Son of God*, and know the same gift of the *Spirit*, and meditate on the same precepts, and maintain the same form of constitution with respect to the *Church*, and look for the same *coming* of the Lord, and wait for the same *salvation* of the whole man— that is, of the soul and body." Elsewhere he says that the catechumens received "the unchangeable rule of the faith" in baptism.

Rufinus, who died in 410, says that in other Churches changes were made in the "Apostles' Creed" to meet the heresies sprung up there; whereas in the Roman Church, where no heresy had arisen, the Creed remained in its original form. It terminated—so far as we know it from Rufinus—with "the Resurrection of the Flesh." The words "eternal life" were added in the fifth century. The words, however, and the truth they express, were formally revealed by our Lord Himself in St. Matthew, xxii, 40.

‡ St. Luke, xx, 35-36.

"Yet a little while, and the world seeth Me no more. But you see Me, because I live, and you shall live. He that hath My Commandments, and keepeth them, he it is that loveth Me. And he that loveth Me shall be loved of My Father: and I will love him, and will manifest *Myself* to him." *

"Father, the hour is come, glorify Thy Son, that Thy Son may glorify Thee. As Thou hast given Him power over all flesh, that He may give eternal life to all whom Thou hast given Him. Now this is eternal life: That they may know Thee, . . . and Jesus Christ whom Thou hast sent." †

"As Moses lifted up the serpent in the desert, so must the Son of Man be lifted up, that whosoever believeth in Him may not perish, but may have life everlasting. For God so loved the world as to give His Only-Begotten Son, that whosoever believeth in Him may not perish, but may have life everlasting." ‡

Hear St. John the Baptist: "The Father loveth the Son, and He hath given all things into His hand. He that believeth in the Son hath life everlasting: but he that believeth not the Son, shall not see life, but the wrath of God abideth on him." ‖

"Whosoever drinketh of this water shall thirst again: but he that will drink of the water which I shall give him, shall not thirst for ever: but the water that I shall give him will become in him a fountain of water springing up into life everlasting." §

"My sheep hear my voice, and I know them, and they follow Me. And I give them life everlasting; and they shall not perish for ever, and no man shall pluck them out of My hand. That which My Father

---
* St. John, xiv, 19-21. ‖ Ibidem, iii, 35-36.
† Ibidem, xvii, 1-3. § Ibidem, iv, 13-14.
‡ Ibidem, iii, 14-16.

hath given Me is greater than all: and no one can snatch *them* out of the hand of My Father. I and the Father are *One*." *

"When the Prince of Pastors will appear, you will receive a never-fading crown of glory." †

"Wherefore, brethren, labor the more, that by good works you may make sure your calling and election. For doing these things, you shall not sin at any time. For so an entrance shall be ministered unto you abundantly into the everlasting kingdom of our Lord and Saviour Jesus Christ." ‡

"Of this one thing be not ignorant, my beloved, that *one day with the Lord* is as a thousand years, and a thousand years as one day." ‖

"You, therefore, brethren, knowing these things before, take heed, lest being led aside by the error of the unwise, you fall from your own steadfastness. But grow in grace, and in the knowledge of our Lord and Saviour Jesus Christ. To Him be glory both now and unto the day of eternity!" §

"Labor with the Gospel according to the power of God, who hath delivered us and called us by His holy calling, not according to our works, but according to his own purpose and grace, which was given to us in Christ Jesus before the times of the world; but is now made manifest by the illumination of our Saviour Jesus Christ, who hath destroyed death, and hath brought to light life and incorruption by the Gospel." °

"By this hath the charity of God appeared toward us, because God hath sent His Only-Begotten Son into the world, that we may live by Him." ¶

---

* St. John, x, 27-30.
† 1 St. Peter, v, 4.
‡ 2 St. Peter, i, 10-11.
‖ Ibidem, iii, 8.
§ Ibidem, iii, 17-18.
° 2 Timothy, i, 8-10.
¶ 1 St. John, iv, 9.

"He that believeth in the Son of God, hath the testimony of God in Himself. . . . And this is the testimony: That God hath given to us eternal life. And this life is in His Son. . . . These things I write to you, that you may know that you have *eternal life*, you who believe in the name of the Son of God."‡

"To him that will overcome, I shall give to sit with Me in My throne, as I also have overcome, and am set down with My Father in His throne."||

THE CONCLUSION.

Such are a few—a few only—of the divine utterances on which repose our belief in the eternity of the heavenly kingdom, of the everlastingness of the life of bliss and glory enjoyed by its inhabitants. It is—from the testimony of revelation, and from the very nature and necessity of the reward itself— a participation of the very life of the Godhead, a most intimate union with the Trinity, which is never to be dissolved, and the continuance of which is to be measured on the duration of God Himself—if, indeed, we can use the term duration in speaking of that Being, whom our intellect cannot conceive of without conceiving at the same time that He can have had no beginning and can have no end.

Wherefore, just as the rank to which men and angels are raised in heaven is divine, just as the life they enjoy is divine; even so must that life be everlasting in order to be divine in its duration.

Only think of it: To be associated with the Three divine Persons in one family, to be indissolubly united to them in oneness of life and joy, and to

---
* 1 St. John, v, 10-13. † Apoc., III, 21.

know that such an existence can no more come to an end than that the very essence and being of the Godhead can be subject to decay or destruction.

To look around on the boundless and magnificent empire which He created, prepared, and firmly established as the material home of His family, and to feel that it is their own, in its length and breadth, in its height and depth, as long as the throne of God is secure in the heavens—such is one element of felicity for the citizens of that empire. Even in the titles by which, on earth, royal families claim the possession of a throne, a principality, a kingdom, an empire, there is insecurity and instability. We see, in every century, revolutions upsetting the most ancient dynasties, and the popular will becoming more and more the only acknowledged source of right. But in that society of the land of the living, the divine Will is the only law, the immovable and eternal basis of possession, the secure pledge of enjoyment never to be disturbed. A thousand times more than home and domains can be claimed, and held, and enjoyed as one's very own and forever here below, can every member of Christ's family on high claim the heavens of heavens as his.

To survey, as the blessed in glory can, all the nine glittering spheres of the angelic world, with their sublime spirits innumerable rank above rank, circling in their ecstatic joy around the throne of Christ and the myriads of His brethren; to see this angelic world, like concentric masses of living light, encompassing round about the scarcely less glorious human world, as if these glorious spirits still continued in heaven their offices of watchfulness and loving care over those who had once been their earthly charge! And is it not one part of the felicity of the angelic world to feel that they have had their share in bringing their pilgrim-brethren to the home and inheritance of the common Father? What a society is that of God's kingdom in eternity? And what a sense of surpassing joy is it to know that all the divine charities, the blissful intercourse, the pure and unalterable love of these multitudes, are treasures which can never fail the possessor!

"Blessed is one one day in Thy courts above a thousand!"

It is in this connection, and while deeply meditating upon eternal things, while the Roman empire was falling around him beneath the assaults of the barbarians, that St. Augustine wrote, upwards of fourteen hundred years ago:

"Such is the beauty of holiness, and the joy of that light eternal, of that immutable truth and wisdom, that although we were not to continue in it above one day, yet for so short a time, a thousand years of our present life, though filled to overflowing with delights and the abundance of all earthly goods, should be rightly accounted as nothing." *

We whose hearts are preoccupied, sometimes by fear and sometimes by holy hope, at beholding the vicissitudes of human society, may cheer ourselves by lifting our thoughts to that society of the blessed, where truth and holiness reign forever, where the Eternal God, seen, known, loved, possessed securely, is the very Soul of Life to all.

The Eternal God possessed *eternally!*

---

* "De Libero Arbitrio."

What more can tongue express? What dream more glorious can fall upon the soul? What higher goal would the heart aspire to?

> "Now to the King of Ages, immortal, invisible,
> The only God,
> Be honor and glory forever and ever! Amen."

[THE END.]

Catholic Standard Publications.

ABBEY OF ROSS AND THE BRIDEGROOM OF BARNA..... $	40
ADVENTURES OF A PROTESTANT IN SEARCH OF A RELIGION	1 25
ADVENTURES OF MICHAEL DWYER........................	1 00
ADELMAR..	40
AGNES OF BRAUNSBERG. By Mrs. J. Sadlier..............	40
ALICE HARMON, AND OTHER TALES........................	1 25
ALICE SHERWIN..	1 50
ALL ABOUT KNOCK...	1 00
ALL FOR THE SACRED HEART. Cloth, red edges..... net	50
French morocco, round corners ....net	1 00
Turkey morocco, round corners.............................net	2 00
ANECDOTES OF NAPOLEON....................................	50
ANNETTE AND HER FIVE DOLLS...........................	40
APPARITIONS AND MIRACLES AT KNOCK. Four illustrations, paper covers	25
ART OF SUFFERING	50
AUNT HONOR'S KEEPSAKE. By Mrs. James Sadlier	1 00
AUGUSTINE. Translated from the French, by A. T. Sadlier....	40
BALMES' FUNDAMENTAL PHILOSOPHY. 2 vols.........net	2 00
BATTLE of VENTRY HARBOR. 48 pages, paper cover.........	20
BARRINGTON'S PERSONAL SKETCHES OF HIS OWN TIMES	1 00
BARRINGTON'S RISE and FALL of IRISH NATION........	1 50
*BATTLE FIELDS of IRELAND, THE.........................	1 50
BANIM'S (JOHN) WORKS. 10 vols., 12 mo, neatly bound in leather, half-morocco, gilt top. Per set,................net	7 00
or sold separately, single volumes, each....................net	75

   The Peep O'Day.   The Denounced.
   The Croppy.   Peter of the Castle.
   The Mayor of Windgap and Canvassing.   Father Connell.
   The Bit o' Writin'.   The Ghost-Hunter.
   The Boyne Water.   The Life of John Banim.

BENJAMIN. By Mrs. James Sadlier...........................	40
BESSIE CONWAY. By Mrs. James Sadlier	1 00
BLAKES and FLANAGANS. By Mrs. James Sadlier...........	1 25
BLANCHE, OR THE EVIL EFFECTS OF PRIDE............	40
BLANCHE LESLIE AND OTHER CATHOLIC TALES......	75
BLIND AGNESE, OR THE LITTLE SPOUSE OF THE BLESSED SACRAMENT. By Cecilia Mary Caddell; new and enlarged edition...	75

Catholic Standard Publications.

BIBLE HISTORY. By Rev. James O'Leary, D. D., with 65 illustrations and 14 maps. 1 50
BIBLE HISTORY. By Rev. Joseph Reeve. Illustrated with two hundred and thirty engravings.......................... 75
BLIGHTED FLOWER, THE... 40
BOYHOOD OF GREAT PAINTERS. Two vols........ per set 1 50
BROKEN FLUTE 40
HOLY BIBLE, THE. Douay Version. Royal octavo, 968 pages.
   LARGE TYPE. Cloth, sprinkled edges......................... 2 60
   Turkey Morocco, flexible, red under gold edges......net 5 00
   Turkey Morocco, padded, red under gold edges......net 5 50
   Divinity Circuit, red, under gold edges....................net 6 00
   Complete Bible and Prayer-book list on application.
*BOG OF STARS. By Standish O'Grady. 16 mo, paper cover 50
BOHEMIANS IN THE FIFTEENTH CENTURY. By Mrs. James Sadlier... 75
BRITISH CATHOLIC POETS. Red line, gilt edges, cloth...... 1 25
BROOKSIANA. Controversy between Senator Brooks and Archbishop Hughes... 75
BROWNSON'S ESSAYS. By O. A. Brownson, LL.D.,......net 1 00
BROWNSON'S LIBERALISM. By O. A. Brownson, LL.D...net 75
BURKES LECTURES AND SERMONS. Complete, 3 vols...... 6 00
   "   "   The same, gilt edges 9 00
   REPLY TO FROUDE 1 00
CALLISTA. By his Eminence Cardinal Newman 1 25
CANNON'S POEMS. Red line. Gilt edge 1 25
CAPTAIN ROSCOFF. A Tale of the French Revolution........ 1 00
CAPTAIN OF THE CLUB, THE 75
CANNON'S PRACTICAL SPELLING BOOK. 12mo, boards, net 10
CATECHISM OF SACRED HISTORY. By Mrs. J. Sadlier. 18 mo. cloth 25
CATHOLIC SCHOOL BOOK, THE. 16mo, boards,..........net 10
CATHOLIC FAITH AND MORALS 50
CATHOLIC EXCELSIOR LIBRARY. 6 vols., per set........... 4 50
   " FIRESIDE " 10 " " " 7 50
   " HOME " 8 " " " 6 00
   " JUVENILE " 6 " " " 2 40
   " PIETY (Prayer Book). Prices upwards from...... 60
CATHOLIC ANECDOTES. 3 vols. in one, complete. By Mrs. James Sadlier. 12 mo., cloth. Nearly 1,000..................... 1 50

Catholic Standard Publications.

CATHOLIC CRUSOE. By Rev. Dr. Anderdon............ .... 1 25
CATHOLIC LEGENDS 1 00
CATHOLIC SONGS OF THE MONTHS. Verses from Father
   Ryan, Father Faber, etc. Full page colored illustrations... net 25
CATHOLIC FLOWERS FROM PROTESTANT GARDENS.
   Gilt edges, steel plate. Red line 1 25
CATHOLIC O'MALLEYS......... 75
CATHOLIC OFFERING. By Archbishop Walsh................ 7 5
CARROLL O'DONOGHUE. By Christine Faber. Imitation half
   morocco, gilt top.................................. .... 1 25
CARLETON'S (WILLIAM) WORKS. Ten vols, 12 mo, neatly
   bound in leather, half morocco, gilt top, per set............ net 7 00
   or sold separately, single vols., each .... net 75

     Willy Reilly.   Valentine McClutchy.
     Jane Sinclair.   The Poor Scholar.
     The Emigrants of Ahadarra.   Fardorougha, the Miser.
     The Tithe-Proctor·   The Black Baronet.
     The Black Prophet.   The Evil Eye.

CASTLE OF ROUSSILLON. By Mrs. James Sadlier 75
CARPENTER'S SPELLER. 12mo, boards ... . net 10
CHRISTIAN MAIDEN'S LOVE. By Louis Veuillot 75
*CHRISTIAN ARMED, THE. By Father Ignatius (Spencer).
   Passionist. Cloth, red edges........ 50
CHRISTIAN POLITENESS FOR LADIES AND GENTLEMEN 1 25
CHRISTIAN AND RELIGIOUS PERFECTION. By St. Al-
   phonsus Rodriguez of the Society of Jesus. 3 vols., 12mo, cloth,
   red edges....... .... net 2 00
CHRISTIAN MISSIONS. By T. W. M. Marshall. 2 vols., 8vo , net 2 00
CHRISTIAN BROTHERS' THIRD READER. 12mo, cloth, net 32
CHRISTIAN'S RULE OF LIFE. By St. Alphonsus M. Liguori.
   Cloth, red edges 50
CHRISTIAN VIRTUES. By St. Alphonsus M. Liguori 1 00
CHRISTIANITY IN CHINA, TARTARY AND THIBET. By
   Abbe Huc. 2 vols., 12mo, cloth .. .. net 1 50
CHRISTOPHER COLUMBUS. By Marquis de Belloy. Large
   type, toned paper, fine satin cloth, bevelled, gilt edges 3 00
CHRISTMAS NIGHTS' ENTERTAINMENT 60
CHANCELLOR AND HIS DAUGHTER, THE. By Agnes M.
   Stewart 1 25
CHATEAUBRIAND'S ATALA. Illustrated by Gustave Doré.
   Quarto, toned paper, fine satin cloth, bevelled. Gilt edges...., 3 00
CHIVALROUS DEED, A. By Christine Faber. Imitation half
   morocco, gilt top......... ....,............... 1 25

Catholic Standard Publications.

CHURCH OF ERIN. By Rev. Thomas Walsh and D. P. Conyngham, L.L.D. Large octavo, illustrated, cloth, full gilt covers and edges............	6 00
French morocco, blocked pattern, full gilt............	10 00
CLOISTER LEGENDS	1 00
CLIFTON TRACTS. Library of Controversy. 4 vols....... net	1 50
CLOCK OF THE PASSION OF OUR LORD JESUS CHRIST. By St. Alphonsus Liguori............	50
COBBETT'S HISTORY OF THE PROTESTANT REFORMATION............	1 25
CONFESSIONS OF ST. AUGUSTINE. Cloth, red edges......	75
CONSOLATION FOR THE AFFLICTED. By Anna T. Sadlier	50
COLLINS' BALLADS, SONGS AND POEMS. Red line, gilt edges	1 25
COMMANDANT LA RAISON. A Story of the French Revolution	1 00
CONFEDERATE CHIEFTAINS. By Mrs. James Sadlier.......	1 50
CONFESSIONS OF AN APOSTATE. By Mrs. James Sadlier...	1 00
CON O'REGAN. By Mrs. James Sadlier............	1 00
CONVERTED JEW. (Conversion of Marie Alphonse Ratisbonne.)	50
CONSCIENCE, HENDRICK. Tales of Flemish Life........	1 25
COUNTESS OF GLOSSWOOD............	75
CROWN OF JESUS (Prayer Book). Prices upwards from.......	1 00
CREED OF CATHOLICS. By Bishop McGill............	1 00
DALARADIA. An Irish Story, by Wm. Collins............	75
DAUGHTER OF TYRCONNELL, AND FATE OF FR. SHEEHY. By Mrs. J. Sadlier, 2 vols. in one	1 00
DAILY COMPANION. 48 mo. (Prayer Book). Prices upwards from	25
DAVIS' POEMS AND ESSAYS, Complete. By Thomas Davis..	1 50
DEVIL, THE. Does He Exist?	60
DEVOTION TO GOD THE HOLY GHOST. Cloth ...... net	10
paper............ net	05
DEVOUT MANUAL. 18 mo. (Prayer Book). Prices upwards from	75
" " 32 mo. " " " "	35
DEVOTION TO ST. JOSEPH. By Rev. Father Patrignani, S. J.	1 00
DIVINE PARABLES EXPLAINED. By Rev. Joseph Prachensky, S. J.	75
DICK MASSEY	1 00
DISAPPOINTED AMBITION. By Miss Agnes M. Stewart.....	75
*DOVE OF THE TABERNACLE, THE. By Rev. T. H. Kinane, C. C............	75

www.ingramcontent.com/pod-product-compliance
Lightning Source LLC
Chambersburg PA
CBHW032354230426
43672CB00007B/695